# Smoke From the Branding Fire

## Hank Pallister's Tales

Hank Pallister

with

Joyce Pallister

## DETSELIG
### ENTERPRISES LTD

Calgary, Alberta, Canada

**Smoke From the Branding Fire: Hank Pallister's Tales**

© 2007 Joyce Pallister

Library and Archives Canada Cataloguing in Publication

Pallister, Joyce

    Smoke from the branding fire : Hank Pallister's tales / Joyce Pallister.

ISBN 978-1-55059-336-5

    1. Ranching--Alberta--History.  2. Ranch life--Alberta--History.

3. Cowboys--Alberta--Biography.  4. Cattle--Marking--Alberta--History.

5. Pallister, Hank, 1925-2005.  6. Alberta--Biography.  I. Title.

FC3670.C6P34 2007          971.23'03          C2007-902244-8

Detselig Enterprises Ltd.
210, 1220 Kensington Road NW
Calgary, Alberta
T2N 3P5

DETSELIG
ENTERPRISES LTD

www.temerondetselig.com
temeron@telusplanet.net
Phone: (403) 283-0900
Fax: (403) 283-6947

We acknowledge the support of the Government of Canada through the Book Publishing Industry Development Program (BPIDP) for our publishing program.

We also acknowledge the support of the Alberta Foundation for the Arts for our publishing program, as well as Doc Seaman for his support of this publication.

Appreciation is also expressed to the Alberta Historical Resources Foundation for their financial support of this publication.

SAN 113-0234
ISBN 978-1-55059-336-5
Printed in Canada on 100% recycled paper    Cover Design by Alvin Choong

Dedicated to future generations of ranching families – that they may appreciate the sacrifices of their parents, grandparents, and great-grandparents – and to Aleesha Faith Pallister (May 6, 2001 to May 9, 2001), the first grandchild of the fourth generation of the Hank and Joyce Pallister family.

# Table of Contents

## Other Stories

## Range Men's Dinner Program

# Foreword

Many friends that Hank and I have in the livestock industry requested that we publish Hank's stories in book form. I kept encouraging him to do this, and when we moved to High River the focus on his ranching heritage became more important, as we were involved with the Bar U Ranch National Historic Site. He continued to write and publish these stories in *Alberta Beef Magazine* and *The Regional* – a newspaper supplement that was published throughout Southern Alberta by the major weekly newspapers and distributed to over 27 000 homes. The writings in this book cover the period of Hank's retirement from the Alberta Brand Office in November 1991, to his death in April 2005. He contacted David Finch, Editor, in March 2005, about the possibility of a book. Hank passed away before he realized his dream. It would have been a shame to leave so much history of Alberta left unpublished; therefore I have brought the project to completion. I trust those who read it will have as many hours of enjoyment as I had in putting it together.

– Joyce Pallister

# Acknowledgments

I wish to thank David Finch, editor, historian, and author, for the many hours of sorting through Hank's manuscripts. David helped bring the reader stories that portray the hardships of the ranching lifestyle and the perseverance and tenacity needed to survive on the open range.

A special thanks to Ted Giles, at Detselig Enterprises Ltd., who had the foresight to envision the final product through my enthusiasm. I am also indebted to Leif Baradoy, who acted as the publisher's liaison and typesetter, for his patience and understanding as he guided me through the editing and publishing process.

Finally, I wish to express my gratitude to Doc Seaman, along with the OH Ranch, for the generous financial support, which helped bring this book to print.

# Brand Inspection Stories

# Livestock Identification:
# Alberta's Heritage

Brands used to identify range cattle throughout Western Canada for more than a century are as old as the livestock industry itself. The appearance of visible brands on the hides of a good herd of ranch cattle can be considered to be similar to a serial number or a private trademark. When applied properly, a brand is more tamper-proof than a birth certificate and most certainly as personal as a business card.

The scar tissue that makes a good brand visible may not be too eye appealing to some folks, but woven in with those old brands is more ranch history and rangeland stories than most people realize. In many cases, over a period of more than a hundred years, numerous old ranch brands have become better known than the people who owned them. Brands and branding fires were a common sight in the early years of ranching, and have remained so among the livestock community. Smoke from these branding fires, scattered by winds of the past, has carried the history of brands and early ranches to a new generation of livestock producers.

Cattle brands have been a part of human culture for centuries. Early history reveals that during ancient times the Egyptians, and later the Greeks, discovered the advantages of signifying the ownership of an animal with a permanent mark by burning a brand on with a properly heated iron. They also felt branding had equal merit for the purpose of identifying human slaves. Western European countries later adopted the practice, and it was not until the middle of the eighteenth century that France stopped branding certain criminals.

With the coming of the Spaniards to North America, branding made its first appearance on this continent in old Mexico and soon extended to Texas and the American southwest as it gradually became settled. The custom of branding cattle in that part of the world did not become a common practice until after the Civil War in 1865. Since there were no markets for beef in the south, herds were put together and trailed north into Texas to market. Branding became necessary when several livestock owners made up trail herds for the long trip north, and the means of brand identification was certainly a beneficial financial factor when they arrived at their market destination. These first brands were called "trail brands."

An Ordinance with Respect to the Marking of Livestock in the Northwest Territories by the use of brands was passed at the Second Session of the Council of the Territorial Government at a meeting in North Battleford on August 2nd, 1878.

This represented the first movement towards the recording of cattle and horse brands throughout the ranching regions of Western Canada. When the term "Northwest Territories" is referred to in this article, it means the portion of the Territories that became the Provinces of Alberta and Saskatchewan in 1905.

The Lieutenant-Governor of the Northwest Territories was given the authority to declare Stock Districts in which the Clerk of the local Magistrate Court acted as Brand Recorder. It was his responsibility to designate a mark or character to interested livestock owners who wished to obtain a brand to mark their livestock, as well as what position on the animal it would occupy. The first brand district organized in the Territories was at Fort MacLeod during 1878 and David Laird was the man you had to locate in order to register a brand.

During 1898, the Legislative Act of Recording Brands became the responsibility of the Department of Agriculture of the Territorial Government. The different stock districts were no longer allowed to register brands, and one recording office for the Territories was set up in Regina. At this point, approximately 3052 cattle and horse brands had been registered.

When the Provinces of Alberta and Saskatchewan were founded in 1905, Alberta established its own office for recording brands at Medicine Hat. During 1923, the office was moved to government headquarters in Edmonton. There is very little evidence on record as to exactly when this move transpired, except for a few scattered dates on aged paper that still exists in the old files.

This same office was located close to the Provincial Legislature in Edmonton for more than five decades, and because of a political platform introduced by the Conservative Government during 1971, the office was decentralized to Stettler in February 1975. During this fifty-year period, a fair number of men had served as Brand Recorders and by this time, more than 50 000 brands had been registered and were in active use by cattlemen throughout Alberta. At that time, the province of British Columbia had registered approximately 8000 brands and Saskatchewan had 28 000 brands registered.

The assignment of finding enough suitable brands during that era, due to the fast growing livestock industry, had become a much more difficult task than it had been a century earlier. The alphabetical letters and numerals of the English language, are used to make up a brand design, can appear similar in many cases, especially when applied to the hide of livestock that are guarded with a heavy hair cover. During registration, considerable caution is exercised in the issuing of brands to prevent conflict and duplication of these letters.

The letter Q was never registered and the letter G is always used in a reverse position. Four brand symbols and four characters, are also part of the makeup of Alberta's brand system. The symbols are: quarter circle, half diamond, bar, running bar; the four characters are diamond, triangle, anchor, and box. Newly registered brands are a combination of two letters or numerals that include any of these signs. Any two letters of the alphabet registered in a horizontal position also have to include one of the four symbols. Two letters registered in a vertical position are satisfactory without having one of the symbols included.

Some letters of the alphabet lend themselves well to a reverse position and others were suitable in a lazy position. Those registered in a reverse position are the type that could have another letter monogrammed or attached to the right on the straight side of the first letter. The letters that are used in a lazy position, are those that would lay to the left and rest satisfactorily on a flat side of the lazy letter.

Letters designed in a way referred to as walking, flying, hanging or running are not used in the current registration system.

Characters interpreted as "Arbitrary" Brands such as Bits, Boxes, Hats and Spurs, for example, have not been part of Alberta's active registration system since 1955. This is due to so many different interpretations of those types of characters, along with the problem of having them indexed properly for reference in a brand book. If these brands continue to be registered or legally transferred, they will have remain in the system. However, when such brands are allowed to expire, they are taken out of the system and not reissued again to any other person.

Brands can be registered on any of six animal positions for both cattle and horses. The cattle locations are shoulder, rib and hip on both the left and right side and horses are also the two sides – jaw, shoulder and thigh. The same set of brand characters applied on two different positions of an animal is considered a registration of two entirely different brands. A brand applied to a position that was deemed to be unavailable was almost certain to duplicate a brand owned by another person.

To "vent" a brand, was a legal procedure whereby the original brand owner could cancel the ownership of his registered brand by placing one character of the brand in a lazy position immediately below the brand. The term "legal vent", in more recent years, seemed to have been an unimportant issue. This is due to the high frequency of times that the majority of livestock are bought and sold during their short lifetimes. Most of today's cattle producers have not been interested in the proper procedure necessary to vent a brand, which was not the case during the early years of the cattle business.

There has been considerable controversy over the disputed issue of how many brand books have been published since the first Brand Ordinance of 1878. There is evidence available that indicates the first Brand Book was compiled in the Northwest Territories during May,1888 by James Henderson and printed by W.T. Walker, a publishing company out of Winnipeg.

This book contained the bylaws of the Alberta Stockgrowers Association, which outlined to ranchers their responsibilities with respect to prairie fires, cattle rustling, unbranded livestock and annual roundups. It also contained the first ordinance to be enacted for the marking of stock, which included a list of early registered brands and the ranchers who owned them.

The Henderson Directory Company, also out of Winnipeg, published the second brand book in 1889 and the third edition in 1894. A supplement to the 1894 book was printed during 1896 and the fourth edition brand book was published in 1898. The Calgary Herald tackled the enormous task of printing the next brand book in 1900. This same company printed another edition in 1903 and a supplement book in 1904.

By 1905, the Government Printers of the Territories had accepted the responsibility of printing a brand book and published a supplement book that same year, as well as another supplement in 1906. The brand book printed for 1907 was a joint effort between the Agriculture Departments of both Alberta and Saskatchewan. Seven years passed before the next book was put out in 1914 that covered the period between 1907 and 1913. A supplement to this book was also printed in 1914 and another supplement book was published in 1915. The King's Printers of the Provincial Government published their first book in 1919, which listed all the brands that had been issued for the three years previous. Another book was printed in 1921 that took care of the new brands registered during 1919 and 1920. The first brand book published after the Brand Office was moved to Edmonton was printed in 1925. Twelve years passed before the next book was published in 1937. Another supplement was printed in 1941 and a large red book was put together in 1947.

During the next decade, the livestock industry in Alberta changed considerably, with an explosion in the cattle population. The number of new cattle brands registered was enormous, and a new style of a brand book was produced in 1954. Since 1958, a new brand book has been published every four years with the same number of supplement books printed during the even numbered years between. Among these is a Centennial Edition printed in 1978 and a supplement to that book in 1980.

Including the first brand book published well over a century ago, there has been a total of 40 books printed up to and including 2002. Among these were 24 official brand book publications, with the other 16 being supplementary editions.

The first brand to be duly registered in the Northwest Territories was "71" on the left rib. Percy Neale and Sam Steele, two retired mounted policemen who had been stationed at the NWMP MacLeod detachment, registered this brand as partners in January, 1880. There were five more brands registered during that same year. Twenty-nine more brands were registered in 1881 and another thirty-four in 1882. The two oldest brands in current use that have been kept registered since they were initially issued are: the Circle brand, O, registered on the left hip for cattle, and the OH brand that was registered on the left rib for cattle and left shoulder for horses.

The Circle Brand brand was registered on June 25, 1881 to David MacDougall whose address was the Morelyville post office, located on the Bow River, west of Calgary. The OH was registered during the month of July, 1881 and both brands have been kept active over the years at the same ranch location where they were initially registered. The oldest brand currently registered that has remained in the same family name since it was first issued is the "70" brand, registered for cattle on the left rib to Charles Kettles of Fort MacLeod on July 9, 1882.

Cattle ranching and brands did not really become a lifestyle in the North West Territories, until the signing of the historical treaty with the American Indians during 1877. The signing of this treaty was a dramatic event for the native people, that later made the way for settlement of the same territory where large cattle and horse ranches were established.

By the time the North West Mounted Police arrived on the Old Man River in Southern Alberta in 1874, the Blackfoot nation had become small and unimportant. The older chiefs could foresee the white settlers coming like snowflakes in the winter, and in order to save even a part of their land for their own people, the chiefs were willing to talk peace. In September 1877 all the tribes of the Southern plains and foothills gathered at the Blackfoot Crossing on the Bow River for the formal signing of the Treaty. For the nominal sum of twelve dollars cash to every man, woman, and child, the leaders of five Indian nations surrendered their rights, titles, and privileges to the Canadian Government.

By this time, the great buffalo herds had disappeared and the lonesome wail of the steam locomotives, often heard in the still of the night as they rolled across the mighty plains, foretold that the cattle herds were coming. Cattle ranching had become a way of life and new ranches, financed mostly with British and American capital, were established. The area of southern Alberta held a natural environment for cattle ranching and ranching syndicates from both Eastern Canada and the United States quickly took advantage of the new virgin grassland.

For more than a century of time, there have been many cattle ranches, some large ranching companies, family partnerships and a multitude of ordinary people who got into the cattle business and, for various reasons, have disappeared. It should be recognized that many of the old-time cattle brands have remained, which are now proudly owned by families or companies who survived the economic disasters of years gone by. These same brands have become somewhat of a legend with the descendants of those early ranching families, and will continue to be recognized accordingly with those generations yet to come.

# The Hazards of Brand Inspection

During the 1970s while I was supervising the Regulatory Services Programs of Alberta Agriculture out of Stettler, my work required a considerable amount of traveling. On one particular trip to Southern Alberta during November 1979, I had reason to visit the Brand Office situated at that time, in the Exchange Building at the old Calgary Stockyards location in East Calgary. Rudy Everson of Millarville was head Brand Inspector at Calgary and Harry McWilson, whose headquarters were at Airdrie, was supervising an area between Olds and Nanton across the province east and west.

McWilson happened to be in the Calgary office the same afternoon I stopped there. He inquired whether I could accompany him the following morning to visit a widowed woman who owned a small ranch near Priddis. Apparently this woman had shipped some feeder cattle to the Calgary market several weeks earlier, amongst which the Brand Inspectors had found an animal that belonged to one of her neighbors. It was policy in most cases to allow stray animals of this kind to be sold, with the proceeds being held until rightful ownership could be established.

The rancher had disputed the fact that she had shipped her neighbor's animal, which was the reason for our personal visit. Our pictures and documents served as evidence to prove to the woman what had taken place. From stories we had heard of people who had visited there previously; we both had reason to be somewhat cautious and concerned about our morning visit.

We met next morning at the Calgary stockyards and traveled together to the woman's ranch, arriving there just after daylight. The ranch house was a short distance off the highway where about eight inches of fresh snow had fallen during the night. The driveway stopped about fifty feet from the east side of the house where two mongrel dogs were tied to an old timber log. Each dog was tethered with about twenty feet of cotton rope that was frayed and half eaten through in several different places. As we left our vehicle and started towards the house the dogs became angry and began barking and snarling while they leaped in the air hitting the end of their tether ropes with every jump. It appeared the front entry of the house was not being used so we made a new trail through the freshly fallen snow and hustled around the north end of the large house to an open veranda on the west side.

As we were removing our overshoes on the veranda, a woman past middle age greeted us and invited us inside to a dimly lighted kitchen area. We were not offered a seat anywhere so we stood stationary along the wall on opposite sides of her kitchen; being careful not to wander too far from where we stood. We were aware of a rumor that had circulated through that part of the countryside, where a previous government official had visited the same women regarding a road allowance that went through her property. According to rumor, the information given to the woman was contrary to what she wanted, so she dropped the government man into a dark cellar of the house through a trap door in her kitchen floor!

The information we outlined to the lady rancher that morning was not in her favor either, showing her evidence that she attempted to sell an animal that was owned by another person. The woman never did agree that she was at fault in any way but the money for the stray animal was paid to the rightful owner at a later date without any theft charges being laid. We both escaped the dramatic shock of the dark cellar, possibly because two of us were present, or perhaps it was the fact we located ourselves properly within her kitchen!

We concluded our business with the lady rancher in about twenty minutes, and left the kitchen as quickly as possible. I was out onto the veranda first, slipped on my overshoes and stepped off into the snow to start back around the house to our vehicle. While McWilson was putting on his overshoes he said to me, "I think I should go first."

I stopped, looked back and asked, "Why?" He said, "If those dogs out there break those old ropes, I would feel awful bad if I had to run over top of you trying to get back into that vehicle before they eat me for breakfast!" Brand Inspectors are a loyal bunch of cowhands!

During the many years of brand inspection work, I always considered it a dangerous occupation. Brand Inspectors never received extra compensation for the hazardous assignments they often performed. As I often think about some situations that happened throughout the years, I am surprised there were not more injury accidents, respecting the nature of their responsibilities.

# Livestock Investigations

During the early 1970s I was administering Alberta's Brand Inspection system, working out of office headquarters with the Animal Industry Division of Alberta Agriculture in Edmonton. The province had recently been divided into six brand inspection areas with a Brand Supervisor appointed for each of the six areas.

K Division of the Royal Canadian Mounted Police had also established four more livestock investigation positions; which were filled with new personnel located strategically throughout the same areas.

Early in 1974 an elderly farmer in the Bashaw-Ferintosh area made a report to the Red Deer Brand Office and claimed his cow was being harbored by two brothers who farmed nearby. The animal was an Angus-Holstein cross, about five years old which showed the Holstein color but had the build and conformation of the Angus breed. When the incident was reported, the brothers had been in possession of the cow for several years. During that period had sold two calves from the cow; with the third one being a yearling heifer that was still on their property.

The Red Deer Brand Inspection Supervisor and R.C.M.P. Livestock Investigator made numerous visits to the area regarding the complaint; without finding any worthwhile solution to the problem. For reasons which I cannot recall, I was requested to take part in the investigation. The disagreement was that both parties were positive they raised the cow and accused each other of illegally branding her. The cow remained on the brothers' farm during the investigation and in order to establish proper ownership it was necessary to compare the size of both sets of branding irons to the size of both brands on the cow. This exercise was evidence enough to determine which of the two brands was applied first on the animal. The size of the farmer's brand confirmed that he had branded the cow when she was a calf and the two brothers must have branded the animal several years later. Regardless of the evidence presented, the brothers continued to claim ownership. In order to settle the matter, a charge of livestock theft was laid against the two brothers under the Criminal Code.

The case was tried later the same spring at a Court of Queen's Bench in Wetaskawin. I was subpoenaed to appear and testify as a professional witness, at which time I simply explained to the court that when cattle are branded at a young age, the size of the brand would increase in size until the animal is full-grown. The farmer's brand on the cow had grown about three times the size of his branding iron, whereas the brothers' brand remained exactly the same dimensions as when it was applied. This satisfied the judge that the farmer's brand was applied first and he informed the courtroom the complainant must own the cow. The type of evidence given surprised the courtroom to some extent and the trial quickly ended. Whatever evidence the defense attorney was going to use in an attempt to claim ownership for his client was never given in court. The farmer obtained possession of his cow and yearling and the accused brothers were ordered to pay market price for the two calves they previously sold.

The evidence I gave at the trial must have impressed the judge. After court was dismissed I was invited to the judge's chambers where he personally congratulated me for my knowledge of cattle brands and the decisive evidence given in the courtroom. The judge had considerable knowledge of the cattle industry but was surprised to learn that proper application of a cattle brand can determine the age of an animal from the size of the brand.

Some years after the Provincial Brand Office had been moved out of Edmonton to the Town of Stettler during 1975; a big man walked into my office one autumn afternoon. I recognized the man, but before I could say anything to him, he said "I'm in trouble and I need your help." As he revealed his problem to me I knew he was in big trouble and that he needed considerably more help than I was able to provide. He advised me that he had to appear in court within several months, and wondered if I could show up to say something favorable about him as a livestock producer. Not knowing the man that well I thought it was a most unusual request, but I advised him that if his lawyer subpoenaed me to appear on his behalf, I was compelled to do so.

I remembered the man from the days when the first High River Auction Market was operating during the 1960s. He was a bachelor fellow with a small herd of cattle who farmed near High River. Sale day was his day to come to town; mostly for fellowship with other people, because he appeared to be a person who had few friends. I visited with him often at High River while waiting for the sale to finish because the man was a pleasant enough person to pass some time with. I moved from Calgary to Edmonton in 1968 and never saw the man again until he walked into my office at Stettler more than fifteen years later.

Sometime during the passing years he moved from the High River area north to the Rimbey district. He remained in the cattle business and farmed enough land to grow his own feed. Apparently he had borrowed a considerable amount of money from the bank that listed all his cattle as collateral. After several years of not receiving their annual interest payments, the bank decided to seize his cattle in order to recover some of the borrowed money. Preparations were made to remove the cattle from the man's farm through a sheriff's seizure and the necessary search warrant. Capable help was hired by the bank, and accompanied by the R.C.M.P. Everyone arrived at a designated location one suitable afternoon. Instead of involving the man who owned the cattle, it was their intention to remove the cattle from the back area of the farm without him knowing about it. In the process, the man heard the cattle bawling and decided to drive over the hill to see what was happening. He was driving an older model truck with a reinforced grill guard made from heavy steel, and had a loaded sawed-off shotgun with him on the seat. When he saw what was taking place he rammed the police cruisers broadside several times with the old truck and then with his loaded shotgun threatened the life of an R.C.M.P. member. The man was finally apprehended and taken to a hospital where he was given psychiatric treatment for a period of thirty days.

When the case was heard in Wetaskiwin during March the following spring, the man faced five charges. I was subpoenaed by the defense lawyer to testify on behalf of the accused, but what I was able to truthfully say about him under oath had no bearing whatsoever on the outcome of the trial. The man was found guilty on all charges and was sentenced to serve a ten-year jail term.

During my long affiliation with the cattle business in Alberta I found the majority of people associated with the industry were good, reputable citizens. Of course there was always a percentage whose integrity could be questioned, but the industry had a natural set of guidelines that would separate those who were inclined to be dishonest. Alberta's cow business has remained a prosperous free-enterprise industry for more than a century because of the genuine, honest producers whose ranches have been passed to the next generation.

# Alberta Auction Markets

Alberta cattle producers both past and present should agree that the public auction method of selling commercial live cattle has contributed greatly to the success of the cattle industry in this Province for the better part of the past fifty years. The construction and improvements of country Auction Markets must also be given equal recognition for the accomplishments gained in the marketing of livestock within Alberta during this same time period.

The old Alberta Stockyards that operated in east Calgary for eighty six years, closed their gates for the last time during December 1989. These stockyards must be acknowledged as being the first market where all types of livestock could be traded on a daily basis. It is now difficult to comprehend that less than fifty years ago, there were only two markets in Alberta that were open daily, to producers of both feeder and slaughter cattle. Calgary began their daily sales during 1910 and Edmonton did not get started until 1916. The Lethbridge stockyards, a subsidiary of the Alberta Stockyards Company at Calgary became a third daily market that began operating in that city in January of 1950. These three daily markets were governed and controlled by rules set down by the Federal Department of Agriculture and were referred to as the "Central Markets."

The Calgary Stockyards functioned as a Central Market until the fall of 1981, when the owners of the Commission Companies and Order Buying Firms, incorporated into a new company called the Calgary Public Livestock Market Ltd. The Calgary Livestock Exchange was dissolved and the new company became licensed under Provincial legislation instead of being regulated by the Federal Government. During 1982, the Commission Companies at the Edmonton Stockyards also amalgamated into a similar company and have since continued to operate successfully under the regulations of a Provincial market. The Lethbridge stockyards discontinued operating entirely as a livestock market in June 1984.

It may be of interest to the current generation of livestock producers that during the early years of this era, there were seven slaughter houses in Alberta that were operating under Federal inspection. Three were in Calgary with the other four in Edmonton. The feedlot business expanded so dramatically during the 1950s and 1960s; that by the middle 1970s there were eighteen slaughter plants operating, with new facilities at Brooks, Grand Prairie, Lethbridge, Medicine Hat and Red Deer. The following decade saw some of these packing plants go out of business as quickly as they began, until where there are currently only three plants operating in Alberta under Federal Meat Inspection.

The Calgary stockyards held the distinction of introducing the auction method of selling commercial cattle at central markets throughout Canada. Although the first sale of commercial cattle by public auction was held at Calgary during December 1950, the same method of selling livestock had been proven successful in Southern Alberta at least ten years earlier. A group of ranchers in the Pincher Creek district decided there was a better method to sell cattle than the old style normally used; where cattle dealers and packer buyers visited farmers and ranchers to make offers on cattle that were for sale. These ranchers were successful in forming an organization known as the Community Auction Sales Association, which officially became licensed to operate during August 1939. Their first sale by public auction was held during September of that year at Bain, a siding on the CPR railroad east of Manyberries. More than one thousand head were consigned, that were sold by two veteran auctioneers Don Ball and Warren Cooper, who are both now deceased.

For twenty-five years this Association operated only during the fall months, to accommodate ranchers selling cattle off grass. Eleven sale yards were built in Southern Alberta, with sales conducted at Azure, Cardston, Claresholm, Fort Macleod, Lundbreck, Nanton, Pakowki, Pincher Creek, Parkbend, Warner, and Whiskey Gap. As the methods of transporting livestock improved, most of these sale points disappeared to where only Pincher Creek and Parkbend were operating in the fall of 1965. This association continued to hold weekly sales at Pincher Creek until April 1993, when those market facilities were leased by the Highwood Auction Company, from Fort MacLeod. After more than fifty years of a practical marketing service to the ranching communities in Southern Alberta, the half dozen men who founded this organization should be remembered as the pioneers of selling commercial cattle by public auction. With James Mailer as President, Lea Park held their sale by public auction and organized an Association also during the fall of 1939.

The cattle ranchers around Cadogan also saw the benefits of selling cattle by public auction, and livestock sales were held at a temporary market near Consort, with Archie Boyce as auctioneer. All future sales of this Association were conducted at Cadogan; which became an annual event each year until their last sale in 1954. Their first sale was held in August of that year at the Lea Park corrals, and has continued each fall since, for the benefit of cattle producers in that area of north eastern Alberta.

The efforts of C. J. Anderson, who was the Manager of the Bow Slope Shipping Association at Brooks for many years, cannot be overlooked. Carl Anderson, along with staff from the Alberta Livestock Commission Company out of Calgary, began holding cattle sales by public auction during the fall of 1944. Anderson recalls the difficulty in organizing these early sales due to livestock transportation. There were no livestock trucks available during the war years, so a sale was not scheduled unless the Canadian Pacific Railroad would guarantee at least twenty-five stock cars to move the cattle from the sale.

The Walsh Cattle Marketing Association began operating during 1947 under the leadership of Bert Hargraves. A scheduled number of sales were held each spring and fall to accommodate the sale of ranch cattle in that part of Alberta and southwest Saskatchewan. The quality of cattle marketed off grass in that part of the country, attracted both Eastern and Export Buyers to the majority of their sales. After forty seven years, their last sale was held during October 1994.

Although the Central markets enjoyed the monopoly of selling the major portion of livestock in Alberta prior to 1950, this avenue of selling livestock soon shifted. Alex and Keith Sims of Red Deer, who pioneered the idea of auction markets in Alberta, held their first sale at a small facility in North Red Deer on November 19, 1949. Additional auction markets were not started until the summer of 1953, when Archie Boyce along with Charlie and Adolph Rosehill opened a market at Olds on August 4 of that year. Another market started at Stettler on the nineteenth day of the same month under the management of Ace Pratt and Charlie McKay. The fourth market showed up at Ponoka during the fall of 1953, and for the following ten years, auction markets in Alberta sprang up like mushrooms on a rainy weekend. Currently, there are approximately fifty five auction markets operating in the Province; many located in or near the larger urban centers.

It is interesting to recall that when auction markets first became another outlet to market livestock; people with authority in Alberta Agriculture did not actually believe they would exist long enough to be concerned about their volume of sales, or regulation of their activities. Most of the new markets began operating without brand inspection, and yet some were inspected by personnel from a Central Market who would travel there on sale days. It was not until well past the middle 1950s that the Government finally realized that several of the new markets were going to remain operating, and a local brand inspector was appointed to that area.

All auction markets in Alberta operated without any health regulations until 1959. During that year some regulations were established which set various health standards as to the construction of new markets in an effort to control livestock diseases; especially brucellosis.

Many of the auction markets that were built during the past forty eight years have not remained in business. Thirty six of these premises that once heard the lingo of an auctioneer weekly, have since closed their doors and disappeared completely at most locations, Listed alphabetically; these markets were situated at Acme, Airdrie, Andrew, Athabaska, Bashaw, Bow Island, Calgary, Castor, Claresholm, Clover Bar, Coronation, Cremona, Daysland, Didsbury, Drumheller, Eckville, Fairview, Hanna, Hardisty, High River, Holden, Leduc, New Sarepta, Manning, Rycroft, Smoky Lake, Strathmore, Taber, Thorhild, Trochu, Valleyview, Vauxhaul, Vegreville, Walsh, Warburg, and Wetaskawin. Newer markets facilities have since been built at High River, and Strathmore, who both operate on a weekly basis. The Hanna market continues to hold several sales each fall to accommodate the marketing of cattle off grass in that area.

For the most part, the cattle business in Alberta has been a thriving enterprise since the hoof and mouth disease during 1952. The public auction method of selling livestock has proven to be more profitable for selling commercial livestock; than the old private treaty system that had been accepted prior to 1950. During the years of this decade and on the threshold of a new century, other methods of marketing livestock have been experienced. Livestock producers now have the opportunity to offer livestock for sale through the use of computer terminals and video screens; situated at appropriate locations in Western Canada. The next generation of livestock producers will be confronted by this method, and newer technology ideas that will challenge the marketing structure of selling livestock throughout North America. At least, the cattle producers in Alberta still have the freedom of choice, as to where, when, and which type of the marketing systems, best suits their operation.

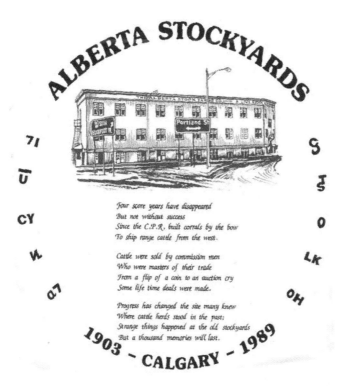

This is a copy of a commemorative plate designed by H.G. Pallister, depicting the marketing history of the Calgary Stockyards. The brands identifying the Big Four, sponsors of the Calgary Stampede, including also other brands of early ranchers who support the public auction concept of marketing cattle. The old stockyards building was a historical landmark in east Calgary and became a meeting place for livestock producers and buyers as well as those who knew it as a place of employment, business and friendship.

# Stories of Early Registered Brands

# Lazy H Brand

ⴄ Left Rib and Left Hip

Since cattle brands were first registered in Alberta's cow country during 1880, less than four hundred of these brands that were registered by the Territorial Government before Alberta became a province in 1905, have since remained active. The majority of these brands have their own story to reveal, which has created more early ranch history than most people realize.

The Lazy H Brand, for example, has been the property of five different large ranching outfits for more than a century.

The single letter H registered in a horizontal position on the left ribs and hip was first allotted to the New Oxley Ranch during July 1888. Reorganization of the original Oxley Ranch took place in the spring of 1886 to form the New Oxley Ranch. The first Oxley Ranch was a ranching syndicate formed during March 1882, who leased 100 000 acres of grazing land on

Willow Creek west of Stavely. Their first ranch manager was a man named John Craig. Craig himself was the original guiding spirit behind the Oxley Ranch. He was born in Ontario and farmed in York County for many years where he specialized in raising Shorthorn cattle. Later, when he arrived in the Canadian North West, he was considered to be one of the best cattle judges who ever went into the ranching business. During the latter 1870s he made plans for a large cattle operation in the North West Territories and organized a company called the Dominion Livestock Company of Canada, with an authorized capital of a half a million dollars. In this venture, Craig and his partners managed to raise about $200 000 among themselves but felt the company needed more capital. With approval from the other subscribers, Craig traveled to Britain where British investors considered cattle ranching in North America to be both a safe and profitable enterprise.

Among the potential investors in Britain, Craig called on Alexander Stavely Hill, who was a lawyer and a member of the British House of Commons. Hill expressed interest in the venture, but only with English gentlemen of his own acquaintance, and he objected to the other people who had subscribed to Craig's company. Hill told Craig he could obtain all the capital needed from his friends, so there was no need for the investors Craig had already gathered. This was appealing to Craig so he decided to consult with the other members of his company. They all agreed to withdraw from such a large ranching gamble, which cleared the way for Craig to work solely with Hill and his English friends.

Having severed all connections with the original investors, Craig suddenly found it difficult to obtain any firm commitment from Stavely Hill. All the English capital that had been promised was never available when needed to carry out the business of the newly formed Oxley Ranch. In order to pay operating expenses, Craig was forced to sell large bunches of cattle wherever he could. This got Craig into trouble in the eyes of the English investors, and he was finally released as ranch manager.

The first brand used by the Oxley outfit on their eight to ten thousand head of cattle was OX on the left ribs. Jim Patterson from the Waldron Ranch was hired as their new Range Boss, who advised the shareholders that they should re-brand all the ranch cattle. This is when the Oxley began using the Lazy H on the left ribs and hip. With the Oxley herd scattered over the open range, one can imagine the amount of work involved with men and horses in order to re-brand all their cattle.

After Craig's departure from the Oxley, Stanley Pinhorne, who was Stavely Hill's nephew became the official manager. Pinhorne was a popular man among some of his ranching neighbors as well as being active in the Stock Associations and showing leadership on the Willow Creek-Mosquito Creek roundups. During October 1892 he was found dead in his bed with a bullet hole in his head and a discharged pistol in his hand.

Since Jim Patterson had left the ranch in the spring of 1889, the ranch obviously needed capable leadership, so Stavely Hill appointed Authur Springett to the manager's position. Springett managed the New Oxley until 1903, when William R. Hull purchased the whole operation from the English shareholders for nearly $250 000. At the time of sale the ranch consisted of about three thousand acres of deeded land, several thousand head of cattle and a large number of horses. The Lazy H brand was transferred to W.R. Hull during July of the same year. Hull had arrived in Southern Alberta during 1883 with a large herd of horses that he had raised on his ranch in the interior of British Columbia. The following year he started the first butcher business in Calgary, which he later sold to Pat Burns. History does not reveal exactly what transpired at the Oxley Ranch after it was purchased by W.R. Hull. Ralph Bartlett and W.J. Budd were separate owners of the ranch for short periods of time before it became the property of the George Lane family during the early 1920s. Descendants of George Lane continue to operate a ranch on a portion of the property once owned by the historic Oxley outfit.

The Hardwick brothers from Gleichen purchased the remnants of the once great Oxley herd in 1912 and obtained possession of the Lazy H Brand during November of that year. Douglas and Shorty Hardwick were Quorn Ranch cowboys who came to Canada from England in1889. They first started a ranch on the Little Bow during 1896 and soon after the turn of the century they moved their camp from their permanent ranch headquarters to where they were the only ranch situated east of Snake Valley. The Hardwicks survived the dry hungry ranching years of the 1920s and '30s with a bit of financial help from Pat Burns. Western Ranches Ltd., a subsidiary of P. Burns Holdings, purchased the complete ranch from Hardwicks during the summer of 1943, which included all the livestock and the Lazy H cattle brand on the left ribs and hip.

Although Burns Ranches had already started selling off some of their ranches by this time, the Hardwick property served a worthwhile purpose for them during the next half dozen years or more. The Hardwick ranch was supervised by the late Raymond Clifford who kept the ranch stocked with dry cows and second cut two-year-old heifers from the Bar U Ranch. Each spring a trainload of cows and heifers were loaded at Cayley and shipped in stock cars and unloaded at a railroad siding called Paget, which was located on the Hardwick ranch east of Lake MacGregor. The same cattle were usually shipped out again and sold as beef the same summer because of the natural hard grass that grew in that area of Southern Alberta. A man named Owen Doyle was Burns Ranches first foreman on the Hardwick ranch. Doyle was moved to their feedlot at Calgary during 1947 and replaced by Mike Burke, whose parents were early ranchers in the foothills west of the Bar U. To my knowledge, Burns Ranches never used the Lazy H brand. Any calves they branded on the Hardwick ranch were marked with Pat Burns's original cattle brand, which was an inverted N monogram L on the left ribs. ⋈L

When Burns Ranches sold the old Hardwick ranch, which consisted of nearly one hundred sections of mostly leased land in 1950, it was separated six different ways. The Melvin Nelson family at High River obtained the largest portion of slightly more than half of the property. The Lomond Community Pasture and William Marks both acquired between eight and ten sections each. The remaining lease was purchased by Charlie Shields, the Voice brothers, and Vic Bertram who were already land owners in that part of the country. Melvin Nelson obtained possession of the Lazy H brand during January 1951 and had it transferred to Nelson's Lazy H Ranches Ltd. in November 1971

Since Melvin Nelson purchased a major part of the Hardwick ranch over forty years ago, his ranch holdings have now developed into a large ranching family enterprise. During 1957 he bought the old TL ranch on Sullivan Creek from Bert Sheppard, which has been managed by his son Laurie. Another son Bob has operated the remnants of the mighty ranch Bar U that was purchased from the Wambeke brothers at Longview in 1984. During the same ranching years, Lazy H Ranches Ltd. were owners of large ranching units at Milk River in Southern Alberta and Williams Lake in British Columbia. The Lazy H has since identified the cattle on the Hardwick lease at Armada and it also distinctly marks their herd that grazes the hilly range which lies north of Pekisko Creek, on the famous Bar U Ranch.

The Lazy H brand has traveled a long journey through more than a century of ranch history, and this journey has not yet ended. Cattle kings, large ranching companies and some ordinary people have directed its course. The majority of these brand owners have since passed on, but the old brand itself will possibly live on forever.

# Quirk's Q

## Q Right Ribs

Some modern day ranching families in Southern Alberta are privileged owners of old time cattle brands that were registered during the early years of ranching in this province. Not many of these current owners realize the amount of ranching heritage that belongs to some of these old brands and others are really not too interested. Some of the early brands were of a better design than others regarding appearance and easy application. Personally, I feel one of the better old time brands presently being used in today's mechanized cow business, is the Q brand, currently registered to Gallup Brothers, who ranch in the Longview area.

This brand was first issued on the right ribs position to John Quirk during October 1882. He arrived at 'The Crossing' at High River, with four hundred and fifty head of cattle that he, along with Mrs. Quirk had trailed north out of Montana earlier that summer. The Quirk's were the first white couple to settle on the Highwood River, where they established a ranch site south of the river among the big cottonwoods, near where the town of High River is now situated. The cattle were turned loose and allowed access to the open range north of the river.

Successive dry years persuaded the Quirk's to move further north and west onto the north fork of Sheep Creek during 1887. Their ranch on Sheep Creek prospered to where the cattle herd increased to nearly two thousand head, running on six thousand acres of deeded land and an equal number of leased acres. By 1910 the country was becoming too crowded for John's liking so the Quirk's sold the ranch and the brand to Pat Burns and moved back to the United States to spend their last years in comfort after so many years together on the ranching frontier.

Pat Burns owned this ranch for only seven years when it was sold to J.F. Dole in 1917 who had been farming in the Vulcan area; but Burns retained ownership of the Q brand. Within a few years this ranch was sold again and became the property of the Kendall Stock Company, who continue to own a portion of the original ranch west of Millarville. During the years Burns operated the old Quirk ranch, his ranch foreman was an Irishman named Jack Dempsey, who was a nephew of Mrs. Quirk. Dempsey arrived in Calgary from Ireland during the fall of 1898 and became an experienced cowhand under the tutoring of John Ware. During 1922 Dempsey went back to Ireland, but was not happy until he returned to the Alberta foothills in 1928, at which time he became ranch foreman on the Q7 Ranch west of Nanton for the following twenty years.

When Pat Burns sold the Quirk ranch and cattle during 1917 but retained the Q brand, it must have been for a good reason. Without any doubt, there must have been someone in the Burns organization at that time who realized the quality of this brand and wished to retain it for further use. It is a difficult situation to understand because the only time and place Burns Ranches used the Q brand thereafter was on their purebred hereford cow herd, between the years of 1930 and 1950, at the Bow Valley Ranch near the south edge of Calgary. Pat Burns acquired the four thousand acre Bow Valley ranch from William Roper Hull during 1902, where the attractive ranch buildings were close to where Fish Creek empties into the Bow River east of Midnapore. Mr. Hull used the beautiful ranch site mostly for the purpose of entertaining Calgary's most distinguished visitors for many years. Burns was certainly not the showman that Hull was, but definitely had more interest in making the ranch pay some returns. He continued to purchase adjacent ranch properties until the Bow Valley Ranch consisted of over nine thousand acres. This prize grass and farm land was in one parcel which laid between the Bow River and the McLeod Trail and extended for nine miles more or less in a north-south dimension along the east side of today's McLeod Trail. The pure-bred cowherd that was marked with the big Q iron at the Bow Valley Ranch was sold by auction during November of 1950.

Meanwhile, during the years preceding the Second World War there was a rancher named Frank Gallup, who operated a horse ranch along the Red Deer River south of Bindloss, along with his two sons Stan and Wallace. Stan, the oldest, left the ranch during 1928 and became involved in other types of employment, which took him to Longview during late 1937 to manage a grocery store in the early years of the South Turner Valley oilfields.

Due to the drought, wind, and grasshoppers during 1939, Frank and Wallace were forced to sell the ranch at Bindloss and were headed out to British Columbia. On their journey west they stopped over in Longview to see Stan and it was at this time the three family members decided to pool their money and purchase the store that Stan was managing. For the next twenty-nine years Gallup and Sons were the proprietors of a successful grocery and dry goods business that was situated in Longview where the village motel is now located. The store prospered as the time went by, but within ten years the Gallup's wanted to get back into the ranching business.

In 1950 they purchased the section of land at Longview that takes in the big hill, which had been previously owned by Tom Merriman, who had operated a feedlot at High River. Within a few years the Gallup's bought a small herd of Hereford-Shorthorn cross cows from an old time cowman who lived south of the river west of Longview; but they also wanted a good cow brand. Burns Ranches had disposed of most of their ranch property by this time and had a dozen or more good brands that were still registered but not active. The Gallups contacted Tom Farrell of Burns Ranches who offered them their choice of all the brands Burns no longer required. From those available, Gallups selected the old Q brand which was transferred to Gallup and Sons on February 25th 1952. Gallup and Sons sold their retail business in January 1968 and shortly after the store was destroyed by fire and never rebuilt.

The Gallup family has managed a successful ranching operation at Longview for more than forty years and their land base has been expanded since that initial purchase. All members of the original Frank Gallup family have since passed away, but the Gallup name in cattle ranching has been kept alive by a brother partnership of Larry, Neil, and Gaile, who are sons from Stan Gallup's first marriage. The Gallup Brothers obtained possession of the treasured old Q brand on May 29th 1992.

Old cattle brands like the Q are the heritage of cattle ranching in Alberta. Although this brand has been owned by different people and used in other parts of Alberta over the years, it has now run a full cycle with time. The cattle currently seen grazing the prairie wool grass on the big hill near Longview are carrying the same brand and grazing some of the same range that John Quirk's cattle did, more than a hundred years ago.

# The 76 Brand

76 Left Ribs and Left Hip

There are several hundred cattle brands that have remained active in Alberta's brand system since they were first registered prior to 1900. Very few of them have remained registered to descendants of the families or companies who initially registered these brands. Nevertheless, these early brands have remained the foundation of Alberta's ranching heritage. The majority of the people who currently own a brand that was registered prior to 1900 have obtained it through either a legal transfer, with the purchase of certain ranch property; or in some cases, have acquired the brand with a cattle purchase that was identified with a brand of this vintage. The 76 Brand that is registered for cattle on the left ribs and hip fits these categories; and it has created some interesting ranch history during the past century.

The 76 Brand was first registered in the Southern Alberta area of the North West Territories to the Powder River Cattle Company during November 1886. This company was operating in the state of Wyoming and in order to relieve their overstocked range, they moved approximately one fifth of their cattle, which consisted of about 10 000 head, to Canada. They had acquired a grazing lease of seven townships along Mosquito Creek, west of Nanton and the big drive got underway in the spring of 1886.

In order to move a herd of this size, it was common practice to split the herd into bunches of about 2500 head each. Starting out a few days apart, the first three herds were made up of three-year-old heifers and dry cows. Any calves that were born along the way were killed at birth or given away. Experience had taught the old time cowmen that the detrimental effect that young calves had on the progress of a long drive, greatly outweighed their value. The fourth herd were all steers and were allowed to travel at a somewhat slower pace, allowing them to be in market condition at their destination. Each herd was accompanied by its own wagon, trail boss, and horse cavvy, along with a proper complement of cowhands. Upon their arrival at Mosquito Creek, two of the wagons with their respective riders returned directly to the home ranch in Johnson County, Wyoming. Most of the other men that came up the trail with the herd found jobs with other ranches that were already established.

Joe Trollinger who had been an old whiskey trader, was operating a stopping house where the trail from Calgary to Fort Macleod crossed Mosquito Creek. The Powder River outfit purchased Joe's squatter's rights and it was here they proceeded to construct living quarters, a stable, and other buildings to establish a ranch headquarters at that location. Their losses during the hard winter of 1886/87 were much less than those suffered by other Southern Alberta ranches. The cowmen of a later era attributed this to the fact that the Powder River cattle was an "all dry" herd, which perhaps is the reason why weaning calves in the fall became a general practice on ranches after that time.

All was going well with the Canadian operation but it was a different story back on the ranch in Johnson County. Seventy percent of their cattle in Wyoming had perished during the winter of 1886/87, and the directors of the parent company in London, England who had been financing the Powder River Company experienced financial problems and went into liquidation. By 1889, their 7000 head of Canadian cattle were purchased by the Canadian Agricultural Coal and Colonization Company. Along with the Powder River cattle, came the 76 brand; and all the ranches owned by the new company thereafter were referred to as "The 76."

The Canadian Agricultural Coal and Colonization Company was founded by a man named Sir John Lester Kaye, who struck the ranching country like a March snow storm – spectacular for a time without any great lasting effects. He was described also as a dynamic and rather tempestuous little Englishman who possessed the optimism of a big promoter with the courage of a mother bear. Acting on behalf of this organization, he secured ten parcels of land, with each parcel consisting of 10 000 acres. They ranged from different points along the main line of the Canadian Pacific Railway, which extended from Langdon on the west, to as far east as Regina. The plan was to raise livestock, grow grain and promote immigration. European people wishing to farm in the North West Territories could work for Mr. Kaye for several years and then settle on a half section land; with twenty acres under cultivation, buildings provided, and a team of horses with other livestock. The scheme looked attractive, but the fact that most of the land was only suitable for grazing and too uncertain for growing grain; the idea failed.

At the same time that John Kaye was attempting to attract immigrants to farm portions of his large land base, he also was conducting a large ranching enterprise of his own. The headquarters for his ranching operation was at Crane Lake Saskatchewan; and if determination could have achieved success, the 76 outfit would have prospered. Due to one mistake after another, which were costly to the directors and shareholders, along with a couple of severe winters with heavy cattle losses, John Kaye finally admitted failure and retired.

Kaye's ranch foreman at Crane Lake was D.H. Andrews, a cowhand that came up the trail with the Powder River herd and continued working for John Kaye after the cattle were purchased. After John Kaye retired, Andrews went to England in 1895 and found capital to promote a new company known as the Canadian Land and Ranch Company, who took over the ranch holdings of the previous company. The new company took possession of the 76 brand and succeeded until Andrews died during 1906. This left the 76 outfit struggling until the ranch property and famous 76 brand were bought by the livestock firm of Gordon, Ironside and Fares.

Gordon, Ironside and Fares were basically a cattle-buying company who owned several packinghouses in Manitoba and dominated the live cattle export business until it collapsed in 1913. They became involved in the ranching business on a large scale for about fifteen years after the turn of the century; when their firm either leased or purchased large parcels of land in both Alberta and Saskatchewan. They were silent partners with George Lane in ownership of the famous Bar U Ranch from 1902 until 1920, at which time their financial situation forced them to terminate business and their 76 outfit at Crane Lake was taken over by the bank.

There are conflicting stories as to whether the 76 property was bought from the bank by Rod Macleay or whether it was purchased by Pat Burns. The truth of the matter was that the bank asked Burns if he was interested in buying the 76 outfit, but Burns felt the eight township ranch was too large. Burns told the bank that he would locate someone to manage it for them,. This was Rod Macleay, who did such a great job of managing the 76 ranch for the next several years, that Burns became interested in the profit it was making and bought the ranch in 1928. Burns also got possession of the 76 brand at the same time the ranch was purchased.

The number of years that Burns owned the 76 outfit in Saskatchewan has not been established, nor is it known when Burns disposed of it. The 76 brand along with a number of other good brands that Burns had acquired with the purchase of ranch property, were kept registered for many years without being active and were retained as a special file in the Calgary office of Burns Ranches. Eddie Bowlen, who was a nephew of J.J. Bowlen, had a need for a good cattle brand and approached Tom Farrell of Burns Ranches to obtain one of their dormant brands. Bowlen had the choice of a dozen good brands and selected the 76 which was still registered for both the left ribs and hip. Transfer of the brand to Eddie Bowlen happened during March 1952.

Eddie Bowlen was born in Boston Massachusetts, and came with his parents during 1910, to the Meadowbank community located southwest of High River. He became a well known horseman, schooling and training polo ponies and show jumpers, which he marketed in the U.S.A. during the years between the First and Second World Wars. When the United States went to war after Pearl Harbour in 1941, the horse business fell apart. Eddie then purchased a livestock cartage business in Calgary and was kept busy transporting livestock throughout Southern Alberta for the following thirty odd years.

In 1927 he married the youngest daughter of D.P. MacDonald who owned the Mount Royal Ranch northwest of Cochrane, and as a result, this required him to become somewhat involved with the operation of the ranch after D.P. MacDonald's death in 1944. This ranch had an opportunity to increase their grazing capacity after the hoof and mouth disease in 1952, by leasing four sections of the Rabbit Lake Indian Reserve that joined the Mount Royal Ranch to the north. This allowed Eddie Bowlen to purchase feeder steers at the Calgary Stockyards each spring and graze them along with the steers owned by the ranch on the newly acquired lease. The 76 brand was used to identify the Bowlen steers that ran on the Mount Royal Ranch for the following decade.

D.P. MacDonald's oldest daughter remained on the ranch after her father died and managed the ranch until she retired from ranching in 1966. Jaye Bowlen, Eddie's only son purchased her share of the ranch and has operated the old Mount Royal Ranch property since that time. He also became owner of two old brands that the ranch had owned and used since well before 1900. Eddie Bowlen has been deceased since July 1983 and the 76 brand for both positions was transferred to Jaye Bowlen during August 1984.

The 76 along with some other historic ranch brands has traveled through more than a century of time. This brand has marked the hide of countless numbers of good ranch cattle over the years and has survived the prosperous and difficult periods of the cow business. It has always received proper respect of the cattle industry and if the urban society allows the foothills region of Alberta to remain cow country, the old brand may very well be around for another century.

# Courtney and Ware

DC Left Ribs and Left Hip

Cattle brand DC for the left ribs was first registered on June 24th, 1886 to Dan Courtney whose address was High River, in the North West Territories. There is very little evidence as to how and when Courtney first arrived in Southern Alberta, but he no doubt drifted north with a trail herd that was looking for new grass. He disappeared again as quickly as he came and must have left again in the dark of the night on a borrowed horse! Although his stay was short, he remained in Alberta's cow country long enough to put together a small herd of cows and obtain a legal brand to mark them with.

The evidence on file dated December 27th 1887, outlines an agreement between Courtney and John Ware whereby Courtney agreed to sell all his cattle and brand to John Ware for $2700. (see below) The agreement states that Ware was to take possession of the cattle as they were found on the open range and was to be paid for with enough three year old steers at $40 per head. The steers were to be delivered to Courtney in one bunch at the fall roundup of 1888 and John Ware became owner of the DC brand soon after the sale agreement had been honored.

John Ware was a black cowhand who came into the country the same way Courtney did, but stayed around a good deal longer. Ware established a ranch in the Millarville district during the late 1880s. The foothills country became too populated for him, so he moved everything he owned out into the Red Deer River country, north of Duchess soon after the turn of the century.

A few years prior to John Ware relocating his ranch out along the Red Deer River, the Territorial Government proclaimed the Second Brand Ordinance in 1898. Everyone who had been using a brand or mark of any kind had to register them again with the Recording Office in Regina. In the process of having the DC brand registered again, John Ware transferred the brand to his oldest daughter, Nettie, whose later address was Bantry, a rural post office and railroad station, south east of Brooks. When the brand had to be renewed four years later, Nettie Ware had ownership of the brand transferred to include the other five children of the Ware family.

John Ware was killed on his Red Deer ranch during 1905 and the Royal Trust Company in Calgary was appointed as executors of the estate which included guardianship of the Ware children. The Trust Company had the brand transferred during March 1907 to a partnership of Douglas Riddle and Rod and Alexander Macleay. This partnership later purchased the Ware ranch property and all the cattle that carried the DC brand. Riddle and Macleay owned the brand for only eight years when it was transferred to Sam Howe who was foreman on the ranch.

There can be many stories told about the notorious Sam Howe, who is somewhat of a legend with the ranching fraternity, and was possibly one of the best practical cowmen that ever reached the Territories. One fall roundup he was in charge of the Bar U wagon when several other roundup outfits were to meet and camp overnight on the Bow River near Bassano. Sam had a group of riders on a big circle that particular day and by the time they caught up with the wagons late in the afternoon, they had already made camp. The river was freezing ice during the night, and Sam knew if they did not get across before dark, it would be late the next morning before they could get into the water. Sam was angry that the wagons had not crossed while the river was free of ice, and instructed his roundup cook, Frenchy to hook up again, because the Bar U wagon was camping on the other side for an early start the next morning.

Frenchy was most unhappy with the idea of having to move again that day because he was all set up to cook supper, and the wagon horses had been turned loose with the cavvy. It was nearly dark by time the horses were caught and harnessed and Frenchy got everything together to drive off into the cold water. Sam was sitting on his horse all the while and was close along side the wagon when Frenchy pushed his lead team into the fast moving river. Frenchy, being upset with the whole affair and especially with the idea of having to camp that night without the fellowship of the other roundup crews, hollered to Sam in his broken English tongue, "If anything happens this time to me Sam, I'm going to jump." At this point Sam's patience and understanding of human nature completely disappeared, and he hollered back to Frenchy, above the roar of the water, "You SOB, if you jump now I'll make sure you drown." Whatever may have happened that night at the Bar U wagon is not recorded, but Frenchy was up long before daylight the next morning cooking breakfast.

Rod Macleay allowed Sam to build up a herd of cows for himself because the range was big and the grass was free. Sam took advantage of the opportunity and by 1928 he owned 600 head of cattle that carried the DC brand. About that time Sam's financial situation changed and the bank placed a seizure on all the cattle with this brand; and Sam was again out of the cow business. Sam, having the ability to talk a gopher out of its burrow, persuaded the banker to leave the cows on the ranch for him to take care of. Sam wanted to stay in the cow business for himself so he purchased a small ranch north of Duchess. It was also more than an incident that he purchased some cows that were branded P reversed D running bar registered on the same position as the DC brand. Those who understand the application of brands and realize that with some proper brand knowledge certain brand characters can be altered; should not be surprised that Sam again ended up owning the six hundred DC cows.

About the same time the DC brand was first registered, Sam Howe was ranching on his homestead which was situated on the north side of Sheep Creek, about eight miles upstream from Turner Valley. After Sam gave up his homestead, the land became part of the ranch started by John Lineham and later purchased by Pat Burns during 1918. Burns operated the ranch for twenty-five years, with my father, Guy Pallister as manager for Burns; and it was here the Pallister family was raised. Burns sold it in 1943 to Carl Ohlson, a Turner Valley businessman. It appeared strange that Ohlson stocked his new ranch the same year with the last herd of cows and calves that was owned by Sam Howe. These cattle were shipped by railroad from Duchess to Okotoks, and then trailed west, to be turned loose in the exact same field where Sam had raised his first cattle more than fifty years earlier.

When Sam Howe went out of the cow business the DC brand was transferred to a native cowboy named Pat Ward who had worked for Sam for many years. The brand eventually became the property of James McDonal who was Sam's stepson, now living in Drumheller. McDonal had the brand transferred during 1973 to his grandson, Melvin Sandum of Hussar, who has maintained the old brand in good standing since that time.

Locating history on old cattle brands exposes some actions that perhaps those people will account for in eternity. Some brands have remained in existence from generation to generation, and if brands could talk, the information revealed might not be suitable for publication.

# Bar U Ranch History

Ū Left Ribs and Left Hip

In November 1968, the Historic Sites and Monuments Board of the Canadian government recognized the national historical significance of the cattle industry. The board then made recommendations that Parks Canada make an effort to acquire a ranch site to commemorate the ranching industry. An attempt to locate a suitable site within the next decade was not successful.

In the middle 1970s Parks Canada established a criteria on which ranches would be evaluated for this purpose. Issues to be considered in the criteria were historical qualities, historical remains, environment, accessibility to the site, and developmental potential.

In 1989 Parks Canada undertook a survey of thirteen possible ranch sites and identified three that were considered suitable. Preference of the three was given to the Bar U site because the selection committee felt it was best suited for interpreting the ranching industry. Negotiations to purchase the Bar U Ranch for a historical ranch were successful and the headquarters location consisting of two hundred and sixty seven acres was acquired on December 31, 1991.

The choice of the Bar U Ranch as a site to tell the story of ranching was based on several considerations. The Bar U was one of the first and largest of the early ranches in the Canadian west. It was a ranch that operated on the principal of private enterprise and enjoyed a success at a time when many other ranches failed. Possibly the most interesting and important features of this ranch are the people who were associated with it, along with the fact that its history has displayed a great story of ranching for more than a century.

When members of the North West Mounted Police began returning east after their enlistment period, they took with them the news of great ranching opportunities in the Canadian Northwest. This created a sudden burst of financial activity amongst the Montreal business community. About this time, Sir John A. Macdonald's Conservative government was introducing a series of primary incentives for large scale ranching on the Canadian frontier. Regulations with respect to grazing land in the west had been under discussion during the very early 1880s and were finally introduced with an Order-In-Council dated December 23, 1881.

These regulations allowed an individual or company to lease up to one hundred thousand acres of grazing land for a period not to exceed twenty-one years. The rental fee was set at one cent per acre, per year, or ten dollars for every thousand acres annually. The response to this policy was immediate and Central Canadian businessmen joined forces order to obtain some large leases.

William Winder, one of the original North-West Mounted Police who came west in 1873, retired from the police in 1881 and had returned to Quebec. His enthusiasm in the fledgling cattle industry in Southern Alberta convinced his father-in law, Charles Stimson, that they should own a ranch in Western Canada. Since the Stimsons were unable to finance such a venture on their own, they put the proposition to Sir Hugh Allan and Andrew Allan, the wealthiest men in Canada, who owned Allan Steamship Lines.

When the plans were laid before the two brothers in 1881, they suggested that Fred Stimson travel west to scout and select a suitable location. Stimson liked what he saw in the virgin grassland along the foothills west of High River, and wasted no time in taking the information back home. The Allan's moved promptly on Stimson's suggestion and formed the North West Cattle Company, which received its letter of patent during March 1882.

Early spring of 1882 found Stimson on the Highwood River, locating a new ranch site and establishing a centre of operations. He also made arrangements with Tom Lynch to meet in Helena, Montana later that spring to purchase cattle for the new ranch. They were pleased to find cattle in Idaho that could be purchased for nineteen dollars a head; six dollars cheaper than in Montana. They bought three thousand head of cattle and seventy-five head of saddle horses and pointed them north. The leaves of the big cottonwoods along the mountain streams had already turned a golden yellow by time the big herd splashed into the water along the Highwood River, during late September of that year.

By 1884 the North West Cattle Company needed a new ranch foreman so Stimson wrote to the Montana Stock Growers for recommendations for a good man to ramrod their range operation. The Association quickly suggested George Lane, who accepted the offer and headed north into Canada. Stimson met him at Fort Macleod and they joined the general roundup which was then in progress.

One of the first changes Lane made in the operation of the ranch was to do away with their original brand, the Double Circle    This brand proved to be unsatisfactory, due to it's tendency to blotch; so instead, he chose the Bar

U brand. From that time on, the North West Cattle Company became known as the Bar U, one of the most famous brands in the cattle country.

The Bar U brand was applied for in October 1881 and first registered on January 11, 1882 to Fred Stimson for the left hip position on cattle and left shoulder on horses. The brand remained registered in Stimson's name until the new Brand Ordinance of 1898, when brand owners had to re-registered their brands. During June of that same year the Bar U was transferred to the North West Cattle Company and Stimson admitted having the brand registered in his own name was a big mistake.

In January 1902 the directors of the North West Cattle Company sold the company's property, cattle and other assets to a company organized by George Lane. When Lane heard the outfit might be for sale he traveled to Montreal to negotiate a deal. He was given three days to find money for the purchase; and to meet the deadline he interested the meat packing company of Gordon, Ironside and Fares to become partners. The years after the First World War were tough financially for the cattlemen. The cattle market collapsed and Lane's partners in the Bar U ran into financial difficulties to the extent that it was feared that the bank that was financing the meat packing company would also take over the Bar U Ranch. This moved Lane to buy out his partners during 1920, leaving him in sole possession of the ranch property. This purchase left Lane with a heavy debt load but at least he continued to own the Bar U. Herb Miller, Lane's foreman at the YT Ranch, advised him to let the bank take over the ranch. Miller knew the bank would not know what to do with it, and would be willing to dispose of it under suitable terms. Lane did not follow Miller's advice, dismissing the risk of losing the ranch.

When Lane became involved with the administration of the ranch in 1902 he began using the brand on the left ribs in conjunction with the left hip position. He did not bother to register the second position nor did he advise anyone that the ranch was branding all the cattle on both locations. In 1914, the brand recording office at Medicine Hat registered the left rib position to the Hawkeye Farming Company, whose range was north of the Bow River between Gleichen and Hussar.

In the spring of 1915, some Bar U cowhands were riding that part of the country and located some freshly branded cattle with the Bar U on the left ribs. They quickly got the information back to Bar U headquarters and Lane immediately took action. He contacted the Recorder of Brands to advise him of the stupid incident that had taken place, by allowing his Bar U brand to be allotted to another outfit on the same range. Lane threatened to sue the government, and that action got the attention of the Minister of Agriculture, who persuaded the Hawkeye Farming Company to cancel the registration. George

Lane died in September of 1925 and his company finally registered the Bar U for the left ribs in February 1927.

After Lane's death, Pat Burns purchased the Bar U Ranch from the Lane estate during November 1927, and both brand positions were transferred to Burns Ranches. Branding cattle on the left hip was discontinued in 1932 and all their cattle thereafter were identified on the left ribs only. They operated the old ranch successfully until 1950 under the direct management of the late Raymond Clifford. This was the end of a great era for the world famous Bar U Ranch and there is little doubt this brand was placed on more cattle in Canada than any other brand up to that time.

The Bar U Ranch was sold to J. Allen Baker, who took over operation in April 1951. Both brand positions were transferred to Mr. Baker who has since acquired also the left shoulder position. He purchased the majority of the good grazing land along the hills and Roy Henderson got the east portion of the ranch where all the farming had been done. Other ranchers in the area purchased smaller parcels of the ranch, most of which were adjacent to the north fork of the Highwood River. The Wambeke brothers of Longview owned the ranch for a short while, after which it was purchased by the Melvin Nelson family of High River.

The Bar U story did continue after it was sold to Allen Baker in 1950. In some ways the ranch functions initiated some leadership roles that were not demonstrated through the earlier years of operation. It was obvious though that the portions of the ranch sold to neighboring ranchers, along with the division of the largest share between Baker and Roy Henderson, destroyed the glamour of the spread that had been evident since the 1890s. The old ranch took on a different appearance, showing the evolution of modern day ranching.

The Bar U Historical Ranch site is located along Highway 22, ten miles south of Longview, Alberta. This site has the potential to attract a wide range of local, regional and out of province tourists. However, to ensure this market, the Bar U site will have to reflect a high quality standard and provide a variety of attractions. With proper planning and working together with small businesses who cater to tourism, government personnel, and the local population, the Bar U Ranch will make an interesting and unique site to tell the story of early ranching in Canada. Parks Canada has repaired and stabilized some of the original ranch buildings. A Visitor Orientation centre continues to welcome guests to this National Historic Site which opened to the public on July 1, 1995, with the complete site available to the public in 1997.

Meanwhile, the old ranch remains situated in the exact location where some of the buildings were erected over a century ago. The big cottonwoods along the creek that runs through the ranch, have seen a multitude of men come and go. Amongst these were some of the most experienced cowmen that the cattle business has known. The ranch site has been visited by people from all walks of life including royalty, native people and ordinary trail hands looking for a hand-out. This historical property, where cattle once fed on the prairie wool grass, will become a centre where ordinary people will come to visit and learn about Alberta's ranching heritage. Nevertheless, even in the years to come, this old ranch will always be referred to as "The Bar U."

# The Mighty Ranch Bar U

There have been many stories produced by different authors about the historic Bar U Ranch since it was first started in 1882. The following poem tells a brief history of how the ranch became established and progressed for the first forty five years of operation, until Pat Burns purchased the outfit in 1927. Burns Ranches, Allen Baker, Wambeke Brothers and the Nelson Family each owned and operated the old ranch until the ranch headquarters were purchased by Canadian Heritage of the Federal Government during 1991.

There was a mighty piece of grassland between the Belly and the Bow,
Along the hills and watershed from where these two rivers flowed.
A hundred years and more have passed since this grassland was found,
When the Missionaries and Mounted Police came to protect this virgin ground.

The buffalo had disappeared and their trails were growing dim.
The mighty Indian nations of years gone by, had agreed to be fenced in.
The scarlet coats of the Mounted Police were sent west in '74,
And the iron rails of the CPR, were being laid from shore to shore.

Winder of the North West Mounted Police, went east to tell the news
Of ranching opportunities in the west, and how the native grass would cure.
The Allan Steamship Company in Montreal agreed to finance a chance,
Who sent Fred Stimson to the Canadian west to start a cattle ranch.

The spring of 1882 found Stimson in Idaho,
Along with Lynch they bought 3000 head of cows to go.
Trail boss Lynch, along with Ware, headed north across the line,
And reached the Highwood river just before the snow, in time.

Stimson was a character who they called the Great "I Am",
Who was friendly with the natives because of his bread and jam.
When Lane and partners bought the ranch; Lane came to run the show,
Which made the cowboy's laugh and sing, when old Stimson had to go.

To hear the rest, as the years progressed, the Bar U had world wide fame,
When ranching economics prompted George Lane to make a change.
Along with ten thousand cattle that were marked with the Bar U brand,
Nearly a thousand Percheron horses also grazed the pasture land.

Lane's partners had financial problems during World War One,
Because of retail butcher sales from when the partnership begun.
To save the ranch from being lost, through a debt of a major size;
Lane found some cash and kept the ranch, which was no surprise.

Lane's courageous foresight of ranching, finally got some recognition,
But because of age and failing health, he was not in good condition.
In September of '25, paper headlines announced, George Lane's death,
And with a large funeral in High River, his tired body was laid to rest.

The bank that supported Lane, came to claim the Mighty Ranch Bar U,
Because of the borrowed money; and the payments that were too few.
They sent for Frank McLaughlin to manage their large cattle ranch,
And waited for a buyer who was willing to gamble with a chance.

Now, months went by, and on the sly, Pat Burns appeared on the scene,
With wealth already in cattle ranches, the Bar U had been his dream.
What transpired between the bank and him; Burns bargained on the price,
And bought the ranch for Lane's debt to the bank, which was a sacrifice.

What happened from then on, Burn's took all the glory,
And what has happened at the Bar U since, has been told in other stories!

# History of the OH Ranch

## OH Left Ribs

The people who venture into the valley that cradles the Highwood River west of Longview, who remained there for any length of time, probably heard stories about early settlers who worked in the valley during the past hundred and twenty years. Among those who hunted for adventure up the valley, were lumber and log men, gold miners, artists, hay haulers, trappers, oilmen, some ordinary cowhands, and some good cowmen. The majority stayed for only a short while and those who left would have had a different opinion of exactly what did happen in those days gone by. Missing from the stories that have echoed off the hills that followed the river upstream is the history of the OH brand and some things about the old ranch this brand represented.

The brand was first registered for cattle on the left ribs to two men named Smith and French during July 1881, and has since been well recognized for good cattle that have carried this brand for more than a century. The brand was the twenty fifth brand to be registered in the Territories (presently Alberta and Saskatchewan) and it is somewhat evident why the OH characters were selected; being Smith's initials. O.H. Smith and Lafayette French formed a partnership in 1878 and established a business of trading food supplies with the native people of the Blackfoot Reservation near Gleichen. The cost of their merchandise became so extremely high, that the federal government purchased their establishment on the reserve and requested that they move elsewhere. The partnership moved onto the Highwood River, purchased some cattle, and during 1881 squatted in the exact location where the OH Ranch headquarters are currently situated

The late Fred Ings said he purchased the ranch along with the brand from O.H. Smith during the summer of 1883. Another brother, Walter from Prince Edward Island, became a partner in the ranch and the brand was transferred to the Ings brothers in May 1884. The two brothers operated the ranch until the late 1890s when Fred decided to leave the partnership, and the brand was again transferred to Walter Ings during September of 1900. In 1908 Walter Ings hired a man named Johnny Brown to assist him in managing the ranch. He remained there for 32 years as ranch foreman for both Ings and Pat Burns. Ings sold the ranch to Pat Burns during 1918 and the brand was transferred to Burns in August of that year. Burns owned the ranch and brand for only a short while, until it was sold again in the same year to Mayer and Lage, a steamship company out of New York City.

This company had acquired a contract with the Belgian government to supply beef to all of Western Europe, after the First World War. In order to do so they had to own ranch property in Canada, so they became incorporated as a farming and ranching company with an office in Calgary in order to become involved with the ranching industry of that era. How much of the 20 000 acre OH ranch was actually purchased from Burns was never made public, but they did own the brand for twenty years. Burns continued to manage the ranch and paid all the operating costs under the efficient supervision of Johnny Brown. When the New York company first became involved, they appointed Jack Dillion as its representative; who lived in Calgary and visited the ranch on necessary occasions.

Dillion was an Irishman who came to the United States with his parents at an early age. He became involved with the selection of artillery and cavalry horses in Montana at the beginning of the First World War. Mayer and Lage became aware of Dillion's ability when he was placed in charge of a trainload of horses being shipped to France, to which the steamship company had the contract to transport the army horses across the ocean.

Jack Dillion was only involved with the activity at the OH Ranch for about five years, and later he became known in Alberta as arena director for the Calgary Exhibition and Stampede Company.

The brand was transferred back to P. Burns Holdings during March 1938 and Brown retired as ranch foreman in the spring of 1940. Sandy Neish, who had been employed on the ranch for several years, married Brown's youngest daughter and became ranch foreman after Brown's retirement. Neish ran the ranch during the war years of the 1940s, and was replaced during 1946 by Scotty Rowland who had been on the Findlay ranch located near High River; a property which Burns had recently sold. Rowland was an old Burns employee who had chauffeured Pat Burns prior to his death in 1937 and then drove truck for the company until he was put in charge of the Findlay ranch in 1942.

P. Burns Holdings sold their OH Ranch in the fall of 1950 to Kink Roenisch and Bill Arden, both successful Calgary businessmen, who in turn hired Bert Sheppard as their ranch manager. The brand was transferred to C.W. Roenisch and A.D. Kingsford who were kinfolk of the ranch owners. Sheppard was the son of Henry Sheppard, and was certainly qualified to make major improvements to the old ranch for a new ranching era. The new partnership bought only the property west of Fireguard Coulee, leaving the east part of the ranch available for farmers in the Longview and High River areas.

The old ranch took on a new appearance in regard to fence, fence lines, water holes and grazing areas, including a different quality of Hereford cattle.

Ownership of the ranch changed again when members of the Kingsford family, along with Bert Sheppard purchased the property and the brand was transferred to OH Ranch Ltd. during September 1962. Sheppard retired as active manager in 1963, at which time Warren Zimmerman, a ranch employee, became responsible for the day to day ranch operations. The success of the ranch continued under the supervision of Warren Zimmerman who came to the Highwood country during 1945 and learned the cow business from the bottom up. After being with the ranch for 34 years, he decided he had chased cows long enough so he retired from ranch life on November 30, 1984. Kelly Kingsford, a daughter of the major shareholder of the ranch had worked there under Warren, and by the time he retired Kelly was familiar enough with the ranching business to be placed in charge of the daily ranch functions. She remained in that position until the two shareholders decided to sell the ranch property in 1986.

When the ranch owners decided to sell the outfit, the Canadian government became very interested in purchasing the property as a training base for the Canadian Armed Forces. The matter received immediate attention from the area ranchers, who had maintained their land for ranching purposes. They stopped the sale of the ranch from becoming a training ground for army personnel, and a National environmental dumping ground for defense vehicles. This concern received much publicity from the news and television media and became an issue that was debated in detail throughout the countryside.

D.K. (Doc) Seaman, a Calgary oilman, came to the rescue of the area ranchers and purchased the old ranch, including the brand, during November 1987. Bud Maynard, an experienced livestock man from Cluny was appointed as ranch manager in 1988, also had the brand registered for the other two left positions. The breed of cattle raised on the ranch changed somewhat with the new ownership and Maynard recognized the grassland as a precious resource; again managing it accordingly, with great respect of neighboring ranchers.

The OH Ranch, like many others, has changed with the progress of time and whether those changes are for better or worse each will have to determine for themselves. Faded forever is the promptness that once graced the dinner table at the OH Ranch; which identifies only one change that has occurred on some old time ranches. The cowhands were always fed at the old original ranch house that was situated on the west side of the creek. There are still folks around that can recall the big oak table that sat so stately in the large dining room, always prepared with white linen table cloths, fine silverware and butter plates, to say the least. There was dignity involved during each meal, which had glamour enough for it to appear as a social occasion. The big oak table has now been replaced with a round ranch table where the cowhands quickly slip in and out of the cookhouse to satisfy their appetites.

Regardless of the changes that have taken place, the old ranch has enjoyed some great years of operation and will no doubt continue to have many rewarding years ahead. The ranch has survived the economic disasters, the hard winters, the dry summers, the empty water holes, and the everlasting threat of grass fires that could destroy their winter range. The romance of ranching has been evident at that location, no doubt because of where the ranch site has been situated in the Alberta foothills.

This ranch has employed a multitude of men who came and left again, some leaving their mark of distinction and will be remembered for that reason. Thousands have visited the old ranch for one reason or another, but none left without experiencing the hospitality that was evident to all. Many have returned time and time again to stop and enjoy the location. Some will continue to return, to actually explore the feeling of the days gone by, or perhaps to hear a whisper of the stories that have never yet been told.

# Little Bow Cattle Company

ƆC Left Hip

The glamour years of the cattle business in Southern Alberta were the twenty-five years between 1882 and 1907. Most ranch history written about these years of early ranching mention mostly the larger ranching outfits like the old Circle Ranch, the Cochrane Ranch, the Quorn, North West Cattle Company, the Oxley and the Walrond. Although they were all financed by either central Canadian or European capital, the North West Cattle Company was the only one that remained successful under George Lane and Pat Burns and later became known as the Bar U.

Many smaller ranches also became established during this same period and helped to add some adventure and romance to the ranching community. One of these was the Little Bow Cattle Company, known as the "CC" because of the brand. This outfit was always called the "CC" although the first character of the brand was in a reversed position leaving the two C's registered back to back.

The Little Bow Cattle Company was organized during 1884 by a group of five Englishmen. William Cochrane, from a British naval family, preferred horses to life at sea; and was the dominant figure and resident manager. His cousin T.B. Cochrane, Hugh Graham, and brothers Ted and Frank Jenkins, were the other partners. They took out a lease for 40 000 acres on Mosquito Creek and purchased 1500 mixed cattle from Montana during 1885. Their buildings were constructed of lumber instead of the conventional logs, which perhaps was the first indication to the natives that their manager, Billy Cochrane, was sort of an unusual fellow. While the ranch buildings were under construction the partners rented the 'horse ranch' buildings from the North West Cattle Company. After the hard winter of 1886-87 the less interested partners, one by one sold their interest to Billy Cochrane. Hugh Graham was the son of a well-known family in England. He helped trail in the original herd; then left the ranch, returning afterwards only for a few short visits. The Jenkins Brothers moved to the Jumping Pound country west of Calgary. Tom B. Cochrane and his wife moved to the Big Hill district west of Calgary also, but eventually returned to England where he was made Governor of the Isle of Wight.

After Billy became sole owner of the outfit, he began weaning his calves and built a feed camp at the north end of Chain Lakes; where they would put up hay to winter the calves. He would also purchase seven or eight hundred head of feeder cattle every spring from Charlie Knox who was a cattle dealer out of Winnipeg and would increase their annual cattle numbers to around 3000 head.

According to the "CC" wage book, forty-five different men were employed from 1886 to the end of 1895. The two most important positions recognized were always the ranch foreman and the cook. John McEwan was the first ranch foreman and was paid $40 a month. James Doland was the first cook hired for a monthly wage of $30. "Nigger" Green Walters was their round up cook, but stayed on as general ranch help. He took over as ranch cook when Doland left, but did not last long after Mrs. Cochrane arrived. One evening when Green was hurriedly preparing dinner she found him mashing the potatoes by squeezing them with his fists. She thought his methods were fine for the cowhands on the roundup, but was not suitable for her style of dining. Green was replaced by the faithful chinaman, Mow Gung, who remained cook at the "CC" for the following twenty years. The short-term help hired for roundups, or to put up hay were drawn from a pool of men who moved from bunkhouse to bunkhouse around the district.

The cowboys who chose ranch life as employment found it to be some-what of an isolated life-style. The ranch hands needs were relatively simple, due to the fact that food and lodging were supplied. It depended on the size of each ranch outfit, as to how often someone was sent to town to pick up supplies. It was a common practice to ask anyone who was going to town on ranch business to pick up some personal items. These were charged on the ranch's expense account and debited later against the employee's wages. Most often requests were made for only tobacco, papers and matches, but sometime the shopping list became more complex when items of clothing were involved.

Billy Cochrane and his wife Evelyn spent the winter months in England and would return to the ranch each spring. Evelyn made her first trip to the ranch during 1887. She was an expert horsewoman and was thrilled with the sport of running down coyotes with a pack of hounds, which Billy enjoyed also. One afternoon while he was riding he came across a native who was butchering one of his steers. Jumping off his horse he quickly knocked the culprit out and headed for the nearest police detachment to have the thief arrested. When asked how they would be able to identify the criminal, Billy quickly replied "you will know him anywhere, I ear marked him well."

Billy owned the first motorcar in the district and had many breathtaking experiences from speeding along the wagon trails and he startled the horse-powered community into some rearing retaliation!

The Cochrane's had only one son who accompanied them to the ranch along with a staff of nursemaids and governesses. For the three consecutive years period between 1894 and 1896 Mrs. Cochrane had brought over three different governesses from England, only to see all the young women marry Alberta cowboys. She must have been delighted when he become of the age to finish his education in England at the Dartmouth Naval Academy.

During the fall of 1906 George Lane bought the entire "CC" herd, while Cochrane, Nesbitt and Lane purchased the Waldron calves, half of which Cochrane kept. He ran these until they were three years old, and sold them all for beef in 1909.

The same fall the ranch was sold to Jack Drumheller. The property has been the property of the Hutterite Brethern of the Cayley Colony since 1936. Billy Cochrane passed away during March 1929.

# Y Cross Ranch

Y̶ Left Hip

Good cattle brands that were registered in Alberta before it became a Province in 1905 have been recognized by descendants of early ranch families as legacies to be treasured. In most cases they have been traded, transferred and passed down through family generations for well over a century. The "Y Cross" brand was not one of the first to be registered, but has been recognized by cattlemen on the Highwood River and Sullivan Creek range for more than a hundred years.

The brand was first registered on June 6, 1891, to George H. Carle. He had been a barber by trade; but ventured from his home in England and settled in the High River area during the early 1890s. He formed a partnership in the cattle business with Phil Weinard who had started the Riverbend Ranch; which today remains located over the riverbank from the village of Longview. George Carle later bought out Weinard's interest in the partnership, which included the Riverbend Ranch property.

Carle later decided to get out of the cow business and had the brand transferred to H.P. Aubertin and Kenneth Snowden in August of 1906. Snowden obtained possession of the Riverbend Ranch the same year and operated the ranch on the river until the beginning of the First World War. Ken Snowden left the Alberta foothills at the outbreak of the war and served as an officer with the Imperial Army. Before joining the military, he left power of attorney to A.G. Verchire, who was manager of the Bank of Commerce in High River, along with R. Ballachey, a partner in the Ballachey and Burnett law firm.

While Snowden was overseas he returned instruction to the legal firm in High River for them to make arrangements to dispose of his ranch property and all the livestock. Aubertin's whereabouts was not known during late 1915 and there is no evidence available of his destiny. Some old-timers believe he may have joined the military the same as his partner, Snowden, and was killed overseas without any record of his death.

The records reveal that Ballachey and Burnett handled the sale of Snowden's property and livestock, sometime after June 1915. The Sheppard family of High River purchased the Snowden Ranch at Longview during 1917. The Y Cross brand was renewed in Snowden's name during 1915 and allowed to expire at the year end 1919 because Snowden had not returned from overseas after the war. Ballachey and Burnett had retained power of attorney for the Snowden property, so the brand was renewed again and transferred to James Garson Bews during 1920.

Jim Bews arrived in Canada during 1889 from his homeland in Scotland. It took ten years for him to arrive on Sheep Creek west of Okotoks, where he homesteaded and rode for the Quorn Ranch. He had married during this time, but his bride died two years later during childbirth. Shortly after the turn of the century, he moved further south along the hills to an area known as Big Hill, which was a range of hills that ran parallel with the Highwood River, running east of Longview. He married again in 1904 to a widow who had moved to that area from Kansas. From the second marriage the couple were blessed with three children; Marguerite, followed by James Joseph, and Peter John. Prior to his second marriage, Jim Bews had worked for John Sullivan, who drifted north with a trail herd of cattle during the early 1880s and squatted on some property where Sullivan Creek flows into the Highwood River. He established a ranch on this location during 1888 and became the legal owner of the property during April 1900.

While the Sullivan family was living on the ranch during the 1890s their three small children died of diphtheria and were buried across the creek in a little graveyard that has been kept well maintained by the Joe Bews family for all the years since. Highway 541 now runs by the little gravesite, but it is never noticed by anyone in today's busy highway travels; however it is listed in tourism books that suggest day trips from Calgary. John Sullivan also died on the ranch through a riding accident in 1905 and ownership of the property was transferred to his wife Barbara Sullivan during June of the same year. History does not reveal how long Barbara remained on the ranch after John's death, but she did move to High River with a younger family they started after the older children had passed away.

In the meantime, Jim Bews had sold his original homestead west of Okotoks and was proving up on his wife's homestead in the Longview district. Whether he had leased any of the Sullivan land before the First World War is not known, but he did purchase the quarter section in November 1914 where Sullivan had established the ranch site. The remaining Sullivan Ranch was purchased by Jim Bews in April 1919. During the years that followed, Jim Bews, together with his sons Jim and Johnny, operated the farmland east of Longview in conjunction with the grazing land along Sullivan Creek. Grain and feed were grown at Longview and the cattle were trailed back each summer to use grass on the Sullivan Creek range, which continued until Jim Bews passed away in November 1935.

After their father died, Joe and Johnny continued to operate part of the Longview property with the Sullivan Creek Ranch as a joint partnership. The Sullivan Creek land became the property of the Bews Estate in February 1937 and the Y Cross brand was transferred to both brothers as a joint registration. After Joe and Johnny's mother passed away in June 1941, the partnership was dissolved and the Y Cross brand was transferred to Joe Bews during February 1942.

Johnny lived on the quarter section directly north of the Bews Longview homestead and Joe took up residence at the old Sullivan Creek Ranch. By this time, Johnny Bews had married Pearl Watrin, a sister of the famous bronk rider Leo Watrin. This marriage was favored with four children, none of whom remained in the farming or ranching business.

Joe married Josephine Rimmer of Okotoks during 1937 and they had five children; William J., Lenore, Thomas J., Joe Michael and Cecilia. These three sons have remained involved with the Sullivan Creek ranch. Their father Joe Bews died with his boots on at the ranch in August 1982. The Y Cross Ranch Ltd. has continued to function managed by his youngest son, Joe Bews Jr.

If Joe Bews was still around he would not hesitate to tell you the best days in the cow business have been here and gone. The thirty- plus years after the Second World War until the late 1970s were years of enterprise, and the pride of building the Sullivan Creek Ranch into a family operation.

When I visited the original ranch headquarters on the creek where the Bews children were raised, I found it to be a lonely place.

Tidy looking cow ponies can no longer be seen in the 'jingle field' (a field close to buildings where horses were kept that were used daily) or grazing the grassy hillside near the ranch buildings. No more matched work teams breast the feed mangers in the horse barn, and studded harness no longer hang behind the stalls. The tack room that once protected quality riding gear is now empty, and the smell of good saddle leather and sweaty blankets has disappeared. If one was to listen closely, echoes may be heard of happy children as they busily saddled horses in the early morning to trail the dry herd back into the high country or preparing for a holiday pack trip into an isolated mountain area. The old empty corrals where the saddle horses were jingled each morning are now evidence of a ranching era gone forever.

# TL Ranch

L Left Ribs and Left Hip

## Bull Durham Cigarettes and Centre-Fire Saddles

The majority of the ranches now operating along the foothills of Alberta's ranching country were established well before 1900. Although some have changed ownership many times, it is amazing to realize that some of these ranch locations have continually been referred to by the cattle brand which those ranches have used over the years. A striking example of this situation is the TL Ranch that is located downstream from where the three forks of Sullivan Creek join together approximately fifteen miles west of Longview.

This ranch was started during 1887 by Tom Lynch, a legendary name in Alberta's early ranch history. Lynch registered the TL brand in April of the same year with the two characters always being monogrammed, by having the bottom of the L connected to the vertical leg of the T. Laurel and Penny Nelson, who are descendants of a long time ranch and rodeo family from High River, currently own both the ranch and the brand.

Tom Lynch passed away in 1891 and the ranch was purchased by a man named Henry Schmidt during the summer of 1900. For the next thirty odd years the ranch property was owned by least six or seven different proprietors, mostly for speculation. During the dry 1930s, Eddy Thompson and Brent Macleod from High River owned the ranch for a short time, before selling it to Joe and Johnny Bews, Raymond Patterson and Bert Sheppard; all of whom had ranch property along either Flat Creek or Sullivan Creek. The old ranch was divided amongst the new purchasers with Bert Sheppard obtaining the largest portion along with the ranch headquarters.

The living quarters at the first ranch site were burned down during the summer of 1939. New headquarters for the TL Ranch were started within a year's time at a different location a short distance down the creek. A new log house was built along with a workshop made of logs also and a good set of horse corrals. Other corrals and buildings were built as the years progressed. The following decades saw the TL Ranch develop into a beautiful ranch location. It was strictly a bachelor outfit and most of the time any cowhands were difficult to locate, except at mealtime. Those who visited the ranch whether by vehicle or horseback were greeted first by an old 'jingle' mare that had free access to a well fenced paddock which surrounded the ranch buildings. Every visitor was greeted also by a big friendly black and white tomcat that would show up from behind the workshop looking for some attention.

Some strange and peculiar happenings have occurred on these ranches during the years that have passed, and some of these events have become a part of Alberta's ranching heritage. Several years ago while in High River I met my good friend, the late Omar Broughton. He had been carrying with him an old riding spur that showed some rust and had been eaten away to some extent by mineral soil. Omar indicated that he had the spur for several months, hoping to locate someone who could tell him a bit of history as to why it showed up where it did.

Apparently he had visited the TL Ranch several months earlier, when the ranch owners showed him the old spur that their children had found partly visible above the ground north of the old horse corrals at their current ranch site. As soon as I saw the spur and heard where it was found, the scenario quickly came to mind. The incident took place over several weeks and although I was not a member of the cast, I knew all the players involved. The scene unfolded at the TL ranch during late summer of 1947.

During the war years, satisfactory ranch help was difficult to find. About the time the war ended in 1945, a teenage lad named Joe Wallace left his home in Ontario and came west looking for harvest work around High River. He found a haying job near Longview, and later that same fall became employed at the Riverbend Ranch, also owned by Bert Sheppard. Winter came early in October of 1945 and Bert took his new hand and another lad to his Sullivan Creek Ranch to split firewood and cut pine rails for a larger set of corrals. Within the next several years Joe Wallace adapted well and became quite interested in ranch life. Sheppard saw the potential in him becoming a good hand and by 1947 Joe had advanced far enough in Bert's opinion to have the ability to break horses, because the TL Ranch had a half dozen head of young saddle stock that needed to be rode and schooled as cow ponies. Several of them had been started previously and turned out again, which did not make it any easier for someone with no experience.

The third person in this drama was an old time open range cowboy and bronk fighter named Rod Redfern. Rod had drifted out of Montana during 1897 with a herd of horses, heading for George Lane's ranch located on the Little Bow River. He had ridden rough string on the roundup wagons, drove stagecoach, homesteaded in the Peace River country, and hunted for gold in the Yukon when there was nothing better to do. During 1947 he purchased a small house in Longview to live out his remaining days. Bert knew of his ability in breaking horses and invited him to the TL Ranch for several weeks to help and teach Joe Wallace the secrets involved in handling green horses.

The bronks were gathered from their summer range and the stage was set. Rod and Joe worked for several days handling the horses on the ground, because Rod knew this was necessary to properly start young horses. Finally it was time to crawl aboard with Rod as the instructor and Joe, the cowboy; who was prepared to crawl on anything for another lesson in becoming a top ranch hand.

Joe owned and was riding a narrow A-fork saddle on a white river tree, but for riding bronks Sheppard insisted that Joe use the same saddle as he used while breaking horses during some years previous. Sheppard's saddle was somewhat the same style with a narrow fork, high cantle, and a deep seat manufactured by the Visalia Saddle Company out of California. This saddle was equipped with narrow iron stirrups inside heavy tapaderos that Joe had not been used to riding with. One unique feature about both saddles was the way the rigging was built onto the saddle tree. There was equal draught from over the forks as there was from behind the cantle brought together to a large rigging ring slightly ahead of the centre of the tree. These were referred to as 'centre-fire' saddles because they had only one cinch. Often they were preferred by some old time bronk men when riding tough bucking horses, instead of saddles that were equipped with a double rigging with two cinches.

After handling the horses for several hours each day, Rod would suggest they stop for a smoke. They would both sit on the ground, resting against the lower rails of the corral with their legs apart for balance. Rod rolled his own fine cut tobacco, and nearly as much would fall on the ground as he would get into the cigarette. After lighting it he would chuckle away and tell stories of the days when breaking horses was his livelihood, and how them "old boogers" would "chuck their heads with flaring nostrils daring him to come any closer."

Joe always carried a sack of Bull Durham tobacco with rice wheat papers. He would sit along side Rod, trying to get out of the wind to roll a cigarette, because his Durham tobacco was finer than sawdust and would disappear with the slightest breeze. This type of tobacco was purchased in a small cotton sack and kept closed with a pucker string that hung out of his shirt pocket.

Working the horses in the corral progressed very well. Each horse was ridden several times inside the corral before they were taken outside around the 'jingle' pasture. A chestnut gelding, which was one of the older horses was taking more work than the others. He had bucked Joe off several times in the corral before going outside. On one occasion after Joe picked himself up out of the dust he noticed he had one spur missing. The remainder of that day was occupied by them kicking around in the corral dust looking for the missing spur. They had not realized that it might have been pushed underneath the bottom rail, or thrown over the top one from all the action happening that day inside the corral.

Within a few days following, the sorrel gelding bucked Joe off again to the extent of injury to his lower back and broken ribs. Joe had to quit riding, and left the ranch for sometime, in order for his injuries to heal. Rod retreated back to Longview and Sheppard continued riding the young horses until they were turned out for the winter.

Rod Redfern has since gone to a place reserved for tough old bronk men. Joe Wallace left the ranch permanently in the summer of 1948 and moved on to doing better things. His dream of becoming a top ranch hand had been short-lived, realizing his cowboy days were over. He is still around hoping to make a fortune searching for gold, and reminisces with me often about those youthful years of his life spent on Sullivan Creek.

Bert Sheppard sold the TL Ranch to the Nelson family more than forty years ago and lived out his remaining years in dignity until he passed away nearly reaching his 98th birthday.

More than 100 years have disappeared since the original TL buildings were established downstream close to where Blue Ridge drops off into Sullivan Creek. Considerable ranching heritage has been lost with the passing of some cowmen who settled the foothills area of Alberta's ranch country during that early ranching era.

Information reveals that towards the end of the last century some drifters with a disputed reputation occupied the TL buildings after Lynch's death. South and east of the buildings towering high above the creek bed was a lofty summit from where all trails leading to the ranch were plainly visible. This high point of land is still visible from the current ranch location, and has always been referred to as the "Camel's Hump" by the ranchers of the area.

Periodically, many years ago, well-bred saddle ponies would show up in the horse field just before daylight and disappear the same day after sundown, without any riders ever being seen. Smoke from the branding fire could also be seen from the lookout point and if any activity appeared along the trail, a message would be sent down to those in the corral. The cattle that had been gathered would have then been quickly driven up the creek, which no doubt carried freshly applied brands that were not familiar.

Incidents of this kind that happened at the TL Ranch have long been forgotten, and if any illegal activity had taken place, all evidence has completely disappeared with the passing of time.

# The Circle Ranch

O Left Ribs

The great cattle empires that invaded southern Alberta during the 1880s were established soon after the North West Mounted Police arrived on the Oldman River in 1874. The signing of the historic Blackfoot Treaty in 1877 was also another significant event that led up to the access of a new country of virgin grassland. The romance of cattle ranching then became a major way of life as new ranch sites sprang up that were financed mostly by either British or American capital. The area of southern Alberta held a natural environment for raising cattle and ranching syndicates from both central Canada and the United States quickly took advantage of the new rangeland north of the International Boundary.

The Circle Ranch was one outfit that saw an opportunity and moved part of their American herd north into Canada. The original Circle Ranch was located on the Marias River about forty miles north and west of Fort Benton, and was one of the first large ranches in Montana. The ranch was owned by the Conrad brothers, who were major shareholders in the I.G. Baker Company; which held contracts with the Canadian government to supply beef to Indian reservations. The biggest percentage of the meat supplied by the I.G. Baker Company came from the Circle herd.

The Circle cattle that ranged up to the Canadian border and beyond were branded with a big O on the left ribs. During 1885 the Canadian government placed a twenty percent tariff on all American cattle crossing the line into Canada. It then became in the company's best interest to officially move part of their herd north of the border, which was done in 1886. In order to distinguish the American herd from the Canadian herd, the figure 3 brand owned by I.G. Baker had to be placed high on the left shoulder along with the big O on the left ribs. This was a regulation ordered by the government to control the smuggling of livestock back and forth across the border.

A man named Howell Harris was selected to manage the Circle operation in Canada. Harris was born in Missouri and came to Montana in 1868 to go into the business of freighting supplies. He went into the cattle business with the Conrad brothers at Fort Benton before coming to Canada with the Circle Ranch in 1886. Howell Harris picked the site where their ranch headquarters were located at the mouth of the Little Bow River about twenty miles east of

Lethbridge. Their cattle grazed all of the southern Alberta range, which extended north to the Big Bow that flowed east from Calgary.

Through wise management, the Circle Ranch in Canada operated with less expenses and made more money than any other outfit in Alberta. Their cattle were big, wild and thrifty, and even though their calves were never weaned or fed, good Circle beef could have been gathered most any month of the year. All the cowhands were paid off in the fall except one man, who was left to take care of the ranch headquarters. Harris decided that about ten ton of hay was all that was needed; just enough to feed two saddle horses over the winter. Harris wintered in Lethbridge, but would often make trips to the ranch to make sure that his ranch hand was not wasting any hay. When the Circle Ranch quit operating, Harris ranched for himself for some years near Lethbridge, and then returned to Montana, where he passed away during 1921.

The late Chris Christianson, of Duchess, was a Circle man who rode with the Circle roundup wagon during the latter years they were on the Alberta range. Anyone who never had the experience of meeting Chris Christianson missed an opportunity of knowing a fine gentleman, a person who could keep you entertained for hours with stories of his life on the range. I was traveling north from Brooks one day during the middle 1960s and stopped to have lunch with Chris at his ranch. He had just recovered from an eye operation for cataracts and was outside repairing some fence. Inquiring as to how he was, he replied, "I'm better than I've ever been, I can now see right through the hills."

One experience Chris used to like telling about, was one summer when the Circle wagon was camped on the Little Bow east of Nanton. One of the cowhands was late getting back to camp in the evening and the cook refused him supper because all the food had been put away. The cook and the cowhand got to scrapping over the situation and the cowhand pulled out a knife. The remainder of the crew was lazing around camp after supper watching the excitement and when they saw the knife come out, several of them jumped in and stopped the fight. After things had settled down again around camp, the cowhand said, "Well now, if you fellows had not stopped me, I would have enough guts laying around here to build myself a rope corral." Some of the men who found employment with the early cow outfits in Alberta were tough characters.

When Chris Christianson joined the Circle outfit in 1905, a fellow named Bally Buck was ranch foreman and wagon boss. Chris described Bally Buck as a big fine looking man who weighed over two hundred pounds, well educated and a good cowman. The Circle roundup wagon covered hundreds of miles of country every summer, and always trailed from 180 to 200 head of saddle and harness horses with them. Their roundups ran from the month of May, when the grass got green, until the fall when they could no longer drive tent pegs into the frozen ground. The nature of their work was "throwing cattle" back onto their own range and branding calves many times without corrals at locations where firewood was hard to find.

One fall the Circle outfit had finished their fall roundup and were holding a beef herd of about 1600 head of four and five year old steers. They were camped at the old Blackfoot Crossing on the Bow River south of Gleichen, waiting to move the big herd across to load at Stobart, a siding where the C.P.R. had a stockyards and loading chutes. The river was high, and Buck the wagon boss hated to put any of his men into swimming river water, even though the Circle outfit had several good swimming horses. There was a small full-blooded Blackfoot Indian named "Cupi" who was recommended to Buck as being the best river man on the reservation. Buck sent for Cupi to come help cross the herd. Cupi showed up riding a small roan pony without any saddle or bridle; just a rope looped around the roany's lower jaw. As soon as he arrived, Cupi motioned to Buck that he wanted something to eat. After a big feed, he went to a willow patch and cut a long thin willow, leaving a tassel of leaves at one end after trimming off all the branches. He then took off all his clothes except a thin loincloth and signaled to Buck that he was ready.

Cupi smiled and grunted when Buck handed him a five-dollar bill which he stuffed in his hair at the roots of one of his long greasy braids. When the lead steers hit the water, Cupi slid in beside them downstream on his roan pony that swam very low in the water, leaving not much showing except part of Cupi's back. When the steers tried to mill or turn he would slap the water with the willow switch, always about twenty feet from the cattle. When they tried to mill upstream, Cupi would cut through just behind the lead steers and use his willow again. Cupi proved himself a master in swimming water as he swam back and forth through the long string of steers that were being pushed into the water from the south bank until they were all across.

Christianson considered the Little Bow River country the best natural cow country that laid outdoors, before the settlers moved into southern Alberta. He felt it had everything needed for the cow business; lots of good upland grass, some good shelter and water, with chinook winds that really removed the snow, without leaving glare ice like it did on the big Bow River and further north. This was the heart of the Circle range and the heyday for the cow business in that part of the country. After the Circle outfit closed out all their holdings in Alberta, Chris started a little ranch of his own on

Matziwin Creek a short piece north of Duchess and ranched there until his death in 1978.

During the years between 1906 and 1910 settlers moved into the country like snow flakes in the winter and cow ranches with large herds, had to continually move on and on in order to find new range. Like many others of the big ranches, the Circle moved the remnant of their herd onto the Red Deer River north of Brooks. During 1907 they bought the old Lord Beresford horse camp near where One Tree Creek empties into the Red Deer River, about ten miles east of Steveville. There was a small log shack and some corrals on the property, which became the headquarters for the Circle Ranch. They operated here until 1910 when they sold the ranch, cattle and horses to Pat Burns, who also took possession of the Circle brands. Bally Buck stayed on as foreman for Burns for several years, or at least until C.J. Duggan, Burns ranch superintendent saw that old Bally figured the Circle cattle did not need any feed! Mr. Duggan thought otherwise, so Burns arranged to have Bally Buck hired on as a Brand Inspector at Kamloops. Bally Buck spent his last days in Helena, Montana and went to his last roundup over the great divide in 1943.

Pat Burns sold the Circle cattle and brands to Rod Macleay during 1919, but kept the range along the Red Deer, with George Crooks as ranch foreman. Both of the old Circle brands are currently owned by grand children of Rod Macleay.

The Circle Ranch was sometimes called the Big Ring Outfit and when they sold their property along the Red Deer River in 1910, it seemed to be the end of the old time cow outfits. Also, the old style cowman was becoming a thing of the past. Many of them left the country at that time, and others carried on by starting a small ranching business for themselves.

# Cochrane Ranch

## C Left Ribs and Left Hip

Long before Alberta became a province and preceding the time when the white man explored the Canadian west to any extent, the different tribes of native people thrived on the buffalo that ranged the western plains by tens of thousands, for a food supply. It is not definitely known when the first range cattle were brought into the same territory, but after the North-West Mounted Police established themselves at Fort Macleod in 1874 a few settlers were brave enough to bring small herds of cattle and horses to the new land.

It was not until 1881, through an Order-In-Council, that new leasing regulations were put into force, which gave the ranching industry a birth in Western Canada. By these regulations, individuals or companies could lease large parcels of rangeland at the cost of one cent per acre per year. The maximum to one lessee was set at 100 000 acres and it was stipulated that one head of stock to each ten acres, had to be on the range within three years. Almost immediately large ranching companies were formed that were financed by British, American and central Canadian backing.

One of the most famous of these pioneer ranches was the Cochrane Ranching Company, that was headed up by Senator Matthew Cochrane from Compton, Quebec. Their lease of 100 000 acres extended from Morley on the west and as far east as to within five miles of the police post at Fort Calgary, on the north side of the Bow River. The late Colonel James Walker, of the first troop of Mounted Police who came west in 1874, was made their first manager. Their ranch was established at the Big Hill, near where the town of Cochrane is currently located.

The Cochrane Ranch purchased six thousand head of cattle in Montana in the spring of 1881, at a cost of sixteen dollars a head, delivered to the Canadian border. The I.G. Baker Company had the contract to deliver the herd to the ranch west of Calgary, for a further cost of two dollars and fifty cents per head. Frank Strong, foreman for the I.G. Baker Company was in charge of the drive from the boundary north, with a complement of thirty cowboys and three hundred horses. The cattle were divided into two separate herds in order to speed up the travel and make the trip as rapid as possible. The steers and dry heifers made up the first herd, and were pushed along at a merciless rate of eighteen miles each day. The cows and calves followed in the second herd at a pace of about fourteen miles a day. Both herds were kept on the move daily from daylight until dark, and were usually so weary when darkness came, that they preferred to lie down and rest instead of grazing for something to eat.

The worn and weary cattle were jammed across the Bow River near Calgary and turned over to Major Walker and his men who were waiting there. After the counting took place before crossing the river, Walker sent the herd west to become located on their new range. Winter came before the stock could recuperate from the long days on the trail, and hundreds died before they had found any shelter or water. Before green grass appeared on the Bow River range the following spring, the Cochrane herd had diminished to about half of what had arrived the previous fall. The drive did impress upon the early cowmen the power of endurance of the different breeds of cattle that were being used during that era of ranching. It was found that the Black Angus cattle survived the best, the Hereford cattle rated second, and the Shorthorns suffered the most.

The I.G. Baker Company had also contracted to have the cattle branded before they were turned over to Walker at the Bow River, but the speed in which the cattle were driven made this impossible. The cattle were accepted on the 'hair brand' that had been applied as a 'trail brand', but when they finally arrived it was so late in the season, a proper branding was postponed until the following spring. The hair brand on the cattle had completely disappeared after the warm spring days removed their shaggy winter coats.

In the spring of 1882, the directors of the company ordered Major Walker to round up every critter not branded on the Cochrane range and mark them with the big "C", that had been newly registered to the Cochrane Ranch. Several settlers volunteered to help gather the Cochrane herd, but when they discovered their own unbranded cattle were being identified with the Cochrane "C" they quit helping and got busy gathering unbranded livestock to place their own brand on. Had the settlers not seen what was happening and gathered some cattle for themselves, many would have faced financial disaster. Hundreds of cattle were identified with the wrong brand and many settlers ended up with a somewhat disputed herd.

Due to the heavy losses the Cochrane outfit experienced during their first winter along the Bow River, Major Walker again went to Montana to buy more cattle. He arranged to purchase five thousand head from Poindexter and Orr, large ranchers in that State. As the deal was being finalized Walker, was informed by telegram from a company official that the I.G. Baker Company was again handling the purchasing of more livestock. Major Walker traveled on to Fort Benton, only to learn that the I.G. Baker Company was not at all interested in buying more cattle for the Cochrane Ranch in Canada. Walker hastened back to Poindexter and Orr to renegotiate his original deal, only to be informed that the herd he first wanted would cost an additional twenty five thousand dollars. This caused Major Walker to tender his resignation, effective as soon as a suitable replacement could be located.

After the purchase was finalized, the Poindexter and Orr outfit agreed to trail the herd to the Big Hill west of Calgary. The late purchase of the cattle prevented them from starting the long drive until nearly mid-summer and meant they had to be pushed along at an excessive speed in order to reach the Cochrane range before winter. The weary, exhausted cattle were stopped at Fish Creek south of Calgary by a bitter snowstorm in late September. Poindexter, being an experienced cowman, suggested leaving the cattle there for a month and wanted to hold his cowboys for that length of time in order to watch the herd . Walker did not think this was necessary as his orders were to get the herd on their new range as quickly as possible. Poindexter reluctantly decided to continue on, and pushed the weary cattle through mighty barriers of snowdrifts to their destination. When the herd finally reached the Big Hill on the north side of the Bow, Poindexter informed Walker that he should quickly count them, because before tomorrow half of them might be dead.

The fall and winter of 1882-83 was the most disastrous time for the Cochrane Ranch Company. Frank White, a railroad man with little livestock experience was appointed to replace Major Walker. W.D. Kerfoot, who had handled cattle on the Montana ranges, came that winter to act as an adviser to White. By the time White took charge, the company directors in central Canada knew the condition of the Cochrane range. The starving cattle continually wanted to drift to where there was better winter grazing, a distance no further than along the Bow River east of Calgary, yet White received telegraph orders to hold the cattle there. The work involved holding the cattle on the Cochrane range became an enormous task, with White having to establish camps of cowboys at Calgary and at the mouth of Fish Creek. The cowboys worked day and night all winter but the number of dying animals continued to increase daily.

It was June before spring finally arrived in 1883. When it was seen how terrible the losses had been, leaving dead livestock heaped in every coulee after thousands had perished. Out of twelve thousand head that had been purchased and placed on the Cochrane range over a two-year period, there remained now only four thousand, which included also the natural increase. Frank White resigned his position as ranch manager shortly after the spring and early summer had shown the fatal results of following orders from ranch owners in central Canada, who knew little about the practical side of ranching.

Discouraged by the results of two winters in the Calgary district, which seemed to strike only the Cochrane herds, company officials located and leased a new range near Waterton Lakes, southwest of Fort Macleod. The remaining cattle were moved to the new lease at Waterton that summer, and horses were pastured on the Cochrane lease for the remainder of 1883.

The ten years following saw the Cochrane lease along the Bow River used for raising horses and sheep. During 1884 they trailed in 8000 sheep from Montana, which also turned out to be an unsuccessful venture. Mr. Kerfoot resigned from the Company during 1887, being dissatisfied with the company directors who continued to ignore his advice.

The last of the Cochrane property along the Bow west of Calgary was sold during 1894 and the lease and livestock at Waterton was disposed of in 1906; which ended all of Senator Cochrane's interests in Alberta. The site of their original ranch headquarters today, is the location of the Provincial Park just west of Cochrane along Highway 1A.

Stories of the early range men of Alberta have formulated fascinating chapters in the history of this Province. They were the men who first braved an unknown frontier in an effort to establish that raising cattle and horses could be a legitimate business. Men who gambled with the idea that cattle ranching promised a special lifestyle with great opportunities.

# Early Roundups

The territory between the American border and the Bow River was open range country for the period of twenty five years between 1882 and 1907. Large herds of cattle and horses grazed this virgin grassland on a year round basis. If it were possible to turn back the calendar for a complete century or more, the larger ranches throughout this area of southern Alberta considered the annual round-ups an important function of their existence. Two general round-ups were held each year. One in the spring to brand the calves, and another held during the fall to gather the beef that were mostly three and four year steers. The old time round-up outfits became a way of life and a necessary operation in order for the ranches that were established to remain in business. Since cattle ranged over millions of unfenced acres, the ranchers saw it necessary to form an Association that would set dates for the round-ups and take care of other important issues like prairie fires, stray animals, brands not registered and stolen livestock.

The writer of this chapter has a heritage that relates back to this same period of time; when my late father, Guy Pallister experienced the freedom and life-style of an open range cowman; the lifestyle of an era that will never again return. I can recall many stories told by him and other early cowmen which have inspired me to write on this subject, explaining some of the equipment used by the old time round-up outfits during their days of the open range. Modern day technology has helped the livestock industry to take advantage of new practices that differ greatly from the open range method of handling livestock. Meanwhile, the range men who pioneered the raising of livestock in Alberta over a century ago, should be acknowledged for their ability and knowledge of how to handle large herds of cattle in open country without the use of portable corrals, mechanical chutes and pick-up trucks.

The first general round-up was held during 1886, with most spring round-ups thereafter, being interesting and colorful affairs. Round-up wagons came from six or eight different ranches and met on a specific date and location set by the Association. This location was usually above the forks of the Bow and Belly Rivers, or else near High River. The Association decided which ranches needed to send "reps" or representatives to help on certain wagons. Ranches not represented on any wagon were charged one dollar per head for every animal gathered.

Every outfit used a chuckwagon, sometimes called the mess wagon, a bed wagon, a wagon boss, a horse wrangler, a night-hawk, who herded the horses at night, a cook and about eight or nine cowhands. The most important man on most outfits was the cook, who was paid ten dollars a month more than the cowhands; ten dollars that was well earned.

It was not unusual to have more than a hundred head of cow ponies in the cavvy, ( a term used to describe the herd of horses used by the cowhands.) Each cowhand had the use of eight to ten horses in his string, some of which were green broke or bronks. Each man was given several tough circle horses to make long rides to gather cattle, a well broke horse for working the herd, a rope horse to heel calves at brandings, a gentle night horse, and a strong horse for swimming rivers.

Round-up outfits went out each spring about the first of June, after the horses had lost their winter hair and their backs were free of warbles. The wagon boss always led the outfit along with the cowhands, followed by the chuck wagon and bed wagon, while the horse wrangler trailed the procession with the horse cavvy. The wagon boss would decide where to make camp, which was usually near good water and sheltered from the wind. The cook drove the chuckwagon with four horses, and the night-hawk followed behind with the bed wagon.

When the wagons reached a suitable campsite, the wagon horses were unharnessed and turned loose with the cavvy. The cook tent was set up first, directly behind the chuck wagon; close enough for the mess box on the back of the wagon to be inside the cook tent when the weather was not favorable. Otherwise, there was room left between the mess wagon and the cook tent. The chuck wagon was nothing more than a traveling cookhouse where meals could be thrown together in a hurry. The mess box that was built into the back of the chuck wagon served as a cupboard that held granite cups and plates, knives, forks, salt, pepper, sugar, all types of spices and other things such as jam and syrup pails. The door to the cupboard was hinged at the bottom and let down to form a table with a hinged leg to support it.

The night-hawk had additional duties of helping the cook unload the grub and set up camp. The rope corral was set up next, so the horse cavvy could graze near camp during the day. The rope corral was made of two-inch hemp rope that ran through metal rings which were attached to the top of wooden posts and driven into the ground. The posts were allowed to remain above the ground about four feet – a height that allowed the rope to touch a horse about chest high. When set up it could be made any shape or size, but usually assembled large enough to corral the complete horse cavvy of over a hundred head. One end of the rope was tied to the hind wheel of the bed wagon for stability. The rope corral was set away from the wagon in a circle, having the rope coming back to the other hind wheel where a gate was made that could be dropped and tied up again when necessary.

Then the bed tent was set up for those who wanted to use it. The horse wrangler also packed water and cut firewood for the cook. The night wrangler was able to sleep all day if he so wished, except during the days when camp was being moved. Both wagons were equipped with hardwood bows attached to both sides of the wagon boxes to carry wagon sheets made of heavy duty canvas, necessary to protect the food supplies and bed rolls from the weather when it rained or snowed.

The chuckwagon carried a large wooden barrel of fresh water on the near side with a platform built on the off side for the cook stove. Dry firewood that was slung on ropes under the running gear was usually carried from camp to camp to help the cook get meals ready at locations where wood was scarce. Beans, flour, and sugar were purchased in one hundred pound sacks. Various kinds of dried fruit which was always part of the dinner menu, was bought in twenty-pound boxes. Salt pork was purchased in the slab and plenty of fresh beef was always available for the cook. The cook would inform the wagon boss when he was out of fresh meat. Two cowhands were always appointed from the crew to select an animal out of the herd, which was usually a fat dry heifer. The critter would be butchered where the grass was clean and fresh and taken back to camp in quarters. Both men were most likely representing different ranch outfits and very seldom did they butcher a beef critter that was owned by the outfit either of them worked for! The meat was kept fresh in burlap sacks by hoisting it with a lash rope to the top of a thirty-foot pole that was tied to the hind wheel of the chuckwagon. This would keep the meat high enough to be kept out of range from the blowflies, and safe from spoiling.

The bed wagon carried all the extra food supplies and heavy cooking utensils that were not needed daily by the cook. The tents were rolled and thrown into the bed wagon along with the rope corral every time the outfit moved camp. Each cowhand was responsible for his own bedroll and his personal belongings that were carried in a bag called a war sack. They rolled their beds every morning after crawling out and left them in the bed tent so they could be quickly thrown into the bed wagon in case the wagon boss decided to move camp anytime during the day.

The night wrangler corralled the horses before five o'clock breakfast. The cowhands, who were on circle gathering cattle, would take ten to fifteen minutes to eat dinner at eleven o'clock or when they got back to the wagon. A fresh horse was then roped out for them to make a "second circle", or day herd duty. Supper was at five o'clock, after which a fresh horse was caught and saddled for a shift on night herd. Two men worked together on each two-hour shift throughout the night. They would circle the herd in opposite directions until it was time to change shift, then one would ride into camp to wake the new guard.

The beef roundup usually got underway each fall about the first of October. Most wagon boss's plan of action was to have two experienced men work out about fifteen miles from each side of the wagon, picking up the bigger steers that were wanted without disturbing the rest of the cattle. These men worked very slowly and brought these steers into the herd that was being held close to water. The men with less experience rode along each side of the herd to keep them moving in the right direction. Most of the time the herd would be strung out for several miles, but was never allowed to move any faster than a slow walk.

If things were going well, the "line riders" could quit the herd and ride into camp, giving the steers a chance to get a drink, graze or lie down. Sometimes the men gathering beef would be away from the wagon all day, not getting back until evening. The "line riders" would go back to the herd about three o'clock in the afternoon, and slowly drift the herd along, just enough to keep them moving into new territory. At supper time the herd was left to their own until the following morning, because night herding was not a common practice on most beef roundups. When working the range, no one was supposed to ride ahead of the man-leading circle. Everyone followed the boss until told otherwise by the wave of a hand as what to do. When riding into camp, everyone was careful to approach downwind from the fire and cooking pots. The space between the fire and the mess wagon was "sacred ground" occupied for the cook only! The general routine on any of the old time roundup outfits was not actually what anyone would consider easy work.

With the work finished in the fall, all but the regular hands were taken off the payroll. Some would spend the winters at an isolated cow camp, others got jobs tending bar in some cow town, while others rode the grub-line. These grub-line riders rode through the country, stopping at different ranches for a week or more. They were usually welcome guests as they brought bits of news, as there were no radios, newspapers or telephones on the early ranches. A very pleasant winter could be spent in this manner by a cowhand who was willing to lend a hand with anything that had to be done.around a ranch.

A book could be about the men who rode with the roundup wagons; most of whom wanted no other life. Many had been raised on the back of a horse with a rope or gun in their hand. Some had come up over the trail with the herds out of Texas while others were born in the cow country of the North-Western States. There is no doubt some had crossed the line on a tired horse, looking back because of a reward on their head. Most were lean-flanked weather beaten cowhands who were loyal, dependable men to the outfits for which they worked.

The general roundup of 1907 told the death of the open range days, when the wagons scoured the country to gather the remnants of the once thriving herds. Homesteaders were fast fencing the country and the disaster of the previous winter had killed over seventy percent of the range cattle. When the wagons pulled into their home quarters that fall, the glamour year of the open range, the general round-ups and the old time cowmen had become a thing of the past. It was left as history to remember.

# Hardships at the Early Bar U Ranch: Phil Weinard, Oxen Driver

Fred Stimson had decided to move the Bar U headquarters from its first location near High River to the middle fork of the Highwood River, now know as Pekisko Creek. The move may have intended to escape the invasion of the homesteaders, as well as take advantage of better water and shelter offered by the foothills. Possibly, more important was the fact that the original headquarters were not on the lease, which was offered to the Northwest Cattle Company in September 1882, but the new headquarters were.

When Phil Weinard first arrived at the Bar U Ranch shortly before Christmas in 1882, there was a hay corral and the only building at the new ranch site was a log cabin about 14 x 18 feet in size. The building was partly furnished without any windows in yet, and doors were not yet hung. At suppertime a canvas was put on the floor where the food was placed, as there were no tables or chairs. Some of the men squatted around the canvas while other filled their plates and sat on their bed-rolls. The only light was from some candles, and saddle blankets were hung over the doors and windows for the night.

Phil Weinard was born in Prussia and his family immigrated to the United States in 1872. He ran away from home during 1879 and headed for Indian country in late summer of '82. When he left Fort Benton on the Whoop-up Trail he drove eight yoke of oxen pulling three wagons loaded with flour, for the North West Mounted Police. After unloading in Fort Macleod, he quit the freighting company when his outfit was sold to the I.G. Baker and Company.

While in Winder's store at Fort Macleod, a clerk asked him whether he was returning to Montana or remaining in Canada. Weinard's reply was that he might stay if there was any work. Fred Stimson, who was in the store making a food purchase for the Bar U Ranch overheard the conversation and said "You can come with me to High River and I'll be leaving here about four this afternoon." After Stimson left the store the clerk told Weinard that Stimson had just purchased 3000 head of cattle and that he would have a good winter job. On the strength of a job Weinard purchased a Hudson's Bay blanket, some heavy underwear, a fur cap, mitts, socks and overshoes.

Stimson arrived back at the store to load his supplies with a good team and covered wagon that looked almost new, and was also leading a fine looking cow-pony. Leaving town that time of the day, Weinard thought they would be stopping for the night at some ranch or road-house. After crossing Willow Creek about four miles north of Macleod Stimson said, "We will camp here for the night." Weinard thought it was strange that a man who owned 3000 head of cattle would camp outside, in sight of a town. After supper, which consisted of bacon, crackers and tea, Weinard realized he was traveling with a very unusual man.

The next morning they followed the trail north that ran parallel with the Porcupine Hills and they camped on Willow Creek, where the Oxley Ranch was later located. While the team was being unharnessed, Stimson noticed that he had lost his overcoat and told Weinard to take the saddle horse and ride back to look for it. It was beginning to get dark so he rode back until he ran into the lead cattle of the second Cochrane herd that was coming north to the Bow River. Weinard was asked to join their crew for supper; which he quickly accepted, because he had only some cold bacon and crackers for dinner.

After they were on the trail the next morning for about three hours it began to rain and snow. Stimson had Weinard drive the wagon so he could ride and walk sheltered from the storm by the wagon. Weinard nearly froze before they arrived at the lower

Bar U in time for supper. John Ware and Al Deeves took care of the horses while Weinard was told to go inside and get warm. While he was standing beside a small kitchen stove trying to warm his hands, the old cook told him to 'get the hell out of the way' because he was trying to make some supper.

The following morning Weinard asked Tom Lynch what his job was and Lynch replied there was no job; and he wondered why Stimson had brought him up the trail from Fort Macleod. While Weinard was waiting for the stage to take him back he was given a team and wagon to haul firewood off the gravel bars in the river. He worked at this until a big snowstorm happened at the end of September. The big Bar U herd had already arrived, and had been turned loose on the range, while the Bar U bulls were being well taken care of at the new ranch headquarters on Pekisko Creek.

The snowstorm lasted for three days and nights. Andy Bell, who had bought a team and wagon from the Bar U, was going down to Smith and French's farm; offered Weinard a ride. Smith and French operated a stopping house at High River called 'The Crossing' where the stagecoach crossed the Highwood River. The snow was so deep that the trip took them all day, leaving after breakfast and arriving at dark, a distance of only four miles. It snowed intermittently for a week and when a chinook came, it only melted the snow south of High River. When the stage went through it traveled on wheels to High River and used sleigh runners after crossing the river, on to Calgary.

Old Joe Bowers was the cook at the stopping house and had gone on his periodic spree to Fort Macleod, and Weinard was asked to take over until Joe returned. Weinard cooked there until a few days before Christmas when Tom Lynch and John Ware drove to The Crossing to ask Weinard if he would take Ware's job of driving three yoke of oxen at the new ranch headquarters, where the bulls were being fed.

John Ware had quit and there was no one else who could yoke up and drive oxen. They gave Weinard a horse and directions and he reached the upper Bar U in time for dinner. That afternoon Weinard yoked the oxen, and along with George Emerson they hauled a load of hay. The oxen understood Weinard's method of handling them using a whip. By contrast, John Ware had driven them on horseback.

December had been quite warm without any snow. Jim Meinsinger and Cal Morton were getting out logs for a stable, Emerson had been hauling hay and Herb Miller was the cook. Living conditions were tough because they were always short of grub, and Miller was not much of a cook. One night supper was only some bread and dried applesauce. When Jim Meinsinger came in and saw what was for supper he grabbed his gun and went and shot one of the yearling bulls, after which they all enjoyed a good feed of fresh beef liver and brains! They were so low on food that Weinard volunteered to ride down and get what they needed the most. Luckily the saddle horses came into the hay corral. He caught two and rode to the lower camp, and brought back fifty pounds of flour, twenty pounds of beans, some sugar and dried prunes. The first warm day in March, both Weinard and Meinsinger quit. Weinard went to Calgary and joined the C.P.R. survey crew as a dispatch rider. Phil Weinard spent the best part of his life up and down the Highwood River. For twenty years between 1890 and 1910 he owned and operated the Riverbend Ranch located over the bank from the Village of Longview. During 1926 he bought property at Salmon Arm, British Columbia where he retired and passed away in September 1941.

# Oldtimer Biographies

# George Emerson of
# Southern Alberta Ranges
## P Left Ribs

The signing of the historic Blackfoot Treaty during 1877 and the liquidation of the vast buffalo herds before 1880, led up to the establishment and romance of the great cattle empires in the Northwest Territories. There was a multitude of early cowmen and ranchers who found their way into Alberta's cow country during this era, where many of their names can be found in community history books that have been written more recently. One of the earliest men who came was George Emerson, and he was considered 'The Grand Old Man of the Southern Alberta Cattle Ranges'. His accomplishments, courage and pioneer spirit have long been forgotten within the annals of modern day technology of the ranching industry.

Emerson was born in 1841 and raised at Danville, Quebec. He left Danville as a young man, and it was not until he settled on the Highwood River twenty years later, that his family heard from him for the first time. George claimed on a homestead at Council Bluff, Iowa and got to Montana in 1865. Stories of the wild and exaggerated tales of gold to be found in the Saskatchewan River, brought him to what is now Alberta in 1866. It was the lure of gold and high adventure that first started him and so many other young men during those times, towards a land where little was known other than worthless rumors. He found he could make $8 a day panning gold with some hard work, but only during the low water season.

Seeing that this was not a paying proposition, he went to work for the Hudson Bay's Company in charge of their freight shipments, where he remained for a number of years. Charged with the responsibility for many Red River carts, he delivered large volumes of cargo to destinations, traveling across endless miles of trackless prairie; often through hostile Indian country, and swimming rivers when necessary. This type of work developed the characteristics that in later years won the respect and confidence of the pioneer cattlemen, with whom he became associated. A thorough knowledge of the country with its fast changing climate, his ability to defeat difficulties, coupled with physical and personal courage, made him a leader of his time.

On one occasion while his cart train was camped on the north side of the Saskatchewan River, the bull teams swam the river during the night, and left his crew afoot. It was early winter and the river was full of floating ice but instead of calling a conference or asking for volunteers, he jumped into the icy water himself, gathered his bulls and swam them back across to be harnessed for another day's travel.

During 1877 Emerson formed a partnership with Tom Lynch to trail cattle and horses into the new ranching areas, when they became open after the buffalo had disappeared. In 1879 Emerson and Lynch trailed in 1000 head of Montana cattle for themselves and picked the north side of the Highwood River for their range. Their buildings were located four miles west of the present town of High River. During 1883 Emerson moved his headquarters onto Pekisko Creek, about half way between where the Bar U Ranch is located and their hay camp, which later became owned by Cartwright and Thorpe. Emerson stocked his ranch with good cows and fine horses; for 22 years carried on a thriving ranching operation with his cattle on the open range. They were identified with the Rocking P brand that he had registered during June of 1885. He was one of the most highly respected men in the territories and also an original member of the Western Stock Growers Association.

His Pekisko Ranch, which he first held by squatter's right, was sold to the Northwest Cattle Company during 1905 and he moved east to the short grass country south of Brooks. Emerson and George Lane leased the same piece of country from the CPR that ran east of Bassano, lying south of their right-of-way. They ran their cattle independently on the lease and paid no grazing fees, because if the railway had charged a fee of any kind, the railroad would have had to pay land taxes.

The same year Sam Howe unloaded at Brooks, 2000 head of steers from Manitoba, at $18 a head; and turned them loose on Emerson's lease. The rains came, the grass grew high, and another 1500 head were turned out in the spring of 1906. A year later, after the hard winter, ninety percent of these cattle lay dead on the range, in the coulees and behind every piece of shelter and cutbank in the country.

When Emerson went into partnership with Rod Macleay during 1909, he moved into the Sand Hills north of the Red Deer River. Both range men were trying to recover from the hard winter by purchasing Manitoba doggies, grazing them on the short hard grass in the summer and then trailing them west in the fall to winter in the foothills, where there was some good shelter. The next spring they were trailed back to the Red Deer and in the fall the beef was shipped out of Brooks. The partners prospered and in 1914 Emerson sold his cattle and the Rocking P brand to Rod Macleay because he did not like the idea of having to run cattle on deeded land.

Like many other frontiersmen, he was a silent man. However, his keen eye missed nothing, and knew by his uncanny sense what everyone around the ranch was doing and thinking. He never gave his friendship to anyone until he had satisfied himself that they were worth it, and when he did, it was for life. George Emerson contributed a great deal to the opening of Canadian west during its most colorful days. His last years were spent in High River where he and George Lane built the Lane and Emerson Block. Emerson used the High River Club in High River as his headquarters, and he could usually be found there with some of his friends from the earlier years. After a short illness he died in September 1920 and his body rests in the High River Cemetery.

# John Ware

ΠΠΠ Left Ribs

Cattle brands have formed a major part of Alberta's ranching history for over a century and their have been told and retold over the years. An example of a situation of this kind is a historic cattle brand recognized as Three Walking Sticks – sometimes mistaken for three numeric nines. The three walking sticks brand was originally recorded in the brand files of the Territorial Government as four walking sticks and was registered to John Ware during May 1885. During 1898 the government of that era proclaimed the second brand ordinance; whereby everyone using brands had to register each brand again with the recording office in Regina. John Ware had realized his brand was too large for the left rib position on cattle so he requested the brand be changed to three walking sticks instead.

John Ware was a negro cowhand and being big in stature and ambition he was hired as a trail hand in Idaho for a trail herd of Bar U cattle that was heading north into "The Territories" with a destination for the Highwood River country near High River. Big John liked the virgin grass that was so plentiful along the foothills, so he decided to stay around for a while. The same year his brand was recorded, he found employment with the Quorn Ranch; whose headquarters were on the Sheep Creek west of Okotoks. During 1889 the ranch manager was a man named Barte, and he sent John one morning to the north side of the lease to instruct some squatters to move on. Barter figured the squatters were homesteading on Quorn property. Big John was not hankering for this kind of duty, but the squatters informed him not to be concerned because they were not moving in any case. The area was soon surveyed and it was found that the squatters had settled a full mile outside the Quorn lease.

By 1890 John Ware had acquired his own homestead, and started a ranch on the north fork of Sheep Creek west of Millarville. Soon after the turn of the century, he decided the foothills had become too populated for his liking, and he decided to move everything he owned into an area on the Red Deer River north and east of the town of Duchess. This negro cowman was killed on the ranch in a riding accident during 1905.

At the time of his death the records indicate he owned nearly 1 000 cattle and 100 horses. The Royal Trust Company in Calgary was the Executor of the estate and had the responsibility of settling all ranch matters as well as guardianship of the Ware children. Royal Trust became owners of the brand for a short time and transferred it during August 1907 to a partnership of Riddle and Macleay Brothers. This partnership had previously purchased all the Ware assets by a letter of tender dated October 9, 1905. The letter specified that the company was willing to purchase the John Ware range including all buildings and implements thereon, near Brooks, Alberta, at a price of $24.50 per head for the cattle and agreed to pay a 5 per cent deposit with their tender and the remaining balance when all the cattle were turned over.

By 1909 Rod Macleay and George Emerson had purchased the complete outfit from the previous partnership. Early ranch history discloses that Emerson was with Macleay on the Red Deer range until 1914, after which Macleay continued to use the brand in that part of the country until the ranch was sold during the Second World War.

When Macleay and Emerson purchased the Ware cattle during 1909 they did nothing with the ownership of the brand, which was recorded in government files as being the property of Douglas Riddle and Macleay brothers. By 1925 Rod Macleay became concerned as to who was the proper owner of the old Ware cattle brand and attempted to have it recorded in his own name. The Recorder of Brands advised Mr. Macleay that this could not be done without consent from the other two previous owners. Rod Macleay informed the Recorder in several informal letters that he did not know the whereabouts of his two partners for signatures, so legal ownership of the brand had to be obtained through a sworn statement of claim.

For a reason not disclosed, the brand was transferred during 1930 to the Lone Star Ranch at Jenner, which was the property of Mike Stapleton. Stapleton owned the brand for only a short time and had it transferred back to Macleay in 1931 and then recorded again in the name of Laura S. Macleay during 1932.

The old brand files reveal that by 1933 Rod Macleay had exported several shipments of cattle to the British Isles. The English buyers were concerned because the cattle were marked all over the left ribs with such a big brand and remarked they would have paid more money if the hide had not been so badly marked For this reason, Macleay inquired whether two walking sticks could be registered on either the shoulder or hip on the same side as the three walking sticks. The request was granted and Mrs. Macleay registered a smaller brand on the left hip position.

Early in 1943 the Red Deer river property along with both brands were sold to George Stringham of Lethbridge. Members of the Stringham family used the old Ware brand in the Duchess area until 1968 at which time it was transferred to the Three Walking Sticks Ranching Ltd. who owned ranching property west of Claresholm. In January 1986, ownership of the brand was again transferred to a similar company name with an address in Calgary but owned by the Robin Chisholm family of Strathmore.

Each old cattle brand can tell a different story. A hundred years ago this particular brand represented a humble ranching family and has since been passed down through different family generations. Old brands have always been a controversial issue to some folk and a matter of major importance to others. However, they have certainly been part of our ranching history and have maintained a definite heritage of this country as the years go by.

# Charlie Knox

The business of raising cattle and horses in Western Canada would have never developed to its current state of success during the last century, if it had not been for early cattle traders like Charlie Knox. He had a natural interest and desire to learn the best methods available to raise livestock under open range conditions, as well as finding outlets to market them. Charlie Knox was the man responsible for the first shipment of grass beef to leave the Alberta foothills during October 1888; destinated to the British Isles.

Mr. Knox was born in Ireland and arrived in High River during the fall of 1883. The first job he obtained was as a cowhand with the HL outfit, which was located immediately south of the Bar U Ranch. During 1885 the HL ranch was sold to the North West Cattle Company and became part of the Bar U. Charlie started his own outfit the same year, located where the Harvey Gardner ranch is currently situated. Knox operated from this location for the next ten years before selling the property to Captain Gardner, the grandfather of Francis and Harvey Gardner. After leaving the Alberta range, Mr. Knox made his headquarters at Winnipeg; from where he shipped cattle and horses to all part of North America as well as to markets overseas.

Another component to the success of our early livestock industry in Western Canada was the Canadian Pacific Railway Company. Although the Canadian railroads are a thing of the past for the movement of livestock, this certainly was not the case during the pioneer days of ranching in Western Canada. There was never any doubt that the CPR made it possible for Western Canada to become developed and settled more quickly, than any other factor.

During the late 1890s Knox was shipping large numbers of horses by railroad, when he received a letter from William Van Horne, the President of the CPR. Mr. Van Horne invited Knox to come to Montreal to see him, as he might have a market for some good Alberta horses. When Knox arrived in Montreal Van Horne had correspondence from the Dutch government saying they would be interested in purchasing one hundred and fifty head of horses. The horses had to be of good quality, well broke, and delivered to Holland; for which they would pay up to thirty five pounds per head or approximately $160 in Canadian currency. Knox told Van Horne he could find the type of horses they wanted, but had no idea as to what they would consider a well broke horse. Knox was afraid he would get horses over to Holland that were well broke for Alberta standards; but not gentle enough to suit the Dutch criteria.

After some discussion on the matter Knox suggested the following proposition to Van Horne. "I will take the risk of putting together one hundred and fifty head of top quality horses, if the railroad company will risk the freight charges on the horses from Alberta to Holland." Knox also suggested that the railroad company hold the freight bill until after he returned from Holland, and if their government took the horses, then he would pay the freight. If they did not buy the horses, he would get rid of them the best way he could and the Canadian Pacific would stand their own freight costs. Van Horne thought the proposition over for some time and finally said, "It's a fair enough deal."

Having reached this agreement, Knox took along with him one man to ride the horses, and left Calgary six weeks later with one hundred and fifty head of as fine a bunch of horses that had ever been assembled in Alberta. They left Montreal on one of the last boats down the river for that season, sailing the Atlantic for nineteen days before arriving in Antwerp, Holland with the horses in fair shape.

Officials of the Dutch government met the shipment of horses as they docked on the Holland coast, where they were loaded onto another railroad and shipped inland to be lodged in the government stables. Knox knew within fifteen minutes that his venture had not been successful, because of the fact they were scared to death of the horses. The veterinarian inspection of the horses proved they were physically sound and satisfactory as far as conformation and type was concerned, but not gentle enough for the culture of the Dutch people. They informed Knox he had use of the stables until he could make some arrangements as to what he was going to do with the horses.

Leaving his man in charge of caring for the horses, Knox went back to the coast to advertise a large auction sale. All the horses were sold at auction, with exception of twenty-five head, which were hunter-type horses that were purchased from the Quorn Ranch. These were shipped back to London, England and sold as hunter prospects which all developed into well-known hunters, from the letters that Knox received during later years. The complete deal had averaged Knox about thirty English pounds for each horse, or one hundred and fifty Canadian dollars.

Upon Knox's return to Montreal, he contacted William Van Horne again and was prepared to show him what had been accomplished. In the meantime Van Horne had already received a letter from the Dutch government saying they were very impressed with the shipment of horses; but could not accept them because they were not domesticated enough. Van Horne inquired as to whether Knox had been able to sell them and he began explaining to Van Horne the details of his sales when Van Horne interrupted and said, "I don't want to know. Our deal was that the Dutch government was to take one hundred and fifty head of horses for thirty-five pounds each, which they did not do. So, according to our agreement the Canadian Pacific Railway will have to stand the shipping charges on the horses. I'm glad you were able to dispose of them," he said to Charlie, and that was the end of the conversation.

Charlie Knox had many more deals with the CPR during the years that followed, while he was engaged in the feeder and stocker cattle business out of Winnipeg. From his headquarters in Manitoba he shipped thousands of cattle annually by railroad to points in Western Canada. The largest train load of feeder cattle shipped out of Manitoba was during 1905, when Knox shipped twenty eight carloads of cross-bred shorthorn cattle to George Emerson of the Anchor P Ranch; which were unloaded at High River. Over the years Knox shipped over thirty five thousand head of cattle to his friend Emerson without even a scratch of a pen between them, or any word of difference in all their business transactions. Like many other old time range men, their word was sound and considered as good as their bond.

Charlie Knox finally retired in Vancouver on the Pacific coast, after a most interesting life of being part of pioneering the livestock industry in Western Canada. While Knox was living out his sunset years of retirement he was firmly convinced that the great Canadian Northwest would have never developed into the country it did without the Canadian Pacific Railway and the great men that headed-up their operations over the years; men who had vision to see the country grow. He considered it a great benefit to Western Canada that railroad officials were able to establish suitable freight rates that not only assisted early settlers to settle up the country, but continued to provide them with excellent service as the years went by.

The current players in our modern day livestock industry in Western Canada should continue to remember men like Charlie Knox, Pat Burns, George Lane and George Emerson. Even later men like Harvey Adams, George Dennon, Art Adams and Lee Williams, each played an important role in the different livestock activities. They brought Alberta's quality livestock to where it has been recognized and available, to buyers of export markets throughout our western world.

# Charlie Blazier: Trader and Trapper

The majority of those who were associated with the livestock industry in Alberta during the past century were honest, reliable people. A good example of this statement was a man named Charlie Blazier, a trapper by nature and a man who knew the country better than anyone else. He had some experience in handling rough horses and was a crack shot with a Winchester rifle as well as a six-gun. He usually traveled and worked with interesting people; of which there were many around Brooks during the early days. In later years he made a living catching young antelope, and taming them for sale to wildlife reservations and museums throughout the United States.

While the homesteaders were flocking into that part of the country during 1908, horses of any kind were selling for a good price. Charlie and his crew were working the Bow River country south of Brooks, where he met two brothers named Hamilton. These brothers had thirty-two head of better than average stock horses for sale. The Hamiltons were leaving the country, and offered Charlie a clear bill of sale for the horses at a price of $2700. They informed Charlie there were four head harness broke, two were well broke saddle horses and the rest were bronks. However, they put a two week time limit on the offer, and payment had to be all cash.

Charlie rode into Brooks the next day and applied for a loan at a bank, which had been recently built and was open for business. He explained to the bank manager that if he could get a loan he would break the horses over the winter and sell them to the homesteaders in the spring for a good price. Charlie came out of the bank without a loan; and disappointed because he had been refused; due to the fact that he lacked security because he was not a landowner. The same day in Brooks one of Charlie's friends informed him that possibly the only person around that would have that much cash would be a man name Jim Pearce, someone Charlie didn't know.

Jim Pearce had come to Brooks with a fine bunch of cattle and horses, from the pothole country south of Brooks several years before . Pearce had been considered to be a hard-boiled businessman, someone who was hard to deal with. He had built a home in Brooks near the stockyards and established a feed and livery stable business, which everyone knew as "Pearce's Corrals."

The next morning Charlie decided to go and see Mr. Pearce, but found he had left for Lethbridge several days earlier; without Mrs. Pearce knowing exactly when he would return. He was traveling in a specially made buggy and driving a small team of Indian ponies that could cover eight to ten miles an hour. Charlie was beat again, but as he was leaving Mrs. Pearce told him to come back in a few days if his business was urgent. Charlie stayed around town for several more days but when he went back, there was still no Pearce. This time he told Mrs. Pearce that he wanted to borrow $2700 until he sold the horses he intended to purchase. He left again thinking to himself that the horse deal was off because he had only three days left to raise the money.

Later that fall and before winter set in Charlie and his trapping crew had covered the country and were camped near Sullivan Lake, situated between Hanna and Castor. Charlie had forgotten about the Hamilton horse deal over on the Bow River; and heard that someone from Lethbridge had bought the horses. While at Sullivan Lake a native boy that no one knew rode into camp and asked for Charlie Blazier. He told Charlie he had been trying to locate him for more than two weeks, always getting to the place where he had been and left again. He said he was working for Jim Pearce and that he had a parcel from Pearce to be delivered to him and no one else. Reaching behind his saddle, and from inside an old coat that was tied there, he handed Charlie a small package wrapped in oilskin paper. Charlie took the bundle into the tent and counted out $2700, all in large bills. He offered to pay the young fellow for delivering the package but he said he was working for Pearce. Charlie put the money back in the oilskin, threw it under his bedroll and slept on it all winter.

The following spring Charlie and his crew were camped at a big spring west of Brooks when Jim Pearce drove into camp, just as they were cooking some dinner. Pearce was invited to unhook and stop to eat; while everything was talked about except the money. Charlie was helping to hook the team again after dinner when Pearce asked Charlie how he made out with the horses he bought. When Charlie answered, "I never bought any horses, " Pearce replied "Oh, is that right! Then you must have had a good time this past winter." Pearce started getting in the buggy and Charlie said, "Hold it a minute Jim, I just remembered I have something that belongs to you." Charlie got the cash that was wrapped in the oilskin paper out of the tent and while handing it to Pearce. Charlie said, "Thanks Jim for your kind help. It was my fault that it arrived too late."

Pearce took the bundle and stuffed it inside the buggy seat, reached for the whip and took off like a coyote that had been shot at! As he was leaving Charlie shouted, "Aren't you going to count it Jim?"

The old time cowmen trusted most everyone but at the same time always maintained that if a man's word was not any good, a signed agreement from him was not worth anything either.

# Lee Brainard: A Lonesome Death

There has been much written with reference to the disastrous and brutal winter of 1906-07, when seventy five percent of the range cattle in western North America either starved or froze to death. Nearly a century has passed and it is very doubtful if there is anyone living who can relate to the experiences of that terrible time in ranching history. The following story unfolds a dramatic incident of a respected rancher from Montana who came to Alberta and lost everything except his own life during that same dreadful winter.

Lee Brainard was born in Minnesota during 1859 and by turn of the century, he had established a successful cattle ranch at Bozeman, Montana. For years the ranch prospered; but soon settlers started crowding in and took up rangeland that Brainard regarded as his own. He was also getting tired of the work that was involved in having to stock pile large amounts of feed each year to carry his livestock through the long cold Montana winters.

From time to time Brainard heard stories of a country that was truly a rancher's dream. A country where warm winds from the Pacific Ocean would sneak through the mountain passes in the dead of winter, melting the snow from the hills and plains as if by magic. Stories where men with courage, some capital and livestock of their own, could carve a cattle empire from the thousands of unfenced acres where the grass grew tall enough to roll the rowels of their spurs. It was the stories of this nature that inspired Lee Brainard to move all his livestock north into Canada.

During mid-summer of 1906 he outfitted two covered wagons and with his twenty-year-old son Albert, and a faithful old cowhand named White. They pointed a herd of seven hundred cattle and one hundred horses in a northwesterly direction. Brainard hired several extra riders to get the herd started and after they left their home range, they managed with one additional man, who went back when the drive was completed. The herd made an impressive sight as they wound their way through the hills, leaving their old range behind them forever.

The livestock were allowed to graze along in the general direction of a new range to which they were now headed. The herd entered into Canada at Wild Horse, then on to Pakowki Lake, before skirting the lofty Cypress Hills on their western side. Occasionally they would meet a rancher or some rider on the trail who would help them correct their course of direction. Suddenly one day they saw before them the mighty valley of the South Saskatchewan

River and by evening they were all able to ride into the frontier town of Medicine Hat.

At Medicine Hat, Brainard's onward progress was nearly stopped. When the Mounted Police heard that he was going into a new country so late in the season with no feed supplies or buildings established, they were prepared to stop him from going on. The Government Land Office was another disappointment, when he learned that all the land had been taken up along the South Saskatchewan, the Bow, and the Red Deer Rivers. However, north of the Red Deer was a vast piece of country where only a few brave settlers had made any claims.

After their wagons had been restocked with supplies, the herd was gathered and forded the river to continue their journey into the unknown. It was a long climb out of the river valley but finally the land leveled off again to rolling prairie country. At this point Brainard was becoming concerned about the obstacles that lay ahead, not realizing that they were traveling out of the chinook country that he had heard so much about. Only a few more days had passed before the herd reached the wide deep valley of the Red Deer River.

They followed the river up-stream until a suitable ford was found, and saw a few established ranches from time to time. After crossing the river, Brainard decided to follow the first large creek northward in search of a location where a ranch could be started. This proved to be Berry Creek, and the spot selected was where the creek widened into a large meadow, located about three miles north from where the town of Richdale was later located, east of Hanna. On the large meadow different types of grasses could be found, while on the higher ground, prairie wool grass grew as thick as hair on their dog. Along the creek there was some willow brush for shelter and some firewood, and in the creek was plenty of water for the livestock.

Lee Brainard had found the answer to his dream and he decided to go no further. One of the covered wagon boxes was lifted off of its running gear to be used for their winter home. Someone had to continually day herd the livestock to keep them from wanting to stray back south. It was now already September and ducks and geese by the thousands could be seen winging their way southward. Brainard actually believed he was in the chinook belt of Alberta and expected to enjoy an easy winter. Instead of making some preparations for the months ahead, he spent much of his time riding around exploring the surrounding countryside.

On one such day he came across a ranch owned by the Hunt brothers, who were situated about forty miles northwest of Brainard's camp and near where the town of Endiang is now located. They talked about the coming winter and the Hunt's strongly suggested that Brainard bring them all his cattle and have them wintered on a share basis, as the Hunt's had put up a good supply of hay. Brainard was somewhat of a stubborn man and refused their offer, for which he was later sorry.

September passed and October came; when large bands of antelope could be seen making their way southward also. Brainard's camp experienced a big shock one morning when they awoke to find the ground covered with a heavy snowfall. As it was only the middle of October, they felt sure a warm wind would come any day and melt the snow as quickly as it came. Instead of a chinook coming, more snow fell and later on still more came. After Brainard made a long cold trip to Brooks for food supplies, the cattle and their camp were moved to the hilly country around Dowling Lake where the wind kept the ridges partly free of snow. There was more shelter there for the cattle from the ever-blowing wind each day. Protection for them also became a desperate situation with only a covered wagon box for cover from the deathly cold. The temperature each day remained at 30 to 40 below Fahrenheit, and by year-end they all had endured enough hardships to destroy the life of any man.

January brought more severe cold and blizzards than they had previously experienced. Some of the cattle were already dying, and if others had not followed the horses that exposed some grass by pawing snow, all would have died. As Brainard watched the drifting snow each day and heard the pitiful call of his dying cattle, he regretted not listening to the Mounted Police at Medicine Hat. He also remembered the offer he had refused from Hunt brothers; and wondered if perhaps it was not too late to save part of the cattle and especially themselves. On January 29th a warm and welcome chinook blew in from the southwest, and immediate preparations were made to move out. Some of the cattle were so weak they had to be shot, but early the next morning they were on the move with high hopes of reaching the Hunt Brothers Ranch within several days.

The loose horses were pushed on ahead to break trail for the cattle to follow, but the going was much tougher than expected. The livestock had to be rested from time to time and allowed to graze a bit. As the morning progressed the sun shone brightly and the warm wind caressed their tired bodies to the point of unbelief. By mid-afternoon the livestock were played-out, and a stop had to be made. The team and saddle horses were turned loose to find some feed while Albert and White gathered some dried willow branches to start a fire. The wind had completely stopped and during the mild calm some frozen beef was being cooked for their empty bellies. While the men were eating a dark gray wall of cloud that towered skyward could be seen moving quickly towards them from the northwest. Within a few minutes the sun was blotted out and the men, realizing their danger, quickly ran to catch their horses. Before they could reach them the blinding storm had already struck, and the horses went with it. Some of the cattle found shelter in the willow brush but most of them vanished in the storm forever.

The three men took shelter in the covered wagon for a while, but the bitter wind blew through the wagon as if it was no more than a picket fence. It became colder by the hour and when they could not stand it any longer, they were forced to get out and march around the wagon in a circle to keep from freezing to death. They tried to make a fire using willow branches, but the hurricane wind and drifting snow kept smothering the flames and whipping away any heat that was produced. By daylight the next morning the temperature had dropped more than seventy degrees from the previous day, and the bitter wind pierced their clothing like a knife. The icy cold made breathing difficult, and their tired legs were playing out. Death hovered over the camp, and it was now a question as to how much longer each one could last.

The ordeal was too much for the older man White, who went limp and passed away suddenly, sprawling in the snow. White had been Albert's constant companion and idol ever since the time he was a baby, and now that White was dead the boy was left with no will to live on any further. His father pleaded with him for them both to try and fight their way against the storm to safety, but he did not succeed. Finally Brainard struck out in the storm, trying to carry his son, but he was too much weight to carry for any distance. Within the hour Brainard was back, laying the lifeless body of his own son down in the snow beside White's corpse. Most men would have given up at that point under such fearful odds, but that was not the case with Lee Brainard.

Before leaving the stranded wagon the second time, he found an axe and chopped pieces of frozen meat from an animal that had recently died, and ate it raw. Then, setting his course in the direction of the wind, he struck out facing the storm in an attempt to find the Hunt ranch. He struggled on for hour upon hour, stumbling often in the deep snow, only to rise again and carry on. By nightfall he had become somewhat delirious from the gray-white whirlpools of snow making everything appear the same. Suddenly he knew he had fallen over a wire fence, which alerted him to the extent that there still may be some hope. Realizing he could no longer stand, he crawled on his hands and knees following the wire past some feed corrals and finally to the Hunt brothers shack.

Dragging his body inside, the Hunt's did their best to thaw out his hands and feet by using kerosene. The deep snow, severe cold weather and distance from the railroad prevented them from getting Brainard to a hospital for the longest time. Only the constant care of the three brothers saved him from dying. His face and hands were in terrible condition for weeks, and all his toes fell off except one. When he could finally be moved, he was sent back to Montana where he spent the rest of the winter in a hospital.

When weather permitted, Harold Hunt rode out and located the bodies of Albert Brainard and White to bury them in the snow in order to keep the coyotes from eating them. Hunt made several trips later in the winter to make sure the two were kept well covered. The winter of 1906-07 was so severe that it was not until the 6th day of May that the Mounted Police from Stettler were able to go out and pick up the bodies for burial. At that time there still remained plenty of snow but Albert's face had become bare and the hungry crows had eaten off his nose.

By early summer Brainard was able to ride again, and he rode back into Canada to see if any of his cattle had survived. He found only fifteen head that had possibly drifted away early the previous fall and gotten into herds of other ranchers who had fed them. He continued to find horses for at least six years afterwards, some showing up in Saskatchewan.

In spite of the crushing blow that fate had dealt him, Brainard brought his wife and a fresh herd of cattle from Montana and built up a small ranch north of Richdale. His new endeavor did not last long either, for in the fall of 1909 one of the largest prairie fires in the history of that country burnt out his empire of grass, and the range was never the same thereafter.

The railroad arrived in 1913 and the country was opened up for home-steaders and Brainard was crowded out much worse than he had been in Montana. The following year was dry, making it impossible to find a sufficient winter feed supply, which he never wanted to be without again. So Brainard took up the search once more for his dream country and found it in the hills around Fort St. John, B.C. where he moved during 1917.

Lee Brainard continued to ranch in northern British Columbia until 1938 when he died at the age of 79 years. During the latter years of his life, his daily life-style involved a resolution he made soon after his close encounter with death. On the windows of his home; blinds or shades were ever allowed to be closed. He wanted his lights to continually shine out at all times for those who might be lost and seeking safety from the darkness, or shelter from a winter storm.

Across the border in Alberta, a post office carries his name, and down around Richdale, a school was named in his honor.

# The Legendary Sam Howe

Much has been written about Alberta's early day range men such as George Emerson, George Lane, Dan Riley and John Ware. Many other good cowmen drifted into Alberta's cow country from south of the forty- ninth parallel between Canada and the United States. Some had come up over the trail with herds out of Texas; and others were born in the cow country of the American southwest. Some no doubt crossed the line on a tired horse, looking back, with a reward on their heads. But the majority of them would were loyal dependable men, and honest to the outfit they work for. One such legendary character was a fellow named Sam Howe.

Sam Howe was born near Nephi, Utah, during February 1865. At the age of fourteen he left home to work out in a country that was wild and rough. He had no schooling, only what he learned himself. He would tell people that he had other things to do during his younger days besides going to school. Before Sam's days ended some eighty odd years later, he had been a prospector, trapper, bullwhacker, freighter, long-line skinner, gold miner, hotel man, soldier, livery stable operator, farmer, a rancher, and first, last and always, a good cowman.

There are two different stories as to when Sam first reached the cow country in Southern Alberta. One story tells that Sam Howe was nearing his eighteenth birthday when he hired out to Tom Lynch, who was assembling a trail herd of cattle to trail north into Canada for the North West Cattle Company during 1882. The other story reveals that Sam trailed in with two thousand head of cattle owned by Emerson and Lynch during 1884, when a man named Joe Johnson was trail boss.

In any case Sam arrived in the cow country during the early 1880s and first worked for Stimson at the Bar U, doing everything there was to do on a cow ranch. Those who knew him considered him a top-hand; never lazy, always cheerful and able to stand a lot of heat in the summer and cold in the winter. During one spring round up, Sam was wrestling calves when it was 85 degrees in the shade. His attire included a pair of long Stanfield black label underwear, the heaviest made. Someone asked him, "Whether those woollies were not kind of hot." Sam replied, "What keeps out the cold will keep out the heat"; and he just kept on wrestling calves.

In about 1888, Sam homesteaded the north half of Section 19 and established a ranch on the north side of Sheep Creek about eight miles upstream from Turner Valley. His nearest neighbors to the south were Fred and Walter Ings who owned the Rio Alto Ranch, situated on the North Fork of the Highwood River. The Ings Brothers claimed all the country between the two rivers that lay west of the big hill where Longview is now located, to be OH range. Near Sam's ranch on the river was an old Indian crossing, where his cattle would sometimes cross to a nice grass meadow on the other side. The Ings threatened to shoot any cattle found south of the river and according to some reports these threats were carried out.

During the same year, Sam obtained a contract to supply the Lineham Lumber Company with fresh meat. Lineham was operating several camps further up Sheep Creek and Sam kept his deal by delivering one beef carcass per week. By the following spring, Ings knew that Sam had the same number of cattle as he had the previous fall. An investigation conducted by the police found no evidence of any hides with the OH brand on the left ribs. After the river flooded that spring, a number of hides were found down stream along the river. The amazing thing about the hides was that each one had a large piece missing from the left side!

Sam soon sold his ranch on Sheep Creek and bought a hotel on Ninth Avenue in Calgary. He and Mrs. Howe operated the hotel for less than a year, when the South African War broke out. Sam joined up immediately and went overseas with the Strathcona Horse Regiment. Sam never wrote home, and while he was overseas an unofficial report reached Calgary that he had been killed in action. As a result the hotel was sold during his absence and when Sam finally returned to Calgary, he was surprised to find out he was without a job. He then went prospecting for gold near Barkerville, British Columbia, but came back to Calgary again with less than he left with.

In 1905, he and his old friend John Ware, went to the Red Deer River country to establish a cow ranch. John Ware stayed, but Sam left to go punching cows again for George Lane. Sam worked for Lane until 1908, when he and Billy Playfair joined forces and started a livery stable business in Bassano, while the Bow River dam was being built. Town was not a good place for Sam, because he spent more money than he made. He went back to British Columbia once again, and got into the freighting business with a fellow named Pete Laport. This venture turned sour within a few years and Sam landed in Calgary once more. He bought some new riding gear and went back to the business he said he should have never left.

For the next eighteen years Sam was ranch foreman on an outfit owned by Rod Macleay, located on the Red Deer River north of Brooks. Along the river was a cow camp that Sam let a trapper use whose name was Scotty Marr. Scotty was trapping up and down the river, looking for anything he could get, and was also cutting water holes for the cattle. Sam gave him a team of horses and a wagon with a sixty-bushel double box. Macleay had shipped a carload of oats to Wardlow and had hired the oats hauled to the old house at the cow camp, which had been half partitioned for storage of the grain.

An Indian boy named Pat Ward, who couldn't read or write, was working at the ranch. One cold day at noon Sam said to Pat, "You ride to the camp and tell Scotty to bring a load of oats in the morning." Pat saddled a horse and left for the camp but when he arrived there was no Scotty. The stove showed he had been there the previous night but was away on his trap line with one horse. Pat rode to some of the close water holes and saw they had been opened that morning. The days were short and the weather cold, so Pat made a smoke and a cup of coffee and waited. Still there was no Scotty. Pat didn't want to wait till after dark, because it looked like a storm was moving in. The fact Pat couldn't write a note didn't bother him in the least. Just before sundown he went to the oat bin and gathered a double handful of oats and put them in a little heap on the table. He then whittled out a hand from a cottonwood stick with the front finger pointing towards the ranch and stuck the hand in the oats. He got on his horse and rode back to the ranch, arriving just as everyone was setting down for supper.

After a time Sam looked at Pat and said, "How is Scotty?" Pat answered "Fine" and Sam said, "Is he bringing the oats." Pat answered again and said, "You bet." That was all that was said and no one knew that Pat had not seen Scotty that afternoon at all. About noon the next day the men at the ranch could hear the screeching noise over the ridge, a noise that steel wagon wheels make in the frozen snow. The men wondered what the noise was as there was no trail to follow in that direction. Pat said "That's Scotty bringing the oats." In a while Scotty came in sight with a lathered up team and a big load of oats. They helped Scotty unhitch and everyone went to the cookhouse because dinner was ready. During dinner Scotty kept grinning at Sam. Scotty didn't know that Pat couldn't read or write, but he did know that Sam could not. Scotty figured that Sam had been at the cow camp the previous day and left the oats on the table. Finally Sam said "What's tickling you Scotty, what is so funny?" Scotty answered, "I saw your sign last night and figured it needed some quick action. Sam was quick to catch on and said, "That was not my sign you saw Scotty, it must have been an Indian sign." Pat was a half-breed native, so Sam's comment kind of hit the spot. Pat was listening to the conversation but said nothing; he just sat there and grinned.

From about 1929 to 1947, Sam Howe lived on his own ranch five miles north of Duchess. He built up a herd of cows again after the dry hungry years of the 1930s. He continued to face the winter blizzards and never spent a winter in any place where he didn't half freeze to death. Sam passed away in Vancouver during May 1947. His body was brought back to Brooks for burial, after the largest cowboy funeral ever held in the west. Twenty mounted men followed the casket to the grave of one of the greatest cowmen who ever rode into Western Canada.

# Slippery Bill McCombe

During the years that Alberta was open range country, people came into the new territory hoping to find employment of some kind, while others were looking for adventure. For those who were in trouble with the law south of the border, found that it was sometimes convenient for them to hire on with a trail herd that was heading north across the International Boundary. The authorities on the American side were usually content in letting things be, as long as the guilty did not return, and no questions were asked in Canada either; as long as they behaved. While the majority of newcomers that came into the country were good reputable citizens, it was only natural there were some that were not.

One such person was a man named Bill McCombe who became better known throughout Alberta's ranching country as "Slippery Bill." Not that old Bill was a bad fellow by any means; but early range men that spoke of him, indicated his nickname suited his character very well. It seems interesting that Bill did not get his name from being dishonest, but from a young chap who worked for Bill on the roundup wagon. Bill was continually picking on the kid, if not for one thing then for something else. Finally, one morning at breakfast while Bill was picking on the young fellow without reason, the kid grabbed a frying pan from the fire pit and poured the contents onto Bill's head. The warm bacon grease ran over Bill's face and down his neck while the other men of the crew expected the kid to be promptly fired. Instead, all old Bill said was "Well now, you are a spirited young fellow aren't you!" He treated the kid with respect after that.

There was little known of Bill McCombe's past, except the he broke jail in Texas and managed to ride as far north as Sheep Creek. Here he obtained work in a coal mine west of Priddis and remained underground for about one year. When he finally came out of hiding he got a haying job at the Quorn Ranch, where it was witnessed that he was more familiar with riding and handling livestock than he was about anything else. He was recommended to Herb Miller at the Bar U Ranch, where it soon became evident that McCombe was an experienced cowman. He rode for the Bar U until about 1900, then went to work for Pat Burns as range boss during the summer months, and managed one of Burns's feed camps during the winters.

Bill was a medium-size man who was always well dressed from a good Stetson hat down to his Mexican spurs. He always carried a knife, and a six-gun in a shoulder holster. His soft voice was occasionally witty, but had a tone of sarcasm most every time he spoke. Some of the early cowmen that worked for McCombe said that Bill had always treated them fine, but most of the range men actually did not like him. However, they all agreed on one thing; he was a top-notch cowman, good with a rope, but mighty touchy to carry on a conversation with.

One evening during roundup the crew was scattered about the camp after supper when a stranger rode in. The newcomer wanted a job, and Bill hired him without looking at the fellow or the saddle he was riding. The man's name was Walter Kesee, whom McCombe has double-crossed south of the border years before. Kesee was long and lean with sharp features and spoke with a Texas drawl. He left an impression with most everyone that he had been an outlaw south of the border. Both Fred Ings and Jack Glendenning described him as a man worth watching, a fellow who had a good mind without any morals.

Now that old Bill had been found, he knew that all that could save him were the Mounted Police and the surety of British Justice. All during the roundup, there was never a word or a look between the two that led anyone to suspect that these two men had met before. When the roundup was over Bill kept Kesee hired on, each afraid to let the other out of his sight. Kesee knew that he could do nothing to old Bill in Canada without the consequences of a hanging loop or a long term behind bars. Things went on quietly enough for the next several years with these two men never being too far apart.

The Irish temperaments of McCombe and Pat Burns finally collided during 1906 when Bill went to work for Gordon, Ironside and Fares. Knowing that McCombe was an excellent judge of cattle and wishing to purchase some good cattle for himself, William Fares gave McCombe a large sum of money to buy some better than average cows. Kesee soon learned of McCombe assignments but did not want to alarm old Bill as to the information he had found out. Leaving his horses with the roundup, Kesee slipped unnoticed across the border for a few days and enticed a fancy lady to make a quick trip to Fort MacLeod. The woman soon found McCombe and persuaded him to accompany her back to Montana. Realizing that McCombe had disappeared, Fares quickly contacted the stock detectives to investigate the situation in an attempt to get his money back. Kesee also disappeared from Southern Alberta within a few days after McCombe had left.

Jackson, the stock detective followed them through Montana to Seattle where he lost their trail. It was here that Bill McCombe was done away with and no one ever saw him again. Fares never saw a penny of his money either, nor did he have any cows to show for the agreement that he had made with "Slippery Bill."

# Wilkinson and McCord

By the year 1900, all the ranch country in Southern Alberta where cattle and horse ranches both large and small were established; had either been purchased or leased. Those who came later were referred to as newcomers and settled for grazing land north of the Bow River or farther east, out along the Red Deer River and beyond. Stories continued to go back south into the American States of the great opportunities still available for cattle ranching north of the forty-ninth parallel.

Two American men named Wilkinson and McCord formed a ranching partnership of that took advantage of a later ranching opportunity in the Canadian North West; though it was short lived. Bud Wilkinson and Tom McCord were ranching together in the south-west part of Texas and New Mexico, but were seeking new range to take part of their American herd elsewhere. Early in the spring of 1902, Bud Wilkinson set out from his home at Boswell, New Mexico, for a destination in Canada at Medicine Hat. On arrival he proceeded to find an old friend named Bill Greathouse, who had worked for the Wilkinson – McCord outfit in New Mexico. Greathouse had come to Canada many years before and had been employed as a ranch-hand around Medicine Hat since December 1899.

During the first week in April the two men struck out north across the prairie with a team and democrat, a tent, camping equipment, groceries, and the services of an Indian guide. Their team was eager, pulling their light load and within less than a week after leaving Medicine Hat, the two explorers found themselves in the Neutral Hills. From the high hills ahead they scanned the country to the north with field glasses and there below, vivid in the morning sun, was Sounding Lake. Traveling a few more miles northward, the hills stopped abruptly at the edge of a large piece of level open country. Stretched before them was a big hay meadow with a stand of hay waist high to a man and a large lake shaped like a horseshoe, both located on the floor of a rich fertile valley. They were satisfied with the fact that there was an abundance of hay for winter feed and enough prairie wool grass for summer pasture, stood in sight in all directions. Wilkinson began thinking about enough timber for a building site. The Indian guide assured him there was sufficient timber for building logs, corral rails and fence post just beyond the hills to the north.

Wilkinson knew his quest for a Canadian ranch had ended, and that he would not find anything better. Parting with their guide back at Medicine Hat, Wilkinson and Greathouse found the fastest transportation back south. Wilkinson's partner Tom McCord anxiously awaited Wilkinson's return and the traveler's enthusiastic report expelled any doubt about a great cattle drive to the Canadian Northwest. The cattle that were to be moved to Canada were scattered over the southwest corner of Texas. These were to be gathered, trailed to a central point to be wintered, ready to be shipped north for the drive the following spring. Bill Greathouse was somewhat familiar the Wilkinson-McCord ranch in New Mexico and was given the task of gathering the cattle and organizing the drive. Thirteen men responded to a call for experienced riders who understood the work of gathering, trailing and holding large herds of cattle at night in all types of weather. Added to the thirteen were the two who were launching the enterprise; and their cook, making sixteen men who came with the outfit to Sounding Lake.

The large round-up was completed in the fall of 1902 under the leadership of Bill Greathouse and arrangements with the railroad companies were in the hands of the two partners of the ranch. Railway regulations demanded that livestock traveling long distances had to be unloaded at certain intervals to be rested, fed and watered. Some careful planning was required between the livestock owners and railroad officials to establish these unloading points well in advance. On April 15th 1903 three thousand six hundred head of cattle, two hundred cow ponies and work horses, along with saddles, harness, tools, wagons and camp equipment were loaded onto railroad cars at Canyon City, Texas; billed for Billings, Montana. The shipment consisted of eight trainloads that took two weeks to reach its destination. Two men, whose duty was to unload the livestock for feed and water about every four hundred miles, traveled with each train. After the last train was unloaded at Billings, more than a month had passed before the big herd reached Sounding Lake, a distance of about five hundred miles. The weary cattle that were at last able to feed on the virgin plant-life located in the big basin of hills around the lake and showed little need to stray elsewhere. The tired cowhands faced a different situation; having the mighty task of completing warm living quarters and gathering some feed before winter set in.

The whole crew hung up their ropes and saddles and now became proficient with axes, hammers and saws. They gathered logs from the finest grove of timber and raised them one upon the other until a cabin, a storehouse, a stable and blacksmith shop were constructed. Some corrals were still needed and the haying had to be done, for contrary to common belief these men were not foolish enough to believe that livestock could survive the winters in

Canada without some feed. Due to the mighty effort of the whole crew, the work was done in time. The storehouse bulged with winter supplies brought in from Medicine Hat and haystacks were ready for the blasts of winter.

The first two years of ranching at Sounding Lake were good ones. The winters were relatively mild and the amount of moisture and sunshine during the summers were ideal. The cattle thrived and although the ranch hands were always busy, there was no longer the urgency and pressure of having to complete things so quickly. On November 16, 1906, a big blizzard struck with a force that had not been equaled for many years. Snow driven by a harsh north wind began to fall and continued to do so for three days. The cattle were still on the open range, so they turned their tails to the icy blasts and drifted with the storm. By time the storm subsided the majority of the cattle had traveled far from their home range. The snow, now three feet deep on the level was covered with a hard icy crust. There have been many accounts written about the terrible winter of 1906/07 where men suffered, and cattle perished by the thousands. Nearly seventy five percent of the cattle died from either freezing or starvation; which ended the ranching business for some early cattlemen and the glamour years of the open range.

When the Wilkinson-McCord outfit moved north into Canada, Dick Ellis was one of the cowhands involved with the drive. After ranch headquarters were established, his wife came north also and became their ranch cook at Sounding Lake. The dreadful winter weather continued for months into 1907 when the thermometer dropped as far as it could go and stayed there. One morning the other lady of the house, that was presumed to be Mrs. Wilkinson, came to the men seated around the breakfast table and reported that Mrs. Ellis was very ill. Unless she got a doctor's advice and some medication immediately, she feared for her life. A deadly hush fell over the table and outside the thermometer hovered near the bulb with a fierce biting wind. The nearest doctor was at Stettler, one hundred miles to the west where the snow laid deep and crusted. The men left the table in silence and dressed with their warmest clothing to face the deathly cold. Out in the stable Bill Greathouse proceeded to saddle the best horse in the barn and the grim and determined look on his face indicated as to what he had in mind.

At the house he told the lady he was going to Stettler and for her to order whatever she felt was required. Hastily she wrote a letter for the doctor telling of the symptoms and asking for advice and some medication. The letter was placed in an envelope and pinned inside Bill's shirt pocket. Dressed as warm as possible, he pointed his horse the best he could towards the next ranch in his path, for they were few and far between. Where conditions permitted he pushed his horse as hard as he dared, changing horses four times along the route. At every ranch in his path he traded horses for the best one each ranch-er had to offer, and left his tired horse behind to rest and to be fed. Ignoring invitation to stop, eat and warm up, he plodded onward. The closer he got to his destination, the easier traveling became because of the people who would have traveled the route before him. At last, numb from the cold and dull from the lack of sleep he reached Stettler in nearly twenty hours. At this hour it would have been well past midnight in the newly corporate town, where the majority of its citizens would be sound asleep on a cold winter night.

During the early months of 1907, the town of Stettler consisted of four hotels, two banks, a dentist, two practicing doctors, two druggists, a lawyer, a feed store, several livery stables, and numerous real estate agents and insur-ance men. Greathouse first found a livery stable to feed and rest his horse and inquired from the livery keeper where he could contact a doctor, whom was soon located. The doctor quickly scanned the hand written paper and told Greathouse he would need a couple of hours to get the medication ready. He told him to go to the hotel and get something to eat and rest. Greathouse ate heartily, after which he dozed at the table until the doctor returned. Carefully storing the doctor's written instructions and the medication in a safe pocket, he stumbled back to the livery stable to face the cold long trail back. Following the same route home, he changed mounts again at each place he had left a tired horse. Having a trail to follow on the ride back, he was able to complete the two hundred mile mercy ride in thirty-six hours without hurt-ing any of the horses. Mrs. Ellis soon began to recover and was on her feet again cooking for the ranch crew. The snow banks lingered long into the next spring and amongst them were the decaying carcasses of thousands of cattle owned by Wilkinson and McCord. The partnership decided that the Wilkinson family would pack up and go back to New Mexico, never again to return.

Tom McCord was left with the task of building the herd again, back to the original number. After several years of having other events intervene, McCord sold the outfit in 1911 and returned also to his native state. Bill Greathouse got into the ranching business for himself around Sounding Lake, but was never content in staying in one place for any length of time. He was recognized as being a good cowhand and an expert man with a rope and became somewhat of a legend in that part of the country. There has been some dispute as to where he spent his latter years, but indications are that he died in Calgary and was buried there.

The cow business has changed considerably during the past hundred years. Ranching people are still as enterprising as ever, with the same chal-lenges being evident over a century of time. Although the oceans of open grassland are gone forever, the knowledge and sacrifices of the range men, has made our land a better place to live for those generations still to come.

# Guy Pallister: Cowman

The men who started the cow business in Southern Alberta well over a century ago were individualists, and each was a character in his own right. Amongst these were a large number of good cowmen who were rated by what they could do, instead of by the clothes they wore, or the money they were supposed to have. I had the opportunity to know some of these same men during their latter years, from whom my life was molded to some degree. My father, the late Guy Pallister was one of these men; who came to Canada from Sheffield, England at the age of sixteen.

My father was a man of few words and seldom spoke of the days he was punching cows with the round-up wagons on the open range, unless some old cowhand of that era came by for a visit, or to stop for the night. While I was home for Christmas one year during the mid-1950s, I got him talking about his early life on the range, and other cowmen he had worked with over the years. Although he was getting up in years by that time, his health was good and his mind was still coherent. This was his brief story as he related it to me many years ago.

He was raised in the same English village as Bert Sheppard's father, which was the reason he came to Canada and to the High River district as a young man. Harry Sheppard met him in Calgary in May 1888, and they traveled by democrat to the Sheppard ranch located at that time, on Hay Creek that is now part of the Spruce Grazing Association west of Nanton.

His first job in Canada was with Harry Sheppard, until the spring of 1892, at which time he was hired as nighthawk for the Bar U round-up wagon; when Henry Arnett was wagon boss. Some other men working on the Bar U wagon that summer were Charlie Miller, Ted Hill, George Scott, Bert Wilder and Dave Bryant. Bryant came in late one evening and was refused supper by the cook. Without any argument Bryant "wiped up the ground with the cook," a phrase my father often used to describe men fighting. The cook asked for a horse and left camp the same evening! Charlie Miller took over the mess wagon for the remainder of the roundup.

That winter Guy went to work for Jack Crawford who was constructing a set of ranch buildings, that later became known as the 7U Brown Ranch. The following spring found him working for Charlie Knox, breaking horses with Ed McArthur and Charlie McLaughlin at the ranch currently owned by

Francis Gardner; now named the Mt. Sentinel Ranch. He said this is where he learned to ride bad horses, which were peddled throughout central Canada.

In the fall of 1895 Guy was with the Oxley round-up wagon with Jimmy Johnson as wagon boss. That winter he went breaking horses for Bill McCombe who was foreman for Pat Burns at a ranch on the Little Bow, out of High River, which was later owned by George and Arthur Broderick. The next summer he was on the round up with the Burns wagon run by Bill McCombe. Several other men who rode with the wagon that summer were Frank Heslip, Marvin Sexsmith and Dave Baird. That winter took him back to the High River place, breaking horses; which W.R. Hull brought over from the central part of British Columbia.

During 1897 and 1898 Guy worked for George Emerson, whose ranch headquarters were established several miles up stream from the present day EP Ranch on Pekisko Creek. He hauled hay for Emerson during the winter months and represented Emerson on the Bar U wagon during the summer. Herb Miller was wagon boss both years. After roundup of 1898 he worked for a man named Flucough who then owned the property that is now the Eden Valley Indian Reservation. Bert Wilder was foreman on that ranch and along with Fred Anderson they built the big log barn that stood for many years on that location.

For the years between 1899 and 1905, he was back working for Emerson and 'repping' on the Bar U wagon each summer. During the winter of 1904/05, he took his only trip back to his homeland; with two trainloads of cattle shipped by boat to England for the Gordon, Ironside and Fares Company. During the summer of 1905 Charlie McKinnon was boss of the Bar U wagon when Guy was riding a good string of horses, all gentle and well broke. One morning early, George Lane showed up at the wagon and asked Guy to catch a good horse to help work the herd. McKinnon sent half the riders on a big circle, including Guy Pallister. He told McKinnon he would not ride circle on that particular horse; and after helping to work the herd all day, McKinnon fired him that evening. For the remainder of that season he went to work for the Mosquito Creek wagon which was run by Charlie Anderson.

In 1906 he was back with the Oxley wagon working for Billy Playfair. During the hard winter of 1906 and 1907 Guy worked for Burns near High River trying to keep 1000 head of mangy steers alive, with only a slab fence for shelter. He was back at the Oxley in 1907 and while loading a trainload of beef at Cayley, Guy was putting up the bull bar on a loaded cattle car when a wild steer struck with a horn that gored his stomach. As the train was nearly loaded, he held in his intestines; while they put him on the train, which quickly headed for High River to get him some medical attention! Being tough, he survived the ordeal and was back with the Oxley outfit the following year under George Crooks.

During the summer of 1909 Guy was boss of the Oxley wagon. My father was foreman for Pat Burns on the Mackie Ranch from 1910 to 1917, which was situated eighteen miles west of Milk River. This was one of Burn's largest outfits and ran over 5000 head of cattle and 600 horses. During the winter of 1912, all the cattle were fed on the river ice at Milk River. Baled hay was shipped from northern Alberta on the railroad, and hauled directly out of the boxcars, with teams, to the feed ground. When this ranch was sold, the cattle were trailed to the Waldron Ranch north of Lundbreck where Einer Nielson had taken over as foreman.

In 1915 he married Evelyn Metchette in Calgary, a bride who had came over from Ireland. On their way back to the ranch after the honeymoon, the Milk River was in full flood. Gordon Hall, a ranch hand at the Mackie Ranch at that time, had taken a team and light democrat to Milk River to pick up the newly married couple. Gordon Hall told me many years later that Mrs. Pallister was nearly lost in the floodwaters on their trip back to the ranch!

Guy worked for the High River Wheat and Cattle Company at the TL Ranch on Sullivan Creek during 1918 and 1919, which he mentioned, were possibly the most enjoyable years of his long ranching career. During 1920 George Lane sent him to Bow City to work for the two Lane brothers, Ernie and Roy. When the Bar U held their last round up during 1922, Guy was the cooking for the roundup crew at the mess wagon.

In 1923 Burns hired him again to run the Lineham Ranch, which was up wind, about four miles west of the town of Turner Valley. This is where the majority of the Pallister children were raised, before that ranch was sold in 1943. He was foreman for the following four years on a smaller ranch for Burns, south of Priddis, named the Bradfield. Burns Ranches retired him during 1947 and Guy was one of very few men who received a pension from the Pat Burns Estate. He enjoyed eleven more good years of retirement before passing away during April 1958.

There were thirteen children born to the Pallister family with the oldest born in 1915 and the youngest during 1937. Never at anytime, were all the children at home together. By time the youngest child was born, the oldest had already left home during the depression years of the 1930s. Only six of the thirteen children are still living. Four sons served in the Second World War, however Joe, who was the sixth child, never returned; and is buried in Belgium. Twenty-eight grand children can claim the name of Pallister who have increased their generations with thirty-three great grand children.

(Note:This statement has changed since Hank's death, and the birth of many more Pallister grandchildren.)

This is only one story that has been written about the early days of ranching; those days which often told about old cattle brands, the open range days, and round-up wagons. If it were possible to turn back the calendar for only a half a century, when Guy Pallister and many other early cowmen were still living; they would be asked a thousand questions about their lifestyle of initiative, courage, and independence; a lifestyle that has long been forgotten. This lifestyle was the way of life, and it can now be appreciated by many generations that have a ranching heritage, including the great grandchildren of Guy and Evelyn Pallister.

# A.J. (Archie) McLean,
# Cypress Cattle Company
## CY Left Ribs

The Calgary Exhibition and Stampede, held annually and advertised as the greatest outdoor show on earth; has become well known world-wide. The first show, held in 1912, had an interesting beginning when a young American rodeo promoter, Guy Weadick, interested four Alberta ranchers of that era to sponsor that first stampede. The annual Exhibition and Stampede has become a universal attraction; and these four ranchers, now deceased, are still referred to as the "Big Four." Three of these ranchers, who were also successful businessmen, have received much publicity over the years in the development of Alberta's livestock industry.

Pat Burns has been remembered for his ranching empire and packing house business throughout western Canada. Alfred E. Cross was known also for his ranching interests and a brewing business in Calgary, while George Lane made the famous Bar U Ranch known worldwide with his registered Percheron horses. The fourth member of the big four fraternity was a man named Archie J. McLean, whose name has been seldom mentioned in livestock circles of the past.

Archie McLean was born and educated in the county of Aldboro, in Ontario. After gaining a considerable amount of knowledge about livestock, forage crops, fruit growing and hard work on the practical end of a hayfork and garden hoe, he headed west into the setting sun, with little money and some good ideas. He landed at Winnipeg during 1881 and established a small farm in the Pipestone River district of Manitoba. McLean's second business of purchasing workhorses in Ontario and selling them to construction crews that were building the Canadian Pacific Railway westward; ended up being a profitable venture.

His involvement of dealing in live horseflesh gave him experience for another plan he had in mind; becoming involved with the cattle business on the western prairies. Several years before Archie McLean arrived in Manitoba, there had been another youthful newcomer from Ontario who had almost parallel ambitions. This man was Patrick Burns, who even during the early 1880s was well on his way towards an industrial cattle kingdom. Burns and McLean, one of Irish descent and the other Scottish, made a companionship that lasted through good times and bad, which included successes and failures right to the end of their careers.

By the time McLean had reached Alberta's cow country during 1886, the possibility of getting into the cow business was not that encouraging. The summer months that year were dry, and prairie fires had eaten up large tracts of the range country. That winter was a tough one and many of the livestock turned loose on the open range did not survive to enjoy the green grass the following spring.

A census of the livestock population was taken in 1886 and reported 104 000 cattle, 11 000 head of horses and 25 000 sheep in the Calgary district alone, which caused a problem of over-grazing for the ranchers of the area. On top of other things, mange had developed in the ranch country and the government raised the price of new lease land to $20 for a thousand acres and placed a twenty percent duty on cattle from the United States. The situation was not exactly cheerful for any newcomers, but looking past the gloom of things, the price of beef continued upward.

Overlooking the problems of 1886, Mr. McLean came to Alberta with not too much knowledge of cattle ranching. He went to work in the southern part of the province as a rather green cowhand, carefully watching and learning the cow business. Within several years, still in his twenties, he was promoted to a managerial position with the Cypress Cattle Company, which was located about twenty miles out of Taber.

About the time McLean arrived in Alberta, experimental shipments of beef to the British Isles had begun, which indicated there was money to be made on a project of this nature. With this idea in mind, McLean organized the export firm of Bater and McLean. Bater being the selling end of the business overseas. For some years the business flourished and many good steers identified with the CY brand made their first and last trip across the Atlantic Ocean.

By 1905 the Province of Alberta had become incorporated; and the ranching business appeared to have settled on a more even economy. The decade preceding saw many new developments, one being the relentless advance of dirt farmers with a determined intent of growing wheat and utilizing great tracts of virgin grassland for that purpose. There were symptoms of mixed farming taking place, and the chief of the CY Ranch saw this invasion reaching limits far more extensive than many of the older ranchers ever believed could happen.

With leases being steadily cancelled as the influx of settlers reached flood proportions, McLean quietly started to liquidate the CY holdings. Its livestock was disposed of while much of the fine grassland went into growing grain, and McLean made a temporary exit from the ranching industry.

Between the years of 1909 and 1921 Archie McLean entered the field of politics and became an effective member of the legislature for the Liberal government in Alberta. During his political career he served in three different cabinet positions as provincial treasurer, Minister of Municipal Affairs, and the Minister of Public Works.

It was during this period that McLean embarked on probably the largest and most pleasing venture of his career. In company with the other three members of the "Big Four" he put up one quarter of the funds required to underwrite the first Calgary Stampede. The initial day of the big show brought thousands of people to experience this unusual extravaganza. People continued to pour through the gates for the remainder of the week, firmly establishing the annual rodeo and telling the world that the backers had made a sound gamble.

When McLean's political career ended in 1921, he immediately rounded up a couple of cattlemen who knew the cow business well and started another ranch. The only original item about this new venture was the CY brand. Their range comprised of 18 000 acres on the Peigan Indian Reserve leased at six cents an acre. It was stocked with cattle and did moderately well, because cattle prices were generally good through most of the twenties. It was not until the Depression became apparent in 1929 that McLean sold the second and last of his CY enterprises to Central Canadian interests.

In the meantime George Lane had passed away, leaving his vast holdings in a somewhat of uncertain state. The bank appointed McLean to manage the Bar U Ranch and while he was in charge, he sold it, along with the Flying E Ranch, to Pat Burns for the unofficial sum of three quarters of a million dollars.

In the latter years of life, Archie McLean managed the Namaka farms for the Lane Estate. He journeyed often to Pincher Creek and Fort MacLeod, where he owned two sections of good farmland. While traveling to Fort Macleod one autumn afternoon, he took ill and died in the hospital there on October 13, 1933. He was buried in that town and his funeral was one of the largest in Southern Alberta. All who attended spoke reverently of a man who never made a million dollars, but who had a million friends.

# History of the a7 Ranch Brand and the Cross Family

More than a century has passed since Alfred Earnest Cross, better known to the Ranching Fraternity of Western Canada as A.E.Cross, left his home in Montreal, Quebec and came west into the "Territories" (presently the provinces of Alberta, Saskatchewan, and the Northwest Territories) looking for new adventure. Being young, educated with a new initiative, A.E. Cross easily found employment with the Cochrane Ranching Company as their bookkeeper and veterinarian.

A year later, during the summer of 1885, he acquired a homestead along with a sizeable lease that would handle 500 head of cattle. The money was borrowed to purchase the cattle, which was only the beginning of a great cattle empire.

During the spring of 1886, Mr. Cross quickly realized his livestock that were running on the open range needed to be branded, so he obtained a brand for cattle on the left ribs, and for horses on the left thigh. On May 26, 1886 the a7 brand was registered to Cross Brothers with the Recorder of Brands, located during that era at Fort Macleod.

A.E. Cross had a brother in the "Territories" who had also obtained a homestead. The tough winter of 1886 -1887 destroyed a large percentage of the Cross cattle, so A.E.Cross decided his management policies had to change if he was going to survive in the ranching business. He saw the need to get further back into the hills, to where there was more winter feed and shelter, so he purchased his brother's homestead and started the original a7 ranch, located at the north end of the Porcupine Hills. During April 1900, the brand was transferred from Cross Brothers to A.E. Cross of Calgary. A person may wonder why Mr. Cross chose the two characters he selected for a cattle brand. Those who may have inquired would have found that his first thought for a brand was A1, because he wanted his ranching operation to be first class! Theoretically, his intention must have been more than a dream because the pages of history have told the a7 operation has been a top notch success.

Further to the brand design, A.E. Cross decided not to use the a1, but chose the 7 instead; the "a" being his first initial and the numeral 7 representing seven members of his family. The legal vent for the a7 brand was a lazy on the left shoulder, and ear marks were also registered as an under and over slope on the left ear, and a crop and an under half crop on the right ear. The records would indicate that A.E. Cross did not reside for any length of time on the ranch, but took up residence in Calgary and managed his ranching operation effectively from his Calgary office. He, like many other old cowmen of that era, insisted on having things done properly and with accuracy.

The Brand file on the brand covers a good deal of correspondence between Mr. Cross and the Recorder of Brands with regard to the manner in which the 7 brand was being improperly drawn on brand renewal certificates, and especially in Provincial Brand Books. He was most persistent in the fact that the numeral 7 had to be drawn at right angles.

A.E. Cross passed away during 1932, and the ranch assets were placed in an estate with his three sons as administrators. The ranch continued to operate under the administration of the estate and during December 1939, the brand was transferred from the estate and became the property of the 7 Ranch. For at least the past two decades, the Ranch has been owned and operated by John Cross and family. The Ranch had, no doubt, enjoyed some good times, along with the numerous problems involved with the ranching industry. The ranch survived the dry depression years of the 1930s and capitalized on the great years of the 1950s and 1960s when they were known for marketing their good cross beef cattle and their range management techniques developed years ago.

This Ranch celebrated it's one-hundredth anniversary in 1986, and I congratulate the descendants of the A.E.Cross family for the development of a great cow ranch, and mostly for their management skills in operating the ranch in the same family name for a full 100 years.

> (written by H.G.Pallister in August 1986 to commemorate to one-hundredth anniversary of the registration of the a7 brand.)

# Lane, Gordon, Ironside, and Fares

Since the headquarters of the famous Bar U Ranch became a historical site of Parks Canada in 1991, relevant historic data of George Lane, Pat Burns and Fred Stimson has since been made public and displayed at that location. The partnership role of Gordon, Ironside and Fares, who were major shareholders for nearly two decades during the early years of the twentieth century, has been generally disregarded in portraying the story of this historic ranch. Furthermore, the ranching achievements of this partnership in the annals of Alberta's early ranch history has mostly been forgotten.

The Bar U Ranch was established during 1882 and for the following twenty years it was owned and operated by the Northwest Cattle Company, whose headquarters were in Montreal. The initial company consisted of five shareholders with the Allan family holding more than fifty percent of the shares. Fred Stimson, who was assigned the position of resident Ranch Manager, owned shares of about ten percent. The ranch prospered during the 1880s and paid high dividends to their shareholders, but by the latter half of the 1890s the annual profits had dwindled.

Fred Stimson would have enjoyed owning the Bar U Ranch for himself and to that end he made it appear to the other shareholders that ranching in the Canadian Northwest was a bad investment. The cattle that were ready for sale were held back for several years and left on the open range, leaving the ranch books showing a financial loss instead of any kind of a profit. George Lane had left the Bar U more than ten years earlier, but had been kept well informed of their financial situation and knew very close to how many beef steers there were for sale that carried the Bar U brand.

Exactly why the Allan family decided to dispose of the Northwest Cattle Company, which was a minor part of their investment portfolio, was never actually established. It may have been because of the Stimson scenario, or because of the death of Andrew Allan, the long-time Company president who died in June 1901. In any case, as soon as word reached High River that the Bar U Ranch was for sale during January 1902, George Lane was on the train heading for Montreal. He stopped in Winnipeg long enough to pick up fifty thousand dollars cash money from his partners; Gordon, Ironsides, and Fares and stuffed it in the pockets of his riding britches.

The meeting Lane had with the Allan family in Montreal while negotiating the purchase of the ranch was described as a formal affair. The asking price for the Bar U was $250 000 and Lane offered $220 000 with $50 000 down. After a period of hassling and sparring over the deal, the Allan's laughingly agreed to Lane's price and motioned for the waiter to fill up the glasses. The Allan's reclined their chairs figuring that Lane was bluffing until he dug out the $50 000 and laid it on the table; advising them at the same time the rest of the financing would be arranged while the legal papers were being put in order. It has always been assumed that George Lane never did plan to purchase the Bar U on his own, recognizing that Gordon, Ironside and Fares would be a factor in the negotiations from the outset.

In 1902 a partnership of George Lane, Rancher, and Gordon, Ironside, and Fares, who were Winnipeg cattle buyers, packers and exporters; acquired the assets of the Northwest Cattle Company. The assets consisted of 3000 head of cattle, 500 horses, buildings and approximately 19 000 acres of land; and for the next eighteen years these partners operated it as the Bar U Ranch with Lane as active manager. The association between Lane and Gordon, Ironside and Fares began during the 1890s when Lane was hired as a cattle buyer for the meat packing company. During their first year of operation at the Bar U, the new owners sold enough Bar U beef to pay for the initial cost of the ranch, since Lane knew Stimson held the cattle for too long!

James T. Gordon was born in Ontario during December 1858 and moved to Manitoba when he was twenty years old. He found employment with a lumber company and went into the lumber business for himself in 1882. He formed a partnership with Robert Ironside, a firm that dealt in lumber, grain, and cattle. This partnership was dissolved in 1886 but was reorganized again when James Gordon moved to Winnipeg.

Robert Ironside was also born in Ontario and moved west to Manitoba in 1882 to work as an agent for a company that manufactured farming implements. He formed a partnership with James Gordon in 1884 to supply beef to construction crews working on the Pembina Branch of the CPR, and to the militia forces in 1885. Although this partnership broke up during 1886, both partners continued to deal in livestock and became partners again in 1893. They purchased 5000 head of cattle in the ranching country that year valued at about $200 000 and exported 4600 of them to Britain. The rapid growth of cattle exports was attributed to changes in international cattle trade, which benefited the Western ranchers at the expense of the Central Canadian producers. The export of live cattle to Britain began in a small way during 1874 and by time the first shipment of Western ranch cattle was exported overseas, Canada had exported a total of 63 000 head to Britain in 1887.

W.H. Fares joined the packing firm in 1897, at which time it became known as Gordon, Ironside and Fares. Fares was born during July 1858 in

Lobo Township, Middlesex County, Ontario, the son of William Fares. Trained as a butcher in Sarnia, he moved to Emerson, Manitoba during 1879. While in partnership with George Christie, he became a well-known cattle buyer in both Manitoba and Minnesota before joining Gordon and Ironside. He gradually assumed the responsibility for most of the livestock purchasing, while Gordon took charge of the company's packing business and Ironside handled their export operation. Fares also maintained interests outside of the packing firm. From 1898 he was a partner with James Ryan, of Ryan and Fares, who were livestock dealers in Winnipeg. He was a partner also in the firm of Smith and Fares, Ranchers and Dealers in Livestock at Rush Lake Saskatchewan. Robert Ironside had been a Liberal member of the Manitoba legislature and often wrote the Minister of the Interior regarding ranching policies for Western Canada. James Gordon sat as a Conservative MLA for Winnipeg South from 1901 to 1910. Although his contacts with the federal government were not as close as those of Ironsides, he had connections with the financial world that were useful in financing their cattle purchasing operation.

At some point of operation, Gordon, Ironside and Fares established a working relationship with Pat Burns of Calgary. Burns focused on the domestic market supplying beef to Alberta and British Columbia while Gordon, Ironside and Fares concentrated on the export market. Western ranchers viewed this relationship as a price fixing ordeal and the Beef Commission of 1907 investigated their complaints. Both Burns and Gordon denied any attempts to fixing prices or to divide up the market. The commission found that Burns did not bother entering the export market and that he turned any export steers over to Gordon, Ironside and Fares. Nevertheless the commission found this arrangement to be legitimate because it benefited all livestock producers. Gordon, Ironside and Fares continued to dominate the live cattle export business until it collapsed in 1913.

Similar to Burns, Gordon, Ironside and Fares became involved in the ranching business on a large scale and between 1896 and 1907, and their firm either purchased or leased large parcels of ranch land in both Alberta and Saskatchewan. About 1896 the company acquired a range in the Wintering Hills and established the Two Bar Ranch south of Drumheller. This ranch consisted of only one-quarter section of land without any lease, and for the next ten years they ran from five to ten thousand head of cattle on this range annually. As early as 1903 Gordon, Ironside and Fares owned a large ranch in Mexico with a breeding herd of 12 000 cows, which was sold before 1913.

In 1907 they acquired the remains of the Canadian Agricultural Coal and Colonization Company, which included cattle and land around Crane Lake along with the old 76 brand. Gordon, Ironside and Fares acquired also the remnants of two large American Ranches, the Turkey Track and the T Bar Down Ranch, which were crippled by the severe winter of 1906. For several years, the firm also leased the Blood Indian Reserve in Southern Alberta where they ran another 10 000 head of cattle. These were only some of their ranch holdings before they sold most of their leases to Pat Burns after 1920.

Prior to the majority of their ranching investments, Gordon, Ironside and Fares had built an abattoir adjacent to the CPR yards in Winnipeg during 1898. Their meat slaughtering business expanded steadily, and by 1914 the size of their abattoir had increased its premises to cover eight acres of land. They built another slaughter house in Moose Jaw; including cold storage, with distribution points at Regina, and Kenora, Fort Williams, Port Authur and Sault St. Marie in Ontario

The company prospered during the decade that followed 1907. In 1909 each senior member received a large bonus in addition to their salaries and the company issued a 46 per cent dividend. At the same time their operating capital was increased to four million dollars. Although profits had risen to nearly four and a half million in 1916, Gordon, Ironside and Fares were in financial difficulty by the end of the First World War. Robert Ironside had passed away during 1910, and by 1917 James Gordon, who was the core of the company, was in poor health. Gordon died during December 1919 and his death effectively ended the history of Gordon, Ironside and Fares. Their Limited Company continued to exist until the late 1930s but became inactive, with no assets and extensive liabilities. History does not reveal the destiny of the third partner, William H. Fares.

George Lane was no doubt responsible in having Gordon, Ironside and Fares involved with the Bar U Ranch during the glamour years of its operation. Because Lane was so knowledgeable in the operation of the Bar U, Gordon, Ironside and Fares were satisfied to be silent partners and their association with the ranch was simply financial. Nevertheless, they remained half owners of the ranch until it was sold during 1920. After the death of James Gordon, George Lane purchased their half interest in the Bar U Ranch for three quarters of a million dollars.

The death of George Lane during September 1925 certainly did not end the story of the Bar U Ranch. The old ranch has continued to operate under several different owners since Lane's death. Through more than a century of time, the ranch has employed some of the best cowmen the livestock industry has known. Each has contributed a special part to the tales that have been told in respect to the famous Bar U Ranch. If a complete storybook could be written about the people and changes that have happened at the old ranch location, it would be an interesting and cherished publication.

# Webster Lefthand: Native Cowman

I have always appreciated the native people in Alberta, especially the older generation of the Stoney Indian Tribe at Morley. In 1948 this tribe expanded to a second reservation located on the North Fork of the Highwood River, approximately twenty miles west of Longview. During the 1940s I had the privilege of working with many male members of this tribe, who had the initiative each summer to find employment on the cattle ranches along the foothills, south of Calgary. Many of these native men have since passed away, but I continue to enjoy visiting with those that are still around.

Several months ago I was traveling the upper Highwood Valley on the North Fork and stopped to see Webster Lefthand. Webster is a resident of the Eden Valley Reservation, and has spent the most of his life as a cowhand for the larger ranches within the Highwood watershed. During our visit we talked about both the present and the past and Webster related this story of the years gone by.

Webster is the son of George Lefthand, who has been deceased for more than fifty years; and was a native of the Morley Indian Reserve . His parents were camped along Sheep Creek east of Black Diamond, stooking green feed for the late Harry Thomson, when Webster was born during September 1920. After being raised and educated at Morley he married Dorothy Rider in February 1939. Dorothy is the daughter of Jonas Rider, an old style native cowman who was well respected by all the ranchers along the foothills.

Webster, like all other young native men during the hungry 1930s, took the first opportunity possible to leave the reservation, that was already over-crowded. His father-in-law Jonas was camped at the Bar U Ranch and had possibly been camped there all that winter. Soon after he was married, Webster and his new bride took the train from Morley to High River and were met at the station by the late Lee Alwood and Jonas Rider. They were taken to the Bar U Ranch where several Indian families were camped on the bench land south of the Bar U buildings. Webster soon found employment as a Bar U cowhand, helping Jonas Rider calve the Bar U cows along with Judy Dixon and Eddy Lefthand.

According to Webster, the following scenarios happened each spring for the next dozen years at the Bar U Ranch. The Indian families would move their camp close to the ranch site as it got close to calving time. Jonas Rider was always in charge of the Indian cowboys who were each allowed to keep several grain-fed horses in the saddle horse stable along with the regular Bar U riders. The Indian boys on the calving crew had to get up early to feed the horses they were riding, and saddle them before breakfast. Breakfast was always ready in the cookhouse at 6 a.m. and by 7 a.m. the stable was cleaned, after which everyone was mounted, and on the trail. The cook always gave the Indian boys a lunch.

Jonas and his crew always calved in the winter field where the majority of the Bar U cows rustled most winters. This large piece of country that was kept especially for winter grazing lay North and West of the ranch buildings. The South fence of the field could be reached within a couple of miles from the ranch and then stretched North for another seven or eight miles. The crew would split up in this field and look for cows that might be in trouble calving and meet again at noon at an old cow camp, situated at the North fence. The cow camp was an old vacated ranch house where there was always some tea, sugar and canned milk. The Indian boys always made a fire to heat some water for tea to have with their cold sandwiches. After lunch they would ride back through the same piece of country, to unsaddle and be ready for supper by 6 p.m. Towards the end of calving season they would start moving the cows and calves to the North side of this field where several branding corrals were located. Extra Indian boys were hired for the Bar U brandings, which sometimes took a week or ten days to finish. Mark Lefthand always brought a crew over from the Anchor P Ranch to help at the Bar U brandings, and Jonas Rider took enough native boys back to Macleay's Anchor P to help them brand, so everyone could be finished before the Calgary Stampede.

Webster grinned as he told about the Bar U brandings, and said, "Every morning at branding time was like a stampede." Extra riders needed extra horses so the Bar U cowboys would bring a herd of green broke horses to the cow camp for the Indian boys to ride. Everyone on the branding crew was given a Bar U horse early in the morning. It was better to get bucked off before leaving camp, because there were always riders to help catch your horse again. If you were bucked off after everyone left to gather cows and calves, you were on your own! Many Indian boys had to walk back to camp, which sometimes was a long way!

After the Bar U Ranch was sold in 1950 Webster continued to work for the new owner. While Allen Baker was negotiating the purchase of the ranch he asked Raymond Clifford which of his riders was the best cowman. Raymond's reply was "Webster Lefthand, without any doubt." Consequently, Webster was hired as cow foreman for Mr. Baker and worked there for the next six years, during which time he and his family lived in a log house at the Bar U Ranch site.

Webster indicated that he rode some good horses during his many years at the Bar U Ranch. He talked about one special horse they called 'Brown Dog' that was sired from a thoroughbred stallion that the Bar U named 'Desmond Star'. Brown Dog was a big five-year-old brown gelding about sixteen hands high. The gelding was purchased from Raymond Clifford for one hundred dollars, which was a bargain price for a ranch horses during the 1950s. Webster said with excitement, "The horse could really run, and for several years I raced him at all the races I could get him to. Clem Gardner always wanted to buy him, so one day I finally sold him to Clem, and never saw the horse again."

About 1970 the native Indian Department of Education approached Webster to go back to school. He attended the University of Alberta in Edmonton for three consecutive years followed with two different summer sessions at the Lethbridge College. "That was somewhat of a contrast" Webster said, "from being a Bar U cowhand." After obtaining this further education he was selected as a Gymnastic Instructor and taught gym courses to all classes of children at the Black Diamond, Turner Valley and Longview schools for seven years.

Webster readily admits that his cowboy days are over. He currently lives in a modern home on the Eden Valley Reserve, where he plans to spend his remaining years. The long cold days spent in the saddle, show in his tall slender frame that is not as agile as it used to be. The glisten of his black hair has disappeared and the years have dimmed his eyesight, to where it shows in his facial expressions. He enjoys reminiscing about the years that have passed, but his face will brighten with a big smile, should anyone mention the Bar U Ranch. "It was a great place to work as a cowhand," he said, "I would do it all again if we could turn back the years."

# Barbwire Johnny Speers

During the days of the old time cowmen, the southern part of Alberta was open-range country that was still unfenced and the grass was free. It has now become part of the heritage that is often talked about throughout our ranching environment. Much has already been written about many early cowmen who had the initiative to gamble with the ranching business, and whose life and success is documented on pages of early ranch history.

There were many other good men who drifted into the early range country, looking for work as cowboys on ranches that had already been established. There were those who were just seeking a new experience in life, and became loyal dependable men to the outfits they worked for. Some were cowmen with years of experience and others were bronk men who would accept only a job breaking horses. One of these characters was an eccentric old cowboy, named John Speers, who became well known in Southern Alberta as "Barbwire Johnny." There are several different stories as to exactly how this man inherited the name "Barbwire."

My father worked with him on the round-ups and told many stories about a person the old timers called "Barbwire Johnny." I finally had the opportunity to meet him after he became an elderly man, visiting with him several times during the 1960s when he was a resident of the Senior Citizen's home in Pincher Creek. His mind was still coherent and he enjoyed reminiscing about the past and especially the years he spent working on ranches, the roundups and the days of the open range. He was a short, stocky man and spoke very slow with a deep voice. This is part of his life story as he told it to me many years ago.

Johnny Speers was born in Ontario and came west with his family to Fort Macleod in 1890. His father was a carpenter, and was kept busy building settler's homes between Fort Macleod and the Crow's Nest Pass. Johnny attended school in both Fort Macleod and Pincher Creek, and then at the age of fourteen he went to work. After working for several ranches in that area, he found a job night herding horses for Herb Miller on the Bar U horse roundup during the spring of 1901. While night herding he became tangled in some barbwire that the settlers were stringing around their newly claimed pastures and arrived back at camp one morning a little scratched up. Joe Lamar was riding rough string that spring the on Bar U wagon, and jokingly called him

"Barbwire Johnny," a name which he was known by for the remainder of his life time.

For the next half dozen years he worked for different roundup outfits and was always given the job of "rough string rider," who was the man who handled the entire group of mean horses that no one else could ride. It is doubtful if Johnny ever knew the meaning of real fear, because while still in his teens he was handling horses that some men would not dare lead to water.

Johnny soon acquired the ability and reputation of being able to ride most anything, but also was rather hard on horses. Sometimes he had to defend himself on this issue and would admit he was rather tough on some horses because he never got any that were not mean or spoiled. He would say, "If I'd handled those old boogers with any kindness, they would have killed me."

One day Johnny showed up at the Waldron Ranch just at noontime while the crew was having dinner. He was dressed in some old ragged clothes and was wearing boots that did not match. He told the ranch foreman he was looking for a job, and claimed he was able to handle rough horses. The foreman was wanting to get rid of this persistent kid, so while he was roping out fresh horses for an afternoon gather, he caught an old bronk for the kid to work on. The horse had not been handled for some time and was only kept around the ranch for cowboys who thought they were bronk riders. The foreman left with his crew to gather cattle, leaving Johnny alone with the horse in the corral without providing him with a saddle or other riding equipment.

Johnny, telling about the incident, said, "It did not take me long to figure out what the old outlaw had in mind!" He said, "The old bronk looked meaner than a female grizzly with nursing cubs, and he just stood there at the end of the rope daring him to come any closer." He recalled the old bronk was showing some age; with a chewed off ear on the near side and a glass eye on the other.

After finding some rope, he caught the horse's front feet. Using a piece of rope for hobbles, he then tied one hind foot high up off the ground. He then found a saddle blanket on the corral fence that had been put there to dry, which he used to 'sack out' the old bronk until he quit fighting the ropes. All he could find for a saddle was an old packsaddle that had been used for packing salt, and a couple of old stirrups that were discarded years before. Finding a couple of halter shanks, he rigged up a primitive looking outfit using the halter ropes for stirrup leathers and cinched it down on the horse with the saddle blanket folded for a seat. He found a halter and by using a snaffle bit with some leather lace he was able to build a makeshift head gear with a piece of worn out lariat rope for reins. All this time the old bronk was just standing there anxiously waiting for Johnny to crawl aboard.

But Johnny had other ideas and proceeded to find some pieces of scrap metal that he located around the ranch. He hung these on both sides of the saddle, low enough to swing freely. When he untied the ropes, the old bronk went straight up and bucked around the corral with the heavy pieces of metal beating him pitifully every time he hit the ground. Johnny recalled the horse was no fool and it did not take him long to figure out there was no benefit in beating himself to death with those pieces of iron that hung down alongside his ribs. The old bronk quit bucking and just stood there 'chucking' his head with flaring eyes, just waiting for Johnny to get on top.

Johnny was fixing to do so, but not until he went to the creek and cut a willow club about three feet long and two inches in diameter. Johnny remembered that when he crawled aboard, it was easy to see that the old horse must have had lots of practice.

He went to bucking and really turned on the heat, even after taking a beating with all the hardware. Johnny caught him a good lick over the nose with the willow persuader to remind him the contest was not going to be a picnic, and the bronk soon gave up. After he quit bucking, the horse tried to chew on Johnny's leg but the willow club did some more discouraging. It was not long until the horse showed Johnny some respect and was satisfied to have him on his back using the willow stick for a reminder. Johnny opened the corral gate and went looking for the crew that was gathering cattle. They were mighty surprised when they saw him riding the ranch's most favorite outlaw.

During 1908 Johnny went homesteading, accompanied by his sister Jessie. One evening her clothing caught fire from an overheated stove and she died the next morning from the severe burns. He was married in 1911 and the Speers raised five children. After the family left home, Johnny spent several years with the Cree Indians in the Peace River country. They taught him to hunt and trap; knowledge he continued to use during the latter years of his life.

He came back south again and for several years during the Second World War he had a summer job looking after cattle for the Stock Association up Willow Creek. Several times a month Johnny would have to ride down country to the little store located above the forks of the creek, to get food supplies. He would always arrive at the store during the evening. riding one horse and leading two. He would throw his bedroll out and sleep on the floor of the store and leave his horses tied to the hitching rail outside. One morning the storekeeper remarked about the halters he used to tie his horse with because they were made from old harness tugs clamped with rings that were half an inch in diameter. Johnny told the storekeeper he made the halters himself, "so that when he had to leave his horses tied at night, he knew at least their heads would be there in the morning!"

During his latter years he took accommodation at the Senior's Lodge in Pincher Creek during the winter, and every spring he would hustle back to his cabin, located somewhere along the Oldman River. There he would trap and wander through the mountains for hundreds of miles every year, following the tracks of a certain bear or hunting for signs of the Lost Lemon Gold Mine. He would often stop overnight or drop in for a meal at Macleay's cow camp situated to the west of the Oldman River. He was always welcome at most ranches because of his dry kind of humor, and the stories he told that were full of action. He was somewhat an eccentric individual who enjoyed being alone. This explains why he was found dead nearly thirty years ago, in a mountain cabin somewhere along the Oldman River, a place where he loved to be.

# Bert Sheppard

Some people are somewhat similar to old saddle horses. Anytime they are turned loose they will return to the part of the country where they were raised. These conditions fit this author to some extent; in that I wander back to the Longview and Turner Valley country , whenever there is an opportunity. Anytime I get near Longview, I usually drop around and visit with my old friend Bert Sheppard. When this happens, we most likely get talking about old time cowmen and circumstances that took place in the cow business during the years gone by. This was the occasion during July 1993, when I had lunch with him at his Riverbend Ranch. After lunch we found a shady spot out of the sun and he talked about a horse he rode while breaking horses for the Bar U Ranch.

It was during the early 1930s, and Bert was living at his ranch over the bank and up the river apiece from where the village of Longview is located. Times were tough, and to help things along financially, he was breaking saddle horses in his spare time for Herb Miller, the ranch foreman at the Bar U. Bert would get a half dozen head of unbroke horses from their ranch headquarters on Pekisko Creek; ride them with a snaffle bit for a week and then for several more weeks put them into a curb bit that was well wrapped with cloth. After about twenty days, these horses would be turned back to the Bar U cowhands and another group of bronks would be picked up. Bert broke horses for the Bar U Ranch for approximately ten years prior to 1934.

During these same years, the Stoney Indians at Morley maintained a small bunch of bucking horses, which were used each year at their annual rodeos. Amongst these horses was a big bay gelding, about ten or twelve years old, who had a scum over one eye. Because of his poor visibility, this horse was blacklisted from the rodeos. The horse had previously bucked off Harry Knight, a top-notch rodeo performer. Jonas Rider, a well-respected Indian among the ranchers along the foothills, took the horse and sold him to the Bar U without telling Herb Miller where the horse came from. Herb threw the big gelding in with some bronks that were on their way over to the Sheppard's to be broke. Miller had been recognized as an experienced horseman and a good bronk man himself, when it came to handling tough horses.

Bert remembered getting this particular horse in the spring of the year. The horse was handled and rode in rotation with the others, except that the big gelding could really buck. Bert always rode an 'A tree' slick fork saddle, with long stirrups that were equipped with heavy tapaderos. When riding bronks; his style was to ride in the middle of the saddle, straight up over his stirrups. The weight of the tapaderos helped him to ride by balance and whip the bad ones with a big, shot-loaded, rawhide quirt.

According to Bert, the better old time bronk men relied a great deal on the use of a quirt to discourage horses from bucking. Some men used a chain quirt instead of one made from rawhide, and if a horse looked a little humpy, just the rattle of the chain usually changed their mind from wanting to buck. When horses did buck the quirt was used in rhythm to when the horse hit the ground. A good quirt was long enough to reach down over a horses flank, to the more tender spots located in front of a horse's hind legs. A good quirt man could reach a bronk's left flank with one jump, then up and over to the right flank on the next jump, to maintain a rhythm until the horse stopped bucking. When branding day arrived at the OH Ranch that year, Bert decided to ride the big bay gelding. Burns Ranches were operating the OH during those years and Johnny Brown was their ranch foreman. They branded and bred their cows in a large field they called 'The Basin'; which extended from the Highwood River on the south to Tongue Creek on the north and from Fireguard Coulee to Highway 22, east and west. The branding corrals were located near the centre of the field. Bert forded the river soon after daylight at his Riverbend Ranch, and gathered the cows that were on the flat along the Highwood Trail to Longview. These were pushed up over the bench, to join the cows and calves coming to the corrals from the other directions.

Bert had been asked to heel calves that day, and was sitting on his horse waiting for the branding irons to heat. The big horse felt Bert relax and decided it was the right time for some action. The big gelding went to bucking and Bert rode him straight up without any problem, whipping the buck out of him. By time the action was over, the irons were hot so Bert heeled calves off the horse all day, as some revenge for the rough ride he had received earlier. Johnny Brown had hired a few Indians to help with the branding. The Indians recognized the horse, and after the good ride Sheppard made that morning, the Indians named Sheppard "Bronco Buster!"

Because of the horse's disposition, he had been rode much longer than time spent on any others. The Bar U had a crew working cattle at a cow camp they often used which was located about eight miles north-west of their home ranch. Bert rode the big gelding and led another horse to the cow camp, expecting to see Herb to inform him that someone should keep riding the bay gelding. Herb was not at the cow camp, so instead of any cowhand taking the horse, he was trailed back to the ranch and turned out. Several weeks had passed when Herb decided to send one of the Bar U cowhands to Cochrane to look after their yearling steers that were grazing on land for the summer; that had been acquired from D.P. MacDonald. Amongst the string of horses given this cowhand, Herb included the big gelding that Sheppard had finished breaking. The morning the cowhand left for Cochrane, the big gelding bucked so hard the back cinch of the saddle broke and the cowhand was bucked off. He was riding the big gelding when he left the Bar U horse corrals, but after he crossed the Bow River west of Calgary; he killed the horse. I have inquired since from men who may have known how the horse could have died. The cowhand was a hot-tempered individual who was known to be mean and hard on horses. My informers felt that the horse had bucked him off several times before he reached the Bow. As soon as they crossed the river, he hobbled the horse, blindfolded him, and killed him with a fence post!

I have discussed this with Bert more recently, and asked him why Herb Miller would have purchased an aged horse, especially when the Bar U were raising so many good young horses. Sheppard's only reply was, "I think Herb knew how the horse could buck and wanted to find out if I could ride him."

Several months ago I stopped at the Senior Citizens long term care unit in Black Diamond to visit a short while with my old friend Bert Sheppard. I was traveling behind schedule for a destination further south and intended to stop for only fifteen minutes to say hello. I ended up talking with him for three and a half hours, helping him to clarify in his mind an incident that happened forty years ago. Being ninety-seven years of age, his mind is not as accurate as it used to be, but he certainly enjoys looking back over the years of the better things that have happened during his lifetime.

Bert began ranching on his own at the Riverbend Ranch near Longview after his father's death in 1934. After the oil business moved into that area several years later, Bert found some solitude by purchasing the major portion of the old TL Ranch on Sullivan Creek in 1939, and using the Riverbend only for growing feed and winter grazing. During 1950, he accepted the responsibility of managing the OH Ranch for C.W.Roenisch and Bill Arden; new owners who bought it from P. Burns Ranches. Bert became part owner of the OH Ranch during 1962 and sold his shares in that operation during 1987. The incident that had him deeply puzzled was when he sold his TL Ranch. He remembered the sale happening in 1957 but did not have the slightest idea of what could have happened to the TL cattle. I recalled to his memory that during the 1950s I was reading brands at the Calgary Stockyards, and I took every opportunity to get back into the ranching communities whenever possible. While on annual leave during early September of 1957 I visited the OH Ranch where I had worked earlier for a number of years. The TL Ranch had just been sold to Melvin Nelson of High River; livestock not included. One hundred head of the younger TL cows with calves were sold to the owners of the OH Ranch for a price of $150 for each pair. Frank, Stan and Wallace Gallup of Longview purchased the remaining older cows.

While Bert owned the TL, he held a forest-grazing permit in the high country on both Flat Creek and Sullivan Creek. The year the ranch was sold, about forty head of second cut TL heifers, and a small number of yearling steers were turned out that spring When I arrived at the OH Ranch, I helped him gather these cattle off the forest reserve so they could sell at a sale that was being organized at the OH later that fall.

The OH Ranch, similar to the majority of other foothills ranches of that era, was marketing two-year-old steers off grass, for slaughter. The owners of the OH Ranch decided to sell both their yearling and two-year-old steers at this particular sale. It was conducted by Adams, Wood and Weiller Commission Company out of Calgary and was held in the latter part of October. The yearling steers sold for an average of sixteen cents a pound and the two-year-old steers sold for fourteen cents. The late Art Adams, who always had endless orders for good ranch cattle on the feeder markets in Eastern Canada and the Mid-Western United States; purchased the majority of the steers.

The price obtained for these cattle is one example of how the livestock business has changed in Western Canada during the past forty years. Those who are currently raising beef cattle must contemplate often what changes will be forth-coming in the next forty years.

# The Life and Legend of Warren Zimmerman

During a lifetime, most of us develop an acquaintance with people that suit our nature, and become congenial through interests and past lifestyles. Such a person is Warren Zimmerman, who I have known for more than fifty years. We recently enjoyed lunch together at the Riverbend Ranch near Longview, where Warren and his wife Betty have spent the last sixteen years of retired life. We discussed many things that we have both seen happen in the cow business during the past half-century, and agreed that we have lived through a most dramatic time of Alberta's ranching industry.

Warren was raised on a mixed farm near Sylvan Lake by parents came to that area in 1905. Because of an allergy to grain dust, he left the family farm for health reasons, and came to High River during the summer of 1945. He had heard about the good ranching country in that area and was prepared to begin a life-time occupation of that nature. His first employment was with Henry Sheppard, who owned the property that is now Sheppard Park located adjacent to High River on the south side of 12th Avenue.

Because 1945 had been a very wet summer and fall without any harvesting done, he found work with Walter Hanson, an old timer who built and owned the Chinook Ranch since 1904, south west of Longview. The following spring, the Hanson's were ready to retire from ranching, so they had an auction sale and sold the ranch property to Jim Hughes Sr. After the Hanson sale, Warren went to work for Bert Sheppard, an association that lasted for fifty-two years. My first acquaintance with Warren was branding day at the OH Ranch on June 25, 1946.

For several years Warren spent the summers working at the old TL Ranch on Sullivan Creek and at the Riverbend Ranch during the winters, looking after the TL cows. Bert Sheppard had purchased only a portion of the TL Ranch seven years previously, and was in the process of building new ranch headquarters, at a different location from where the old ranch site had been situated. Warren was very much part of that building program, and the current TL Ranch include some of his fence and corral work built during that era.

Calgary businessmen Kink Roenisch and Bill Arden purchased most of the OH Ranch during late summer of 1950 and hired Bert Sheppard as their ranch manager. This also involved Warren a large amount of the time, as he was called upon anytime cattle work was necessary at the OH. He remembers having to calve their cows in the spring of 1951, when the previous ranch owners allowed their yearling heifers to be bred too early in the season the summer before. This was the beginning of his long association with the OH Ranch, where he learned the cow business from the bottom up. Warren became foreman of the outfit later that summer, and was appointed ranch manager during 1963. He spent an active life on the ranch for the following thirty-four years, retiring in November 1984.

Anyone who was involved with the TL Ranch during the Sheppard era may remember a big friendly black and white tomcat. The TL was always a bachelor outfit, and Warren recalls many lonesome days and nights he spent there alone with only the tomcat for company. His thoughts went back to when he was moving his personal belongings and riding gear from the TL Ranch to the OH Ranch during the summer of 1951. He had put everything together, and was setting on the open veranda of the old TL cabin. The tomcat immediately perched on top of Warren's duffle bag of clothes, expecting to go also, putting up some opposition when he was not included. The tomcat figured he had spent enough time around there by himself and was ready to move elsewhere. Unfortunately, the old cat stayed at the TL for several more years before he became a respected tenant at the OH Ranch; where he lived out his remaining days.

Warren will tell anyone that the highlight of his ranching career was being part of the foothills area, with the opportunity he had to work in some of the best ranching country anywhere. He mentioned the many winters he would move the younger cattle across the river to section seven. The bred two-year-old OH heifers always wintered on section thirteen, which are the open hillsides that can be seen directly west of Longview. The heifers would winter there from November to the middle of March, the next spring, with only some protein blocks to supplement the winter grass. They would be moved back across the river before the ice moved out and were always in fine shape ready to calve.

The largest challenge he experienced during his ranching career was managing the native grass properly in ranching country during the dry summers, and maintaining a sufficient water supply, where cattle have proper access, during both summer and winter. "The threat of grass fires was always a concern during the dry seasons," he said, "which would have upset a ranching operation for several years if it had happened." Warren remembers the big fire during the fall of 1956 on Baker's Bar U Ranch, which could have wiped out everything south of the Highwood River.

Some changes that have taken place during the past half-century in Warren's opinion, include the fact nearly everyone has some type of a motorized vehicle for traveling. No one bothers anymore to saddle a horse or hook up a team to go somewhere. He mentioned that this is now impossible in most cases, because everyone must have their gates locked to stop bikers and overland vehicles from marking up the hillsides and destroying their grass. He remembered how the native people used to travel across country either on horseback, or with their old teams and worn out democrats. He agrees with the new method of travel, recognizing the great job the search and rescue teams do, and the air ambulances in getting people to hospitals that are injured in out of the way places where there is no vehicle access.

Some highlights of Warren's ranching career included the opportunity of attending the World Hereford Tour that was held in Banff and Calgary during 1976, and being able to go with the Hereford Tour that spent a month in Uruguay during 1980. It was never difficult to begin a discussion with Warren about the horses that he remembered. He enjoyed telling of the good horses he had broken and the features of the better ones that he has ridden over the years. He mentioned a large number of special people that he became acquainted with, people that he would have never met, if he had not come to the Highwood country more than fifty years ago. He also told about some of the good men that had worked for him at the OH Ranch during the same period of time.

Warren married late in life, to Betty Colwell in February 1982, a widow whose husband deceased her years earlier. Warren and Betty lived at the OH Ranch for several years prior to his decision to retire in 1984 when they moved to live in High River for a short time. This move left Bert Sheppard at the OH until 1986, when he decided he would build a new home at his Riverbend Ranch if they would live there also and care for him during his latter days.

Warren had left the OH Ranch before all the controversy began with regards to the sale of the ranch to the Canadian Army, at which time he was happy not to be involved. The old ranch will continue to be a special part of Warren's ranching career, recognizing the multitude of men who came and left again, some who have left their mark of distinction and may be remembered for that reason. Some may continue to return, possibly to explore the feelings of the days gone by.

Warren and Betty have enjoyed their sixteen years of retirement at the Riverbend Ranch near Longview but because of health reasons, they have moved to their own home in Black Diamond. Although they have not moved that far, the Longview-Pekisko communities will miss them both.

# Whiskey Ridge Cowboys

Poem written and presented by Hank Pallister for Bert Sheppard's 75th Birthday Celebration in High River, November 10, 1977.

Back in the coulee west of Whiskey Ridge
Where the grass grows stirrup tall
A feller named Sheppard and Zimmerman too,
Had a round-up just last fall.

They saddled up and took their branding irons
And packed a little grub along too.
They made a gather and branded every long-eared calf
That came within their view.

All the young doggies that got in the bunch
That didn't find brush that day
Got their horns whittled and their hides scorched
In the most artistic way.

It was getting about noon, and the sun was high
And the heel flies were out everywhere
So they turned the herd loose and rode to the camp on the creek
For they knew there'd be refreshments there!

The camp on the creek was a quiet place,
Where a fella could just sit and think
But while Zimmerman was building some dinner up
Sheppard found something to drink.

Now he blew the cork and poured a round
And they drank in a gentleman's way,
It was as certain as anything could be
That they both got drunk that day.

It was night when they decided to ride back to the ranch
On a long lope, like they were carrying the mail,

When who should they meet, but the devil himself
A-prancing up the trail!

The devil said, "You ornery cowboy drunks,
You'd better start hunting your holes,
For I've come up from my home in Hell
Just to gather up your souls!"

Now Sheppard said, "Well, devil be damned,
Us two are kinda tight,
But you ain't gonna get no cowhands from here
Without some kind of a fight."

So Zimmerman shook a hole in his rope
And threw it straight and true,
He lobbed it over the devil's horns
And took his dallies too!

Now Sheppard was a Riata man
With his rawhide all coiled up neat
So he shook it out and built a loop
And caught the devil's hind feet.

Now they stretched him out and tailed him down
And while the irons were getting hot,
They cropped and swalled forked both his ears,
Then branded him up a lot.

They pruned him up with the dehorning saw
And knotted his tail for a joke
When they got through, they turned him loose
Necked to a blue-stone post.

If you are ever hunting on Whiskey Ridge,
And you see funny tracks in the snow
You'll know it's the devil wandering around
Still dragging that jack-pine pole.

# Bob Hale and Gordon Boyd

The cattle population in Alberta has more than tripled during the past forty years. One reason for this large increase was because the Provincial Government made pasture land available to be used as grazing leases or community pastures, for cattle owners with small herds. During the middle 1950s, when grain prices became depressed, many farmers in grain growing communities across the Province, began raising or feeding cattle in order to remain solvent.

Some farmers who diversified part of their grain operation into the business of raising cattle were those in the Lomond community. The Lomond Grazing Association actually originated during the 1940s but was enlarged and became an asset to many more farmers of that area when taken over by the Department of Lands and Forests during 1954. The farmers who organized this Association were allowed to obtain long-term leases; operate their own pastures and pay the cost of any improvements.

In the spring of 1951 this Association required a range rider for the north lease and the directors hired a man from the Buffalo area, named Lloyd Williams. Mr. Williams reported for duty and arrived at the camp on the lease with his horses on Sunday, April 15. Several days later, Williams, along with Bob Marquet, who was office clerk for the Special Areas Office in Lomond; left Lomond by truck to mend some fence in the north pasture, a distance of about twelve miles from town. During the afternoon, a raging blizzard hit the area leaving the two men stranded on the north lease with their truck stuck in a mudhole. The two men apparently decided to leave the shelter of the vehicle and started following a fence line back to the cabin on the lease which Williams had already moved into. By Thursday of that week some people in the area began wondering of their whereabouts; and search parties which consisted of one hundred and fifty people, sixty cars and an airplane, were organized by the R.C.M.P. at Lomond. By Saturday the airplane had spotted the truck which they found had been abandoned. The body of Williams was found later frozen to death along the corral fence, only about two hundred yards from the cabin where he had been living. The other man was also found dead; having struggled within two miles of the same cabin before he collapsed from exhaustion.

Bob Hale was the next man hired as range rider on the north lease after the death of Lloyd Williams. Hale was born at Brooks in 1917 and raised in the Duchess area before going to work at a young age. His first experience with ranch life was at the Anchor P Ranch north of Duchess for Rod Macleay. From Macleay's he worked for a large horse ranch owned by Laibin Nelson. His next job was with Alex Gillespie at the Thumb Hill Ranch near Dorothy, until this ranch was sold in 1951. For the next dozen years he was head rider for the Lomond Grazing Association before going to work for Neil McKinnon of LK ranches in 1963. Bob remained cow foreman for the LK ranches until Neil McKinnon retired him from active ranch life during 1990.

The summer of 1951 was a wet season and winter had arrived by the middle of October. The farmers had most of their crops swathed, but no combining had been done due to the bad weather. The snow laid deep in the Lomond farming community and because there was no stubble grazing that fall, the round-up had to be postponed for at least fifteen days. To help with the round-up, Bob Hale hired Gordon Boyd, the oldest son of Frank and Alice Boyd, who were farmers of the Armada district since 1926. Gordon Boyd has since married, has raised a family and continued to raise cattle on a farm in the Hanna district, until his retirement to an acreage on the outskirts of Hanna.

Both Hale and Boyd had been riding together one cold day, and arrived back at camp after dark. Boyd chose to take care of the horses if Hale would cook supper one particular evening. Hale went to the cabin to light the lamp and get the stove started, while Boyd took the horses to the stable. While Boyd was taking care of all the horses, he noticed for the longest time there was no light in the cabin. By time Boyd had the outside chores completed, there was a light in the window, so he went to cabin hoping that Hale had supper well started. As soon as Boyd stepped inside, Hale said with excitement, "You don't know how lucky you are to be able to walk through that door." Boyd was somewhat confused as to what Hale had said, but later learned why Hale was so concerned.

Apparently, Hale had been to town several days earlier for some groceries and bought a large package of Eddy matches, which came as three large boxes wrapped together. He opened one box leaving matches exposed for easy access, and set the box on the table. The other two boxes were left untouched along with the purchased groceries in another room of the cabin. A mouse found the open matches and chewed the head of one which ignited the whole box leaving only a box full of charred match sticks.

The day the two men arrived at camp after dark and Hale went to light the lamp in the cabin, he knew where he had left the matches. He began scratching dead matches for some light, and after not having any success he stumbled around in the dark and found the other boxes, which had not been opened. When he got a kerosene lamp going and saw the box of burnt matches on the table, he knew exactly what had happened. At this point Hale knew that if the box had been left near anything in the cabin or close to an outside wall, their cabin could have been a pile of ashes when they returned. This explained Hale's comment to Boyd, about being lucky to have a door to walk through!

One day, the same fall Hale and Boyd had just sat down for some lunch. The majority of the cattle had been gathered in a holding field waiting to be worked, and sent home for the different owners. Boyd got up from the table and was looking in the cupboard for something to put in his coffee. Hale inquired as to what Boyd was looking for, and Boyd said, "I would like some milk for my coffee." Hale replied, "Milk! There are two thousand cows out there, and if you want some dam milk you will have to go out and get your own!"

Those who knew the late Bob Hale probably noticed there was a good portion of his right ear missing. This happened at a Bassano Stampede before he was married, when he was entered as a calf roping contestant. While positioning his horse properly behind the barrier, the horse reared up and fell over backwards. During the scuffle of the horse getting up again, a sharp hoof hit the side of his head and removed part of his ear. With the injury bleeding badly, several cowboys rushed him into a vehicle and hurried him off to the Bassano hospital. As soon as Doc Scott saw the situation, he asked the cowboys if they had the missing piece so he could sew the ear back together. The cowboys rushed back to the rodeo grounds, and got some help to dig around through the dirt in the roping box hunting for the missing part of Hale's ear. The missing piece was never found, which left Bob Hale well 'ear marked' for the remaining years of his life.

Bob Hale lived a full life as a cowman and friends knew the appreciation he had for good horses. His days ended during March 1994, and funeral services were held at Bassano, the part of Alberta he enjoyed and loved the best. The absence of his friendship has been greatly missed by the multitude of people who knew him.

Although his years with us have ended,

And he has answered his final call,

His time here will long be remembered,

Because of life's ways he rode so tall.

# The Medicine Tree: A Historic Landmark

Before the town of High River began as a frontier settlement during the early 1880s, the first building to be constructed in that part of the country was a trading post built during 1869 by T.C. Powers Company from Fort Benton, Montana. This trading post was built in the design of a fort, and was more elaborate than those usually erected by the free traders during that period. The building was constructed on bench land north of the Highwood River and about five miles west of the present traffic bridge at High River, on the property now owned by the Western Feedlots Ltd. Several years later, the I.G. Baker Company; also with headquarters at Fort Benton, built a second trading post close to where the first one was situated.

Both companies were operating a business of freighting supplies of food and other goods out of Montana for trade with the native people of the North West Territories, in exchange for buffalo hides and other furs. The Highwood River location was selected for the trading posts because it was found to be a favorite camping ground for the powerful tribes of the Blackfoot Confederacy. The ford on the river was an ideal crossing for their travois and the towering cottonwood trees and dense underbrush supplied sufficient firewood and shelter for their camps. Fat buffalo could always be found, because of an abundant supply of grass and water. The historic "Medicine Tree" displaying its lofty branches upward once grew nearby, but has been blown down by the wind and has since been preserved in George Lane Park, High River.

The ranching industry on the High River range first got started from this same location, an area between Willow Creek on the south with Sheep River as a boundary to the north and from the mountains on the west, to the mouth of Mosquito Creek on the east.

The partnership of George Emerson and Tom Lynch built a log cabin as their headquarters in the area where the trading posts were situated, near the Medicine Tree. During 1879 they trailed a thousand head of cattle in from Montana and turned them loose on the range that ran west from their cabin to the big hill where Longview is now located.

The same year Emerson and Lynch established headquarters near the trading posts, O.H. Smith and Lafayette French built a stopping house where the old trail between Calgary and Fort Macleod crossed the Highwood River. This location became known as "The Crossing", where the Fort Benton stagecoach stopped weekly, bringing the mail addressed to that part of the country.

After the Northwest Cattle Company in Montreal obtained a lease of 150 000 acres from the Dominion government, they appointed Fred Stimson as manager to start a cattle ranch in the Canadian Northwest. Stimson arrived at 'The Crossing' in the spring of 1882 and found George Emerson, Tom Lynch and Jim Meinsinger at the cabin owned by Emerson and Lynch. He approached Emerson to help him locate the range boundaries for a new ranch above the forks of the Highwood River. Jim Meinsinger was hired immediately, and started construction of new buildings that would be their first ranch headquarters, near the Emerson-Lynch cabin. He also closed a deal with Tom Lynch for his assistance in selecting the foundation herd for their new ranching company.

During May 1882, Herb Miller arrived at the new ranch site with some bulls that Stimson had purchased in Chicago the previous fall. Stimson and Lynch were in Idaho buying livestock for the new company and by late September a trail herd of 3000 cattle and 75 horses had arrived at the ranch headquarters near the Medicine Tree. By the time George Lane arrived to take over as their range foreman in the spring of 1884, headquarters of the Northwest Cattle Company had been moved from the Medicine Tree range, to above the forks on Pekisko Creek. From that point in history of the ranch this new company became known as the Bar U for the brand that Lane had adopted when he took over as foreman.

Dan Riley took up a homestead near the same location during 1883. By that time the old trading posts had closed, and their remains had decayed with time. Some of the building logs and foundation rocks were used by other people who later owned the property.

After Stimson established the first headquarters for the Bar U near the Medicine Tree, George Emerson moved to a location on Pekisko Creek, west of where the Bar U National Historic Ranch site is currently situated. Tom Lynch also moved locations, and eventually established the TL Ranch on Sullivan Creek, about a mile downstream from where the three forks of that river join.

After the Bar U moved to their permanent location on Pekisko Creek, a ranch outfit owned by W.E. Cochrane with the CC brand moved into the Bar U's original buildings, and occupied the range they left along the north side of the Highwood River. Cochrane remained there only long enough to build permanent headquarters on Mosquito Creek, about four miles west of Cayley.

After the CC outfit vacated the ranch buildings which had been previously used by the Bar U, an Irishman named Walter Skrine made use of them for several years. Due to heavy losses during the winter of 1886-87, and more people moving into that area, Skrine decided to move further to the southwest and purchase some land on the upper waters of Mosquito Creek.

Until this period of ranching, the country around the Medicine Tree was considered open range and any livestock in that area was allowed to graze freely. After Skrine left the area, two old-country gentlemen from England purchased a large piece of the Medicine Tree range, setting up a ranching proposition for both their sons, Duncan McPherson and Colin Ross. Ross and McPherson stocked their new ranch with 700 head of shorthorn heifers from Ontario, and hired a man from England named Keith Douglas to manage the outfit. The partnership of Ross and McPherson did not succeed, so McPherson's father interested Major Eckford, a retired British army officer, to become a shareholder in the ranch.

In the spring of 1887 Duncan McPherson arrived from England to become the new ranch manager. The policy of the ranch changed from cattle to horses, at which time the ranch became known as the High River Horse Ranch. McPherson, accompanied by Tom Lynch, went to the state of Washington and purchased 500 head of horses. The first ranch foreman on McPherson's horse outfit was a Texan named George Baker, who was succeeded by the legendary John Ware.

During the fall of 1887, Herbert Eckford, son of Major Eckford, arrived at the ranch from Manitoba with some farming equipment. He was put to work as a regular hand at $30 a month, to gain some ranch experience. By 1893, Herbert Eckford was managing the outfit and became sole owner of the ranch after McPherson left, because of his father's death in 1896.

Eckford soon went east and married a lady in Ontario whose family was recognized as a leading breeder of thoroughbred horses. On their return to the ranch in 1904, a large house was built on the same location as the old trading fort. The design of the house and the materials used made it one of the most impressive ranch house in the Canadian west. In 1914 the ranch was sold to the Sibley family from Rochester, New York, and the Eckfords moved to Scotland to make their home there.

Fred Bennis was Sibley's first ranch manager and he figured the land near the headquarters of the ranch was ideal for cultivation, so a policy of producing both cattle and grain was adopted. A thousand acres of the native grass near the home ranch was ploughed under for grain and, in addition, the ranch handled about the same number of cattle. Bennis chose the round top T ( ) for a brand to identify the cattle, and from that time onward, the ranch was known as the "Round T." The new owners purchased the TL Ranch on Sullivan Creek during 1917, as well as owning some grassland east of the big hill at Longview. Bennis retired as ranch manager in 1927 and was succeeded by Ellison Capers.

When Capers resigned in 1936, the Sibley's changed their ranching program. They decided to discontinue active farming operations, and dispose of their workhorses and farming equipment by public auction. The cultivated land on the ranch was leased to several different tenants and both the Longview and Sullivan Creek properties were sold. One of the tenants rented the grazing land for five years, and in 1942 the Sibley's closed out their Alberta interests by selling the complete ranch outfit along the Highwood to C.W. Roenisch.

C.W. Roenisch had been identified with the Midland and Pacific Grain Company with headquarters in Calgary; where he also made his home. Mr. Roenisch continued the policy of having tenants farm the cultivated land and using the grazing land himself. After he passed away, his estate retained possession of this valuable property until it was sold in 1978 to Western Feedlots Ltd., the current owners.

This particular parcel of land along the north bank of the Highwood River, upstream from High River has displayed a special role in the history of Southern Alberta. It not only provided an excellent camping and hunting area for the native tribes of the past, but it was also a sacred spot for them to visit because of the Medicine Tree. The double trunk tree was unique in nature; which lead the native people to believe it had great physical powers to heal their sick and wounded. While camped there they felt safe from their enemies, and would give thanks to the divine spirit for assisting them with their achievements of the past and for accomplishments in the future.

The early cowmen and ranch outfits, who first came to that location, journeyed further to establish a successful life-style in the ranching industry. It is very doubtful if many of them would have had much confidence in the supernatural powers of the tree, but being aware of its influence, some might have located there initially for the same reasons as their native brothers.

# Women in Agriculture

Recognizing the daily changes that happen in our modern day society helps me to realize that I belong to a much different time. I was born and raised on an old time cow ranch before the Second World War. Remembering the social and economic customs of those ranching communities during that era brings to mind the work and responsibilities that farm and ranch women preformed, without any proper recognition given for their role in the agricultural and ranching society. The loneliness these same women experienced was also another factor, along with the location of the farm or ranch where they lived. The distance from services in hamlets or towns determined the degree of support they were able to give as mothers and homemakers. The education level, expectations, and dreams of these women also added another dimension that helped them determine what their future would be.

Women who were part of early ranching, and even the war brides, who left modern homes in Europe and came to Western Canada, must have faced loneliness and isolation that was unbearable. A good example was my own mother, who left her family in Ireland prior to World War One, to come to Western Canada, and shortly after married my father. When they were married, my father was managing a large cattle ranch for Pat Burns; that was situated 18 miles west of Milk River. There was absolutely no social activity in the area and the only means of transportation to town, was a three-hour trip with a team and democrat. During more recent times, the common thread that identifies women in agriculture, is the degree of support which a farm or ranch is able to provide, in order to determine their life-style.

It has become abundantly clear that many women in agriculture have already begun to meet the challenges that are available; either through choice, or the pressure created by the crisis in the cost of farm and ranch equipment; compared to the market value of commodities farms and ranches are able to sell. There are some women in agriculture who continue to allow their lives to be determined by the traditional model and adopt their husband's or society's view of a woman's role in that occupation. Many others are no longer content to remain under an umbrella of that nature, and are striving to identify some personal independence.

National records indicate there are fewer farms and ranches throughout the three prairie provinces, but reports say there are more than 115 000 adult women in agriculture, living in this same area. While the number of both men and women in agriculture has dropped; statistics indicate that the number of women involved, has increased both as operators or wives of operators. Another dramatic change is that less women have reported they have no occupation, and more have reported they are employed in agriculture or some type of work elsewhere. During 1971, forty-five percent of women in agriculture reported that they had no occupation, and by 1986 that figure had dropped to twenty nine percent. Similarly during the early 1970s only eighteen percent of these women reported income not related to agriculture; and by the late 1980s, forty one percent had received income not earned on Canadian farms and ranches.

During the past quarter century, there has been several fortunate events that have helped to encourage women in agriculture to play a more active roll in determining their future. These happenings include the 1975 Supreme Court of Canada decision in the Murdock vs. Murdock case. That year the Court decided that Florence Murdock, a wife who had worked along side her husband on their cattle ranch for twenty five year was not entitled to one-half share, because a court judge stated, that she had only done what an ordinary rancher's wife was supposed to do! Those cutting words brought home the potential fate of many women in agriculture after years of labor without pay, and created an outcry among many women groups throughout rural agricultural areas. The Murdock case was one of several which helped to reform provincial matrimonial laws across Canada and now the majority of farm and ranch women have begun to realize the impact those judicial proceedings has done for their future.

Another less noticed turning point was realized when the federal government finally revised income tax legislation during March 1980, allowing deductions from salaries paid to women for work performed on the land. While women in agriculture have always known that they have worked, government recognition added balance to their cause, which was a positive move towards women labor and financial independence. This move helped to reinforce the monetary value of work done by women, even though in many cases the transaction took place on paper only.

The national figure shows that only twenty percent of married women in agriculture receive a salary. Women as spouses in agriculture have been receiving maternity and unemployment insurance benefits for sometime, as well as paying into the Canada Pension Plan. Despite these important factors in many cases, these changes have remained unnoticed. Women in agriculture are now thinking and speaking openly about their rights they have as married individuals. Changes towards equality for women in agriculture have not been rapid and have lagged behind their urban counterparts. They have been different that the women living in urban centres who realized more that twenty years ago that their destiny will be sealed if they continue to depend on their husbands for economic support.

Urban women have no doubt helped to provide strong examples and influences in relationship to the roles which women in agriculture are currently undertaking and in many ways their journey has been much more difficult. Amongst the foreground of their lives, not only tradition, customs and community are involved, but also their agricultural responsibilities. When it comes to their daily lives in agriculture, there are few women who will risk the importance of the farm or ranch for personal advancement. While most women do not see themselves as feminists, their words and actions are bringing about important changes in their lives. Just as their urban sisters did twenty years ago, women in agriculture are seeking higher education to undertake work elsewhere and calling for social services such as childcare. Many are also becoming increasingly involved in agriculture issues and helping to strengthen the tone of agriculture voices by actively taking part and defining their views on employment issues.

While some women are earning income from sources other than agriculture because of personal choices, the major reason for such work is because the farm or ranch requires the income. In other cases where the financial need is not immediate, the risk of working entirely at home can no longer be accepted because of the future being too uncertain. The crisis in agriculture is forcing the women to deal with economic and financial issues. They can no longer allow themselves to believe or pretend that their livelihood is insulated through their husband's earnings or the value of the business of agriculture.

Our agricultural crisis, with stressful foreclosures and bankruptcies, is also opening the door of change for many women in this occupation. Any type of change is always difficult, but change by force is always much more painful. How women in agriculture are able to handle these changes depends on their courage. If they accept the opportunities that become available, organized meaningful change in their lives and the long-term outcome may well be positive for agricultural women in our rural communities

Recognizing the varied and often difficult circumstances that exist in some people lives, there is very little guidance or support available for them to act upon in making proper decisions. There is no road map, no single or correct method to follow; other than common sense. The bravery and boldness of women in agriculture has allowed them to remain part of a democratic process, and as long as they continue to have a public voice, there will always be a destiny for them in our agricultural future.

# Other Stories

# The BX Stagecoaches and Express

During the era when horses were used for the main means of transportation throughout western Canada, there was a stagecoach and express line in British Columbia that nearly equaled the amount of business done by the Wells Fargo Company in the United States. The name of this business was Barnard's Express and Stage Line, which became known as the "BX."

Gold had been discovered on the lower Fraser River in 1858, and when this ran out a few of the gold seekers headed north in search for more of their filthy greed. Although attempts were made to keep the gold strike a secret, news leaked out through the mysterious ways of the wilderness. In the early 1860s word spread that "Dutch Bill" Dietz had made a big find, and had struck it rich. This started a northern stampede of about 5000 miners.

Many were killed by Indians or drowned in the mighty Fraser River, and still more starved to death. Only small quantities of supplies could be moved by pack train over the one route to the north, which was a narrow torturous trail that ran for 100 miles from Harrison Lake to Lillooet. A wagon road that could handle a larger volume of supplies became a necessity.

The only feasible route was through what was considered the impassable Fraser Canyon; a route that would have to crawl along the sides of gigantic mountains and span the mighty torrents of the Fraser River. The relentless James Douglas, governor of the Colony of British Columbia; in a bold imaginative plan sent 150 engineers to bore and blast a road to run from Yale through the treacherous canyon and then north to the gold fields. During 1864, an 18 foot-wide, 400 mile long road was completed, at a cost more than one million dollars. It was considered the eighth wonder of the world, and to this day people still marvel at how it was accomplished.

This set the stage for Francis Barnard who, with his partner, Stephen Tingley, would write a page in British Columbia's history. Born in Lower Canada in 1829, Barnard was a hard working individual who arrived in Yale B.C. during the early months of 1859. Aware of the activity happening up north, Barnard decided there was a future in the business of carrying passengers and freight into the interior. To gather capital for a company, he began walking 360 miles from Yale into the Cariboo, carrying letters at $2 each and a newspaper he sold for $1. Mail from the miners was carried out on the return trip. It took more than two years and several thousand miles of walking to accumulate enough money to start a business called the Barnard Express.

Stephen Tingley was a big asset to the express stages. He was born in New Brunswick during 1839 and arrived in Yale in 1861. After operating a harness shop, he began driving the express stage in 1863, before becoming a partner with Barnard. With the completion of the great wagon road in 1854; four-horse stagecoaches were introduced that ran from Yale to Soda Creek, a journey of 260 miles that took 52 hours and cost $130. In 1865 the road was extended to Quesnel and the Express went also to Barkerville. An expert in handling the six-horse stagecoaches, Tingley drove the Great North Road for twenty eight years.

The venture soon became very successful and was so efficient that most competition was eliminated. During 1865, the BX stages carried 4.6 million dollars worth of gold, 1500 passengers and traveled 100 000 miles.

Horses were vital to the stagecoach business. In 1868 Tingley trailed 400 Morgan horses from New Mexico to the company's large BX Ranch near Vernon B.C. Along with some horses imported from Alberta and Saskatchewan, the finest horses were bred to assure a continuing supply of horse-power for the stagecoaches. Reliability was important to the BX Express and the mail contract it held for thirty three years. The mail had to be delivered on time, summer and winter. When snow made traveling difficult, sleighs were used to make sure the mail got through.

Their beautiful horses were a source of pride to the drivers and handlers, groomed to the extent that reflected the care and attention given to them. On level stretches of travel a brisk trot was maintained with an average speed of six miles an hour. Horses were changed every eighteen miles and passenger stops for meals were made every thirty-six miles. The harness was made from the finest leather, with a ruling that stated every time harness was removed it had to be cleaned. The coaches were kept noticeably clean, with the outer body of all their stages were painted red and the running gears were yellow.

Women were treated as special passengers on the BX Express, and were offered the most comfortable seat on the swaying, bumpy stages. Their code was to recognize women; they were not judged as to whether they were rich or poor, or if they were a society matron or an outcast of the creeks and dance halls.

No story of the stagecoach business would be would be complete without some hold-ups along the trail. Fortunately, the BX Express only experienced five holdups during forty odd years of operation. The largest robbery happened during the early 1890s when $16 000 was taken. The robbers were caught later, and got seven years in jail for their effort. One hold-up, they lost $2000 when the driver was alone. It was suspected that he staged his own robbery because he left the country shortly after it took place. Their last hold-up happened in 1896, which turned out to be an attempted robbery, because the driver whipped the horses to speed, and galloped to safety ahead of the mounted bandits.

For 50 years the stages and freight wagons traveled over the Great Northern Road, the longest uninterrupted stagecoach run in North America. By that time the railroad and improved motor transportation put the BX Express out of business. At the beginning of the First World War it was all over. Besides, Steve Tingley's death had happened in 1915.

Francis Barnard was always interested in politics and strongly supported the entry of British Columbia into Confederation. He was a member of provincial legislature prior to being elected to the House of Commons until he passed away during 1889.

The Barnard Express that provided early transportation and meant so much to the development of British Columbia, disappeared into history. A small reminder is evident today in Vernon, where the main Street is named Barnard Avenue.

# How The West Was Won

It was during 1874 that the Government of Canada finally decided to police the Canadian West, in an attempt to curb the lawlessness created by the whiskey traders. Three hundred scarlet-coated men, called the North West Mounted Police, left Fort Dufferin, Manitoba; to face a barren land, its ways and conditions they knew nothing about. For seventy days they marched westward across trackless prairie of which they were totally unfamiliar. Day after day they trudged along, in tune with the shrieking ungreased wheels of their Red River carts. The summer heat, mosquitoes, and flies combined; added to their misery, but certainly did not discourage their determination.

After the seventy days they were becoming low on supplies and medicine; and their horses were tired and thin. These men had been trained in the military, but were not frontiersmen, and now they were lost. Their first objective was really Fort Whoop-Up, where they planned to have a battle with the illicit traders, drive them out from the fort and take over. The one big problem that faced them at this point was finding the fort!

The first good landmark they saw was the Sweetgrass Hills to the south, and an order was given for the troops to ride directly towards them. They realized at this time that they could not carry on much longer, because winter was not too far away. For them to be caught on this open prairie land when winter arrived, would be destiny for them all. Another concern that faced them, was that they had not been in contact with Ottawa for months.

When they finally reached the Sweetgrass Hills a camp was set up for several days. A conference was held here amongst the commanding officers. They agreed that the Commissioner and his assistant, Colonel MacLeod, would take a few volunteers and make their way south to Fort Benton. Here, some necessary supplies could be purchased and they could inform Ottawa of their whereabouts. They were also hopeful that they might locate and hire a suitable guide. The trail-weary group made their way southward; and it was a cloudy, stormy fall day, when the small troop of scarlet-coated men rode into Fort Benton, Montana.

Fort Benton was the end of navigation on the Missouri River where the I.G. Baker and Company had stores of every kind of merchandise for anyone who wished to venture beyond. The small troop wasted no time in purchasing the supplies they needed and were fortunate in finding a trustworthy guide who they hired for a wage of ninety dollars a month, with everything "found" (meaning: all expenses paid). This man's name was Jerry Potts, whose father was of Scotch descent, and came to America during 1836. His mother was a native woman of the Blood tribe of the Blackfoot Nation. Potts served the Mounted Police for the next twenty-five years with his skills in survival; as a trail guide, interpreter and diplomat in paving the way for different treaties for the native people; and helping to settle numerous disputes.

While supplies were being purchased, the Commissioner hurried to the Army Post headquarters, where messages were awaiting his arrival. Here approval was given to his decision to split his three hundred men into two groups. Within several days the small troop arrived back to their main camp in the Sweetgrass Hills. Immediately Commissioner French took half the regiment of men and made preparations to leave for Fort Edmonton and Swan Hills. Colonel MacLeod was put in charge of the other half who were to establish headquarters in the southwest area of the Dominion to stamp out the illegal whisky trade. Under him were 150 men, none of whom were familiar with the western frontier of which they were to take command. Jerry Potts was assigned to be their official guide and scout.

Colonel MacLeod had intended to take Fort Whoop-Up by force, and as they resumed their journey, MacLeod was the first to recognize the value of his recently acquired guide. The grueling march westward was now about over when Potts reined up on the crest of a hill looking down on the famous whiskey traders hangout of Fort Whoop-Up. MacLeod turned to Potts and asked him whether they should get their field units in position before they approach the gates. Potts replied, "There will be no problem, we will ride on in"! And they did. There was only one man left at the fort, as everyone else had gone to Montana. Their first mission had been accomplished in the line of duty and they had taken possession of this famous fort without a shot being fired. Their trusted guide appeared to have known this long before they got there.

Colonel MacLeod immediately contacted the owners at Fort Benton, asking for a price for the Whoop-Up fort. He was not sure whether the location was right, but it was already built and winter was getting closer each day. At $25 000, the price asked was much too high. Instead of waiting in hopes the price might change, MacLeod asked Potts if he knew of a better location somewhere nearby. Potts quickly replied and said he knew a good place; one, maybe two days from here. So another fast decision was made upon the scout's suggestion, and the troopers were again ordered to quickly prepare and move out. Potts led them west following an old trail that had been often used.

The next day they arrived at an island in the Oldman River, with water on three sides. The location was suitable for protection from attack, and to the men's great satisfaction, there were plenty of cottonwood trees for building and firewood for winter fuel. As soon as the men were rested, everyone became involved in the building of Fort MacLeod. There was great urgency for speed, as all indications pointed to an early winter; as it had already turned cold. When finished, the fort consisted of officer's quarters, men's living quarters, saddle rooms, a hospital, a guardroom, storage, stables, blacksmith shop, as well as living quarters for Potts. All the buildings faced inward, leaving the back walls as the outside walls of the fort. In the centre of everything were the parade grounds where the troops were exercised and trained.

One day Colonel MacLeod got information through a native called 'Three Bulls', that a colored man named Bond, along with two other Americans had a trading post in Pine Coulee, about fifty miles to the northwest. Three Bulls indicated that they were trading liquor, because he had just bartered two good horses for two gallons of rotgut whiskey. Not wanting to tip off the traders with the information they had received, Colonel MacLeod sent Jerry Potts to meet with Three Bulls the following night, in order to get the full particulars. In the meantime, back at the fort, a trooper named Crozier, of the N.W.M.P. was assigned the job of selecting ten men to be ready as soon as Potts returned.

It did not take Potts long to get the information he needed. As soon as he arrived back at the fort, he set out immediately at the head of a small troop of grim, mounted men, and led them through the night to a spot near the whiskey post in Pine Coulee. As they peered down from the hill overlooking the fort, they saw considerable amount of activity around the settlement. Crozier gave the word, and they rushed down upon the unsuspecting traders and placed them all under arrest without having to fire a single shot.

Potts had gauged the timing of the raid well, because the entire group was caught red-handed with the goods. They captured five people including the two traders, their guide and interpreter Bond, and two hired men. They also seized two wagons; each of which contained cases of alcohol, rifles, revolvers, and buffalo robes. All the alcohol was poured into the snow, while Potts stood by licking his lips, wishing it could have been disposed of by other means; which of course would not have been according to regulations.

The troops rested for a short time before making their way back to the fort with their prisoners. Soon after arriving back at the new fort, Colonel MacLeod held a trial, with other officers present. All the men were found guilty. Bond and the two traders were fined $200 each, while each of the two hired men were fined $50.

News of the seizure, capture and trial traveled fast by 'prairie telegraph', and the police did not have to wait long to find out who was backing the traders in Pine Coulee. Within a short time a man of wealth, named J.D. Weatherwax from Fort Benton arrived to pay the fines for all the prisoners, except Bond.

As this was actually the first arrest made by the N.W.M.P. since they arrived in Canada's western frontier, Colonel MacLeod was eager to wrap up the details. The case against Bond needed further evidence, so he sent word to Three Bulls and some of his tribesmen to come to the fort and swear they had in fact obtained liquor from this man. By the time Three Bulls found it convenient to appear, the prisoner had escaped. It was difficult to keep guard on the prisoner while building of the new fort was in progress. MacLeod had ordered a guard of three men whenever the prisoner was moved; as there was no jail as yet to house him in. In spite of the order, the prisoner was moved at night by one lone guard; and as they came near the brush, the prisoner simply made off in the night. A search was made the next day but the prisoner was not found. MacLeod acted upon Potts' advice not to risk a search for the prisoner by horseback, because of the horses' poor condition.

Knowing the country and winters, Potts was concerned about the condition of their horse cavvy. He told Macleod that many of the horses would die if they were not taken to better shelter and grass. The police agreed the force could function during the winter with half of their horses. Macleod agreed with the idea, but was concerned about their safety and whether they would be stolen. Potts reply was "What's the difference, stolen, or dead in a snow bank!"

The next morning found Potts at the head of a column of seventy-five trail weary horses, followed by several troopers who pushed up the drag. Ordinarily horses could be moved fifty miles a day with no problem, but with these horses he planned only fifteen miles at the most. Potts headed for the north breaks of the Marias River valley in Montana, where there was water, shelter and plenty of well-cured grass. Arriving there after a week of travel, the riders sat on a hill and watched the thin animals fan out as they began to graze. Potts muttered to himself, "Enjoy it here fellows, you have earned it, we will see you in the spring!"

# The Range Men's Dinner

For more than six decades, the Canadian Pacific's Palliser Hotel in Calgary, has hosted an annual Old Time Range Men's Dinner every July during Stampede week. At the dinner held in July 1993 the Palliser Hotel made it known to their dinner guests, that it would be the last one the hotel was prepared to sponsor. This annual event was without any question the most extraordinary function that was attended each summer by those who were invited.

During the last dinner, Palliser Hotel personnel and head table guests, gave a brief outline as to why and when the range men's dinner was first held. I have thought since, that the information given, has required some corrections and further clarification from historical data that I have collected over the years. The first dinner I attended was in 1956 with my father, the late Guy Pallister, who was a guest at the original 1929 dinner, and it has been a privilege for me to attend every dinner since.

The first range men's dinner was held on July 9, 1929, at the Palliser Hotel in Calgary; with Andy Hackett, a railway employee as the Master of Ceremonies, for the event. This dinner became a reality because of the vision of the late Guy Weadick. While Weadick was involved as arena director with the Calgary Exhibition and Stampede, he approached officials of the Canadian Pacific Railway to host a dinner to commemorate the old time cowmen of the open range days of ranching in Alberta.

J.J. McGuire, who was manager of the hotel, agreed with the idea after D.C. Coleman, who was Chief Officer for the C.P.R. in Canada, gave the go ahead.

Those men who had worked on a round-up wagon prior to the year 1900; which included wagon bosses, day wranglers, wagon reps, cooks and nighthawks were qualified to attend the first dinner in 1929. Exactly why the year 1900 was decided upon for a cut-off date, cannot be established. The last general roundup in Alberta was in the spring of 1907, and by 1910 the influx of homesteaders had a good portion of the open range under fence.

The Palliser Hotel placed an invitation in both the *Calgary Herald* and the *Calgary Albertan* early in 1929, which specified the requirements for those wishing to attend. (See the advertisement below from the *Calgary Herald*, dated May 18, 1929.) Those who had the proper qualifications were invited to write directly to the hotel, qualifying their reason to be in attendance. There were only fifty-seven old time cowmen who attended the first dinner, whose names are listed in the first two dinner programs. The programs for both the 1929 and 1930 dinners exhibited copies of the letters written to the hotel from old time range men who attended the first two dinners. (See Appendix for this original programme). Due to the success of the original dinners, Grant Hall, Senior Vice-President of the Canadian Pacific Railway, announced the dinner would become an annual event. At the 1931 dinner, D.C. Coleman who later became CPR President, said "There will be a dinner as long as the Canadian Pacific Railway operates." It has since become evident that the railroad company has violated this promise made to the early range men many years ago.

The dinner held during July 1981, was recognized as the Fiftieth Anniversary of this special occasion. The only reason this anniversary does not calculate accurately from the beginning year is because the hotel decided to discontinue the dinner for several years during the Second World War, and the dinner was omitted for the years of 1943 to 1945 inclusive.

In 1981 Ken MacKell, who was Vice-President and General Manager of the Palliser Hotel, forwarded this writer a guest list of the old time range men who attended the first dinner. He also requested my assistance in locating as many of their sons as possible, so that the hotel could extend a special invitation for them to attend this Fiftieth Celebration, and be recognized accordingly. I did considerable work on the project through personal contacts, public libraries and community history books. It was disappointing to locate only thirty-one of these 'native sons'. One interesting fact about the project; was that a number of these men were never married, some had sons who had passed away, and others had families of only girls. There were also those 'whose trail had grown over with time' and any knowledge of their whereabouts had long been forgotten.

The Palliser Hotel was a generous host over the years for this annual get-together. Each guest was mailed a personal invitation well in advance of every dinner and greeted royally upon their arrival. The cocktails that were served prior to dinner, were referred to as the 'watering hole', which flowed like water in the creek during spring run-off. The meal itself was always exceptional, with the main course usually being prime Alberta beef. Their dining room staff heard about it if the cowboys were fed anything different. There was always an after dinner speaker, some being more enjoyable to listen to than others. After the speaker had concluded, along with a few announcements, the 'water hole' was opened again until the stragglers got tired and went home.

At the 1981 dinner roasted chicken was served instead of beef. The Master of Ceremonies explained that chicken was selected for dinner, recognizing the fact that chicken had been served at the first dinner, held fifty-three years earlier. The late Jim Cross was in attendance, and spoke out unofficially saying that the chicken served that evening tasted about that age!

Naturally, as the years went by, the early range men who were here prior to 1900 have gradually disappeared. The criteria to attend the dinner never did change and was intended to carry on with the sons and grandsons of the original range men. It is a known fact that this was not the case, and the guest list over the years became so inflated with city business men, stampede and government officials, news media and farm writers, including a host of others who were not in the least interested in our early ranching heritage.

For a period during the 1960s, the Palliser Hotel appointed Stuart Grayson as a one-man committee to screen any new requests for people wishing to attend this dinner. Grayson was the son of a pioneer family who came west to the Cochrane district in 1886. He later became a member of the Royal Canadian Mounted Police and served as superintendent of the Calgary subdivision between 1959 and 1965. Grayson was a man with considerable investigation experience and reviewed every new applicant with detail. Those newcomers who thought they should have an invitation to this traditional social function had to have a good amount of early ranching heritage in their pedigree before they were allowed to attend. After Grayson passed on, 'the gate was left open' and the hotel allowed the guest list to kind of get out of hand, for this invitational dinner.

Soon after the surprise announcement at the 1993 dinner, the Friends of the Bar U Historic Ranch Association announced it was prepared to take over the responsibility of organizing this special dinner every July. The Palliser Hotel promised them the mailing list they had been using over the years, but when their president traveled to Calgary to pick up the list, the hotel had changed their opinion on what had been promised.

Since 1993 several past employees of the Canadian Pacific Rail have duplicated this prestigious project under somewhat the same format. Anyone is now allowed to attend providing they pay an annual membership fee of twenty-five dollars plus another forty dollars for a meal ticket that includes two drinks. The only resemblance it now has of being a range men's dinner, is that it continues to be held at the Pallister Hotel in Calgary. Being somewhat superficial, it has now become a social function without a purpose; where anyone can attend for the price of an expensive meal. This criterion has discouraged many of the ranching people from attending.

If it were possible to turn back the years for a meeting with the old time range men on this subject, they would humbly suggest that the dinner be carried on as long as their current and future descendants were involved. They would be in agreement, knowing that the open range days of ranching in Alberta and their accomplishments of the past are being recognized.

The once popular rangemen's dinner held annually every July, could again be revived with a bit of proper organization. It is my opinion that the function needs to come under the control and guidance of some livestock organization such as the Western Stock Growers Association or the Friends of the Bar U Historic Ranch Association. If this annual dinner were revived, the important question would be "Who would be allowed to attend?" The question has a simple answer in the fact that the original dinner held sixty-seven years ago involved only men who had worked on a round-up wagon prior to the year 1900.

An annual revived dinner should therefore include only the male descendants and the men married to the female descendants of families who were ranching in Alberta prior to the same cut off period of 1900. This would allow the current generation of cowmen to take the opportunity to retain a piece of their ranching heritage, by carrying on the tradition of an annual range men's dinner. This would properly commemorate and recognize the early range men who laid the foundation of our cattle industry.

# Stampede Managers

The sport of rodeo first became a spectator attraction in the United States, after the Civil War in 1865. Just as the North American cattle industry has its earliest beginnings in the colonization of the new world, the modern stampedes, frontier days and rodeos reflect history made, as the cattle industry developed. The growth of the cattle industry, helps to trace the beginning of modern day rodeos.

Canada's first formal Rodeo or Stampede is said to have happened at Raymond, Alberta in 1903 while other "wild west" cowboy shows toured the prairie provinces during the early years of the nineteenth century. The Calgary Stampede would not have happened during 1912 without the determination and imaginary western spirit of Guy Weadick. It has since been developed into a well polished, highly professional, attraction that has become known across the world. This level of entertainment has been achieved because of the five men who have held the position of Stampede Manager, with their knowledge and ability to make decisions as to what activities and attractions were best suited for their rodeo arena during Stampede Week

Weadick was born in Rochester, New York during 1885 and traveled throughout the United States working as a cowhand, learning the skills of ranch work. In 1904 he worked at the McIntyre Ranch in Alberta, and in 1905 as an agent for Will Pickett, an American who introduced bulldogging as a rodeo event. After their equipment and rodeo stock was stolen in Winnipeg, Weadick joined a wild west show, and soon married Flores La Due. Together they formed their own show, and appeared on Broadway with Buffalo Bill and with other wild west shows in Europe and the U.S.A.

Weadick first conceived the idea of a Frontier Day Celebration as a World Championship Cowboy contest, while in Calgary during 1908. While there he met with various organizations, including the Calgary Exhibition Company but none were interested; all being of the opinion that Weadick's proposition was too big for Calgary. The result of correspondence between himself and H.C. Mullen, who was the livestock agent for the Canadian Pacific Railway; was the only reason he returned to Calgary in the spring of 1912. Weadick had no problem selling his proposition to Lane, Burns, Cross and McLean; four large ranchers of that era, known since as the "Big Four." The result was a contract to finance the first big show, with Weadick as manager and arena director. They rented the exhibition plant at Victoria Park where the contests were staged and paid cash for the privilege. Prize money was the only connection the Exhibition Company or the City of Calgary had with this big affair.

Weadick was invited back to Calgary in 1919, to organize a Victory Stampede to celebrate the end of World War I. He also managed the 1923 Stampede, when chuckwagon races were introduced and he remained Stampede Manager for the Exhibition Company until 1932. Although the attendance was satisfactory for the 1931 show, the Stampede finished that year with a $16 364 deficit. With the beginnings of plans for the 1932 show, there was some doubt whether the show could be held at all when the senior government announced they would cut their annual grants by $14 000. The Board decided the show had to carry on, but in order to do so, wages and prize lists were slashed; with the biggest budgets cuts made to the Stampede events.

When Guy Weadick returned in the spring of 1932 and these decisions were communicated to Weadick, he exploded in all directions. If the management persisted with these cuts, Weadick felt there should not be any Stampede. It took Richardson's persuasive evidence to convince Weadick that he should proceed with the preparations for a 1932 show. He did so without enthusiasm, and with unrestrained feelings towards the directors; even to the point of telling his cowboy friends that he was through with the Stampede. As for the directors themselves, they became dissatisfied with Weadick's behavior and asked each other what they needed him for, since he was paid a salary of $5000 for six months work.

During 1920, Weadick and his wife purchased the Stampede Ranch, located 15 miles west of Longview along the Highwood River; where they lived until they retired from ranching during the spring of 1947 and moved into the town of High River. After residing in Arizona for a short time, they returned to High River where Mrs. Weadick passed away during August 1951. Guy Weadick remarried, but this marriage was short lived, because he passed away in California during December 1953. Funeral services were held in High River and he was laid to rest in the cemetery of that town.

People who knew Guy Weadick will remember him for his great personality, congenial manner, and his ability to talk. Those who never had the chance to meet him missed an opportunity to visit with an impressive man, a person who had a colorful career as a promoter, and a master showman. He was a man that will remain a legend with rodeo in Canada and the ranching industry of southern Alberta.

The best man around to take over the position after Weadick resigned was a man named J.M. (Jack) Dillon who was born in Ireland and came to the

Chicago district of the United Stated with his parents at an early age. After spending considerable time around the Stockyards in Chicago he decided to go west, and found a job on a horse ranch in Nebraska and later to the Dakotas where he 'punched cows'. From there he graduated to a livestock commission firm in Sioux City, Iowa, where he learned that money in the cattle business was not made by working on some ranch for monthly wages.

During World War I, he began purchasing artillery and cavalry horses for the French army throughout the American west. Later being inducted into the French army, he was placed in charge of their remount department that was headquartered in Boston; where he supervised the purchase and training of thousands of horses for the French army during the war years. After the war Dillon came to Alberta where he became involved with Mayer and Lage, an American company out of New York City who had a contract selling Canadian beef to the countries of Western Europe. This company leased the OH Ranch west of Longview from Pat Burns in 1918; in order to have ranch property in Canada. They appointed Dillon as their representative, who lived in Calgary, and would visit the ranch on necessary occasions. Albertans best knew Jack Dillon through his association with the Calgary Exhibition and Stampede where he was their Stampede Manager for 14 years. He retired from that position in 1946. He passed away and was buried in Calgary during March 1948.

In the process of the Exhibition Company selecting a suitable candidate for another Stampede Manager, they considered three different men who had previously preformed well in the sport of rodeo. They were Pat Burton, Dick Cosgrave and Herman Linder. Because Cosgrave had been involved as the person in charge of the livestock at Stampede time, he was selected as their next Stampede Manager in 1947.

Dick Cosgrave was born at the Indian Hospital in Gleichen during 1905. He was the son of William Cosgrave, who was ranch instructor on the Blackfoot reservation for the Indian Department of the Federal Government. His father died when Dick was two years old, but his mother continued to operate the family ranch until she sold the cows and calves to George Lane for $23 a head.

Dick competed at the Calgary Stampede for the first time as a bronk rider during 1920. Working the chute gates for the Stampede during 1925 started his long association of forty-four years with the Calgary Exhibition and Stampede. Winning his first chuckwagon race in 1926, he went on to win this spectacular event ten times before he retired from driving in 1946. The following year he was selected to become Stampede Manager, a position he maintained until 1969. In 1935 he married Olive Flett, a daughter of pioneer rancher Lester Flett of the Hand Hills.

During the early years of chuckwagon races in Calgary, the three wagon outfits of Marvin Flett, Lone Breeze and Dick Cosgrave would gather at Cosgrave's ranch to practice for the races. Since the first races in 1923, the horses and rules have changed considerably over the years. The type of horses has shifted from heavy workhorses to thoroughbred racing types, that are trained to run four together; pulling a chuckwagon. After circling the barrels and racing around the half-mile track, the first outfit to have smoke coming from their stove was declared the winner. The rules have now changed to where a stove and tent pegs are thrown into the back of the wagon; run a figure eight around two barrels and the race is on. For the past seventy years the competition of the chuckwagon races, are still one of the major attractions at the Calgary Stampede.

As Stampede Manager Dick Cosgrave was like an ambassador advertising the Stampede in many parts of North America. Olive always accompanied him when they visited shows at Denver and Las Vegas every winter, scouting for afternoon attractions for the following Stampede. The Cosgraves were also part of the group from Alberta to attend the first Grey Cup celebration in Toronto during 1948. After Dick's death in 1973, Olive and their son Bob carried on their ranch operations for another four years. She then moved to Calgary where she passed away during October 1981.

When Winston Bruce signed on as arena director with the Calgary Stampede on June 1st 1969; his own thoughts puzzled him as to what changes were required to build the annual stampede into a highly polished professional world attraction. Before the annual show arrived in 1970, he had been promoted to Stampede manager.

Winston's ability as a rodeo performer and manager came naturally, as he was born to and raised by a rodeo family who farmed in Central Alberta near Forestburg. The family maintained a rodeo arena at their ranch, in order to train young cowboys for the rodeo competitions that the father would produce each summer. Bruce claimed it was great entertainment when every Sunday after church, they would hold a rodeo all afternoon with friends and neighbors of the community.

His father, Laurence Bruce had competed in rodeos for many years before Winston was old enough to crawl on his first bucking horse. To the Bruce family cowboys and rodeo was a fact of their lifestyle, and a big part of their heritage. Winston Bruce entered his first rodeo in 1952 at the age of fourteen, when he won the novice saddle bronk competition at Calgary.

By the middle 1950s, Bruce was one of the top Canadian competitors. He won the national championships in 1957 and 1958 and was the Saddle Bronk champion at Calgary in 1959. He was the World's Champion Bronk rider during 1961 as well placing within the international top three from 1959 to 1965. By the late 1960s, Bruce had decided to retire being able to avoid any serious injuries throughout his rodeo career.

One main responsibility of Bruce's new assignment with the Calgary Stampede, was to supervise activities at their ranch near Hanna, that they had purchased in 1961. The ranch was purchased years ago in order to establish a solid breeding program to raise bucking horses. This has developed into a successful venture for the Stampede Company, with evidence of numerous world champion horses that has shown up at Calgary and other large rodeos in the U.S.A.

When Bruce became Stampede Manager, Calgary owned about 250 head of bucking horses, compared to over 500 head when he retired. During the 1950s and 1960s two or three would be selected for the National finals, but during more recent years, twelve to fifteen head of their best horses have been picked. Bruce contributed this to their breeding program, which he created with an extensive set of breeding, production and performance records. A solid set of rules has been set on horse care and exercise programs at the Stampede Ranch. Recognizing Bruce's retirement during October 2002, he can be proud of his contribution to the sport of rodeo after a fifty-year career as a rodeo competitor and stampede manager.

With Calgary reaching closer to the 100th Anniversary of their annual Exhibition and Stampede, Robin Burwash, their most recent Stampede Manager, expresses excitement as his rodeo crew prepares for the 10-day celebration of the 2004 Calgary Stampede. Born and raised with a large family on a mixed farm close to Calgary, Robin's dream came true, with his appointment as Stampede Manager for the Calgary Exhibition and Stampede during April 2002.

Robin never did compete in any boy's steer riding events but went straight to riding bareback bucking horses at the age of thirteen. He first became interested in rodeo while attending high school at Airdrie, and went on to win the National High School Rodeo Finals in Sulpher, Louisiana. Winning the novice bareback event at the Calgary Stampede was a major highlight, which took him on to competing in three different Amateur Associations, while riding also on his permit in the Canadian Professional Rodeo Circuit. He first attended Montana's State University in 1978, and by winning their first fall rodeo that season Robin was offered a full scholarship to rodeo for their University team.

Burwash's professional rodeo career has been an exiting drama. Possibly the most impressive was being a two-time winner of Calgary's $50 000 bareback champion. He won the Canadian Bareback Championship four times between 1983 and 1989 and the Reserve World Championship in 1989 and 1993. He qualified for the National Rodeo Finals eleven times and fourteen times for the Canadian Rodeo Finals. Winning the Gold Medal for the Olympic Rodeo held in Calgary during 1988, he was also selected as Canadian Cowboy of the Year, for that season.

Robin retired from riding bareback bronks after the completion of the National Finals in 1994. He will tell you it is wonderful being back involved with the rodeo action, especially having the opportunity to breed and raise the great bucking stock of the Calgary Stampede. As a competitor and winner at the Calgary Stampede, he remembers the thrill of riding at Calgary was a step above the rest. As their newest Stampede Manager, he mentions how he is amazed when the City of Calgary, Stampede volunteer workers and staff, create a charisma that makes the annual Stampede Rodeo " The Greatest Outdoor Show on Earth."

Burwash recognizes that to heighten the profile of rodeo to be uniform with other professional sports, the public has to be shown to what level rodeo competition will rise when elite rodeo cowboys and cowgirls are matched with the greatest livestock in rodeo. He remarks that this may come to be a possibility, with the Calgary Exhibition and Stampede presenting the world's first Million Dollar Rodeo in 2004.

# Calf Branding Contest

Branding the annual calf crop during the spring months has been a tradition carried down from the open range days of ranching, when all the cattle were handled in the open, without the use of any corrals or chutes. Most ranching generations since, have used the same practices in corral brandings that were used on the open range. This may not be as picturesque as branding in the open; but it has been much easier on horses and men, because of not having to hold the herd, and also the ability to use more experienced help to perform the many jobs necessary at calf brandings.

Branding the calf crop while they are from one to two months old; has always been an important job on most cow outfits, recognizing the advantages of castrating, dehorning, and vaccinating calves at the same time . Several different handling methods are used to restrain these calves during the actual application of the brand. Every cattle owner believes that his method is superior; which may not necessarily be the best procedure for the benefit of the calves.

A convenient size calf branding is about two hundred head, for cow outfits which have a large number of calves to brand. It is an advantage to split the cow herd into bunches of this size, and then cut out about a half to one third of those cows; which prevents the possibility of trampling any calves. The size and shape of a corral, sometimes referred to as a trap, is also an important factor; and helps to avoid the necessity of dragging any calves a long distance. Some of the larger ranches with cow herds of six or seven hundred head, corral everything in one large rectangular shaped pen; then split the herd evenly leaving one half at each end of the pen.

The branding crew and fire pots are spread across the middle of the pen leaving cows and calves on both sides of the crew. The calf heelers drag calves to only the middle of the pen, where the wrestlers are located. Instead of reining their horses back into the same herd, they can ride straight through for a catch at the other end of the pen. Having calves coming from two opposite directions in the same branding pen, makes it more difficult for the calf wrestlers who have to continually switch sides to be in a position to handle calves properly.

A proper size crew for large brandings consists of about twenty men. Two capable heelers can keep enough calves on the ground, with four sets of wrestlers. It works better to use one man for each iron for application of the brand, which may include an age brand on the heifer calves. Two knife men are needed to castrate the bull calves , and also mark ears and cut waddles or other markings if necessary. If horns are being removed, two more men are required, plus another two to handle the vaccine guns.

A good person is also needed to keep proper tally count, because the number of vaccine shots that are sometimes used for a head count, do not calculate the number of steers and heifers branded.

Prior to forty years ago women were never seen in a branding corral. During the years since, there are nearly as many women taking part in all the different jobs involved with branding as there are men. Today most ranch brandings have become a social function, with enough neighbors invited for the affair to appear like a country picnic.

Some of the ranches have never used calf heelers to catch their calves at branding time. Instead, these outfits separate all the calves from the cows into a different pen and acquire the help of a bunch of husky young people who do not mind being kicked, trampled on, or run over by some frisky young calves. They are expected to grab the calves anywhere possible and drag them to the branding fire by hand.

To get the calves on the ground, there is usually a wrestling match, whereby limbs and necks are twisted to the extent that much more stress is placed on young calves than dragging them to a branding fire using a horse with a rope on their hind legs. Other cow outfits use nothing but a mechanical calf table where each calf is pushed separately into a small metal chute. Both sides of the chute are squeezed together until the animal is not able to move, pitting steel against flesh and bone. With the use of mechanical gadgets the chute is turned horizontally to about the height of a table. After each calf is branded, and has had other functions performed, the table is turned vertically again and the calf is turned loose.

During more recent times some ranches have used a system where the calves are heeled without using any wrestlers. Apparently this was an idea started in the United States during the Second World War, when the large ranches experienced a shortage of manpower. To accomplish this, a number of short strong pegs are pounded into the ground around the branding fire. A short piece of soft rope is fastened to each peg with a break-a-way hondu tied in the loose ends. A man is available to slip the short rope onto one front leg, as each calf is heeled and brought near the fire. The same man is available to put both hind legs in the heelers rope for those that are caught by only one hind leg. This enables the heeler to restrain the calf using the rope and horse while the calf's front end is tied to the peg. As soon the branding crew is finished with each calf, the peg rope is removed and the calf is able to scramble out of the heeler's rope by itself.

Regardless of the different practices that have been used to handle calves during the past, some of the methods have accomplished the job easier and with much less effort than others. People who have directed a calf branding often have their own reasons to support their branding methods, and no doubt are prepared to debate the advantages of their own actions. I was brought up in the "old school", and convinced that the system which was introduced by the old time cowmen is the fastest and most effective way to handle calves at branding time.

Heeling calves with horses and dragging them short distances along the ground is somewhat a natural position for a calf, because when the majority of them are born, their body and legs are in that same position. Branding calves using wrestlers can be quick and easy, if done correctly. Many people who I have seen wrestling calves were never shown, or were not interested enough to learn, the simple techniques of how it can be done effectively. Going in front of a calf, and turning it back towards the heeler while caught, is an unforgiven error in a branding corral.

A wrestling team consists of two people, one for each end of the calf, and they are more effective if each of them remains on the same end, instead of alternating back and forth. They should always allow the horse dragging the calf to walk between them, with each partner prepared to take hold of either the rope or the tail. The person handling the hind end, must work the same side of the rope that the calves are being branded. When calves are caught by both hind legs, the person handling the hind end should always grab the rope as close to the heels as possible. By the other partner taking the tail with two hands and both giving a quick pull simultaneously, the calf will be flipped horizontally and land broadside on the ground.

The front end wrestler has to quickly position himself with one knee resting on the calf's neck, and the other on its shoulder; while he holds the upper foreleg with both hands doubled back at the knee. The hind end wrestler sits on the ground directly behind the calf, and in most cases should be able to have the rope removed before getting into that position. With one foot he should push the calf's lower leg forward as far as possible, with his boot instep set just above the hock. The other foot should be placed far enough away from the calf, to give himself sufficient balance. The upper leg is held with both hands, and sitting close enough to the calf, so the hoof nearly reaches his arm pit; this will allow that arm to reach around underneath to grab the upper leg just above the other hock. This is a good position for the hind end wrestler to handle big strong calves, which does not allow the calf any leverage to kick free.

When calves are caught by one leg on the side away from the hind end man, the wrestlers can handle them the same as if caught by both legs. Those caught by one leg nearest to the hind end man, must be handled differently by him, switching from the rope to the tail and visa versa. By giving the same quick pull, the calf is completely turned over and lands broadside having the proper side upwards.

A good set of wrestlers should never move too far from one location in the corral, and make the heelers bring the calves to them; instead of them going after the calves. The calf heelers are usually experienced men who usually ride gentle well broke horses. They control the pace of most brandings; which should move along quickly with a proper size crew.

There are two types of heelers; those who tie their rope solid with one half hitch and a half to their saddle horn and those who dally their rope around the horn. Most 'tied' men use about fourteen feet of rope, and throw a small loop with a short quick half swing to make a catch. The other end of the rope is coiled small and tied to the opposite side of the saddle, over top of the front jockey skirt.

The 'dally' man has to control the unused portion of his heeling rope with the same hand used for the bridle reins. A good calf heeler can catch with equal skill on either side of the calf, using a back-hand throw for the other side. Some heelers tie their rope and then dally over top of the tie. These men are good heelers because they seldom allow any slack for a calf to jerk itself by running out and hitting the end of the rope. Most calf heelers attempt to catch both hind feet, which may happen slightly more than fifty percent of the time.

When the first large cattle herds were trailed into southern Alberta during the early 1880s; with them came men who already had years of experience in the techniques necessary to handle wild cattle. These men who had the proper knowledge of trailing cattle; how to move cattle across large rivers, and the practice of working big herds and branding calves in the open without the use of any corrals or chutes. They came from areas of the United States where cattle ranching was an established industry The annual round-ups and branding a new crop of calves each year became a major importance to the operation of every cow outfit. This involved calf heelers who were experienced ropers that could catch calves by both hind feet in order to drag them close to a branding fire.

Calf heelers with little experience often catch calves above one hock, making the job much more difficult for the wrestlers. It used to be a controversial issue in the ranching community of southern Alberta, as to which method of heeling was the fastest. During the past fifty years special branding contests have been organized to establish whether the man who 'tied' was any faster than the man who 'dallied'. The results of these contests bring to my mind the following story.

Many of the livestock practices that came with the American herds helped to establish the ranching industry in southern Alberta which included the skill of heeling calves.

Cattle ranching in southern Alberta had become well established by 1925, and for some reason that has long been forgotten; the topic of calf heelers became a matter of contention in the Lethbridge area. The extent of the concern became an issue; whereby a special calf branding was organized to determine which method of heeling calves was the fastest; a tied roper or a dally roper.

The contest required each roper to catch twenty-five calves without having to "clean the herd." The event was easily won by the man who had his rope tied onto the horn of the saddle, where the other heeler dallied his rope around the saddle horn for each calf he caught. The tied roper won the contest with a time of between fourteen and fifteen minutes Nearly a quarter century had passed when the same issue of calf heelers surfaced again; this time in the ranching communities around High River and Nanton. During early spring of 1948, the rodeo committees from both High River and Nanton decided to include a calf branding contest at both rodeos scheduled for late June and early July. The purpose of these contests was not for the same reason as the earlier event held at Lethbridge, but more as a special attraction for ranching people to attend the rodeos.

Bert Sheppard volunteered to heel calves for a branding team representing the ranchers west of High River and was challenged by the ranchers along Willow Creek who chose the late Jac Streeter as their calf heeler. Both branding teams consisted of four men; a roper, two wrestlers and a man to apply the branding iron. For the Streeter team, Allie Streeter wrestled the hind end, with Rocky Ewashik on the front end, and Slim Sonnie did the branding. This writer wrestled the hind end for the Sheppard team; with Joe Wallace on the front end and Warren Zimmerman applied the branding iron.

Prior to the contest; one interesting feature about the event was that Jac Streeter was a dally man while Bert Sheppard always tied his rope to heel calves. Both teams met first at the Nanton two day rodeo, where each team was to brand fifteen calves on separate evenings of the rodeo. Rules for the contest were few, with no penalty for catching one leg, or having a calf caught above the hock.

A willow wood fire heated the irons that were applied with proper heat, leaving the evening air filled with the smell of burning hair . The heelers tossed a coin to determine who would brand first, and when Sheppard won the toss, he chose to brand his calves on the second evening. It had rained a good amount leaving the rodeo arena quite muddy and difficult for heeling calves.

Both teams ended up with a slow time of over fourteen minutes, with Sheppard having a slightly faster time than Streeter. The same teams met again at the High River rodeo during the first week of July, both to brand fifteen calves with the same rules used at the Nanton show. The aggregate times of each team would determine the winner of the branding contest. Streeter lost the toss again, so his team had to brand on the first evening, branding their fifteen calves in nine minutes and fifty-one seconds; a time that appeared impossible to beat. Sheppard's team branded their calves the second evening in seven minutes and twenty-two seconds, winning the contest, silver belt buckles, and prize money of three hundred dollars.

The Chipman Chemical Company at Winnipeg also donated a plaque with six silver shields; one each displaying the names of the four team members and their positions, the fifth indicated their time with the sixth shield showing the rope horse's name used in the contest. The plaque is a treasured keepsake hanging on my wall, from the Bert Sheppard estate.

The contest appeared to be an attractive event so both rodeo committees agreed to stage a similar contest the following year in 1949. The Willow Creek ranchers challenged Sheppard again with Alfred (Toots) Burton as their calf heeler. Toots chose to brand their calves the first evening of the Nanton rodeo, but had problems during the event in not finishing, because of one calf that escaped from the branding pen. Streeter took over for Burton and in order for the Nanton contest to become a competition, both teams branded the second evening, together with sixteen cows and calves in the same pen. Both heelers went after their eighth calf at the same time, with Sheppard catching and Streeter missing their last loops, allowing Sheppard to again win the Nanton contest.

When the two teams competed that year at High River, Streeter beat Sheppard's time by using a tied rope, with a fast time of seven minutes and thirty-one seconds. Since the evening shadows lengthened at the first calf branding contests held at Nanton and High River fifty years ago, many similar contests have been organized at agricultural fairs and rodeos throughout southern Alberta.

Most of the more recent contests have branded less than fifteen calves, without using a hot iron. The majority of modern day calf heelers have chosen the dally style of heeling instead of having their ropes tied. If nothing else, these calf branding challenges have demonstrated and remained an authentic part of Alberta's ranching heritage.

# Bloody was the Sun

Now that the summer of 2003 has nearly past with shorter days and cooler evenings, it has reminded the writer of a similar summer during 1936. There was no early moisture that year, therefore the whole country was so dry, that the hay and grain crops suffered for moisture long before the first of July. A comparison of these two years shows that, like many decades ago, the extremely hot days this July caused hundreds of forest fires to burn out of control in Alberta and British Columbia. During 1936, the forest country west of High River and Turner Valley was alive with fires during the latter part of July until the third week of August, which burned for at least a month.

Before becoming a teenager, I can remember being in the hay field one stifling hot July afternoon when a large gray smoke cloud appeared in the sky, towering high above the mountains west of Turner Valley. The source of the fire was on the Elk River in eastern British Columbia and another fire started a short time later in the Castle River area of the southwestern corner of Alberta. Smoke from both fires darkened the sun every afternoon and gave a deathly appearance of a small red blotch in the sky. Some days, depending on the wind, ashes from both fires were visible as far east as Black Diamond and Hartell. The ranchers and rural residents that lived along the eastern slopes were not kept informed of the location, or condition of the fires, because radios were a luxury, newspapers were scarce and television had not yet been thought about.

Harry Wileman was forest ranger at the Mount Sentinel ranger station on the Highwood River, and Fred Nash was ranger for the Alberta Forestry Department on the Sheep River. Both men knew exactly what should be done to prevent the fires from burning over into Alberta; and each had contacted the forestry office in Calgary by telephone with a simple solution. They suggested that a couple of men with pack horses, some grub, a tent and a few tools could be sent to a small pass at the head of McPhail Creek, which was the only place along the mountains where the fire could get through. The pass was only approximately two hundred yards wide between the glacier that was situated south of the pass, and Mount McPhail to the north.

They would of had no difficulty in preventing the fire from crossing over into Alberta by back-firing at night time to destroy the grass and some small trees from the meadow, that was situated at the mouth of the pass. Nash and Wileman were told to mind their own business, as they were not involved with the fires burning in British Columbia. Nash later received a letter from the Calgary office, reprimanding him for spending forestry money on stupid phone calls.

During the third week of July the fire came through the McPhail Pass into the Highwood valley and by August the fifth it had reached Upper Flat Creek. There were no bull-dozers or water bombers to help fight fires in those days; the only tools available were axes, shovels, picks and gas engine water pumps. The soup kitchens and streets of Calgary were full of unemployed men who were hauled by trucks to camp locations that were situated throughout the Highwood River and Sheep River forestry areas. The ranchers along the foothills were also recruited to supply teams and plows to build fireguards in areas wherever it was possible.

Very little had been accomplished in controlling these fires, until it began to rain during the third week of August. The heavy rains continued for three days and nights, thoroughly drenching the fires which had been a threat to livestock and ranch sites in the pathway of the fires. Human safety would have been sacrificed if the fires had not been brought under control by this natural element.

The late rains also caused growth of good fall pasture that germinated plant growth which had not developed earlier in the year due to the absence of moisture. All classes of livestock prices were down, and in many cases the market price received did not pay the cost of the shipping.

These two summers were similar because during July 2003, the owners of livestock in Alberta had no confirmation whether there would even be a market price available for their livestock.

Because of low market prices, and the shortage of feed for livestock in 1936, the Alberta government introduced a subsidy program for old cows that were being sold. There was also a livestock freight assistance program available, whereby the government paid the cost to have livestock shipped by rail to areas in Alberta, where feed was available to winter cattle. The subsidy also paid to have the livestock returned home again the following spring. This is evidence that the saying, "history repeats itself", is as true as the history itself.

# The OH Ranch: 1945

In 2005, the Canadian people acknowledged the 50th anniversary of VE day and the end of the Second World War in Western Europe. As the current generation of older men and women who were not part of Canada's armed forces at that time watched the celebrations by television, they no doubt attempted to recollect exactly where they were and what they were doing during that particular time of their lives. I had four brothers who joined the armed forces and if the European conflict had not ended when it did, I would have been in uniform also.

The year of 1945 has remained a vivid memory for me over the years because of some of the happenings that took place, so I share with you some of those recollections. During the year the war ended I was employed at the OH Ranch, which is one of the oldest ranches in southern Alberta, located seven miles up country from the village of Longview.

During that era the OH Ranch was the property of P. Burns Ranches Ltd. whose headquarters were in Calgary. Their ranch foreman was a man named Sandy Neish who has been deceased for twenty years. He married Mary Brown in 1939. She was born and raised on the old ranch and passed away during February 1995. The Neish's were good people and evidence of this can be found in the three sons and one daughter who currently reside in the Dewinton-Okotoks district.

The long cultivated field that lies along Highway 541 going west to Kananaskis country was finally summer fallowed during 1945 after growing a crop of green feed every year for nearly forty years. The big field had been ploughed every spring during previous years with two five horse hitches and two double bottom gang plows. That spring the old plows were allowed to remain in the metal machine shed and the old work teams were not even gathered from their winter range. Progress in ranching was evident, so the summer fallow was done with a spanking new WD9 International tractor, and a one-way tiller disc that was trailed from the Findlay place, a four-section farm that Burns Ranches owned north of High River. The big field was sowed to cover crop about the first of August but the lush crop of green oats was never grazed that fall because of the early winter which came in October.

The High River area enjoyed a relatively mild winter during early 1945 with a cold spring and a very wet summer, however a ten-inch snowfall occurred at the OH Ranch during the early part of August, which totally flattened the two fields of green feed. The crop was heavy because it was sown on two hay meadows that had been newly plowed - one that lay immediate south of the ranch building and the other to the east. The green feed was all cut one way using pick-ups on two horse binders, and was finally stacked with sleighs, digging the stooks out of the deep snow. We finished the day before Christmas!

Prior to the middle 1950s the larger ranches allowed their beef steers to mature to become three years old before they were trailed to market. By 1945 the OH beef herd had consisted of many older steers, which had been allowed to escape the fall gather during previous years. Due to this ridiculous situation, the OH Ranch had great difficulty in gathering their beef herd that same fall. The older steers were big and wild; they knew the best bush patches to hold up in and would move like old range horses as soon as any riders appeared. We began gathering the beef steers around the beginning of October and completely wore out a string of saddle horses before the gather was finished two months later. During those years their dry herd was allowed to range in one large field that extended east and west from the forest reserve boundary to a line fence that ran straight north from the ranch buildings. The north and south boundary covered an area from the ranch headquarters to nearly Sheep Creek.

Quis Johnson, Charlie McGregor and myself gathered the beef herd, along with Dick and Albert Amos two native cowboys from the Morley Indian reserve. These native families had stooked the green feed on the ranch that fall and remained camped there on the bench land about a mile west of the ranch headquarters. They were paid a daily wage and extra money for providing their own horses. Their agreement with the ranch did not include any food for themselves, or feed for their horses. They were both good cowboys, especially in finding a way through the brush and through bog holes. The weather was cold with very little wind, so it seemed there was as much snow on the brush as there was on the ground. The area we rode, consisted of a large amount of willow brush that held the snow, and with the first brush that was encountered each morning, a dump of snow would land in our saddle forks. As the day progressed our body heat would melt the snow enough for it to freeze and turn to ice, leaving the saddles covered with ice for the remainder of the day. Each night our saddles had to be taken to the bunkhouse for the ice to melt in order to have a dry saddle again for the next morning.

One cloudy morning this group of riders were riding northward half way up the east slope of Jim Coulee when a big moose appeared across the valley. The father of the native family asked if we would stop and wait there until he had time to cross over to get within range to shoot the moose with an old his single shot .22 caliber rifle. The native father quietly found his way down through the brushy bottom of the valley and within a half hour we heard one shot and saw the moose drop. A season for killing moose was prohibited during those years for anyone except the native people, and although his weapon was small, the crafty old hunter knew exactly where to aim his shot for a fatal kill. When we saw him reach the carcass to bleed the animal, the remaining riders rode on looking for more steers that had drifted into that remote area.

The riders continued northward to the end of the valley, crossed over and rode back along the west slope to where the moose was shot. The snow was deep and traveling was slow and by time we reached the dead moose, the native father had the carcass already skinned and quartered using nothing but a large pocketknife. After helping the elderly man drag the four quarters of the carcass and pile them under a nearby evergreen tree, the meat was covered completely with the freshly skinned hide. The father's two sons were not surprised but the ranch cowhands were amazed as to how one man had completely dressed a large moose carcass in such a short time with so few tools. Realizing the meat would have to lay there for at least twenty four hours, the native father was asked about wolves and coyotes destroying his freshly killed meat. Without a word said, the elderly man took the colored handkerchief from around his neck, tied it to a tree branch directly above the meat, got on his horse and we rode on. The following Sunday, which was four days later, the native father borrowed a narrow gauge sleigh with a single deck wagon box from the ranch to bring his fresh meat supply back to their camp, a distance of about twelve miles return. With his small team of horses which were not conditioned, he left the ranch buildings about 10 a.m., pushing snow with the doubletrees and arrived back 12 hours later. I never did find out and have wondered many times since how the old man got a team and sleigh into the area where his meat was cached and how he loaded those heavy moose quarters by himself.

Over the years since I have often thought about the endurance of some horses and the native people that I have known during my lifetime. The three OH Ranch cowhands had three horses each and would change horses every day. Our horses were stabled at night and fed all the prairie hay they could eat along with a gallon of good oats morning and night. The native cowboys rode right along with us; traveled the same miles we traveled through the brush and bog holes, sometimes in the lead. When they arrived back at their camp most nights after dark, they would pull their saddles off and turn their ponies loose to paw snow all night for something to eat. Many days they were back riding the same horse the next morning and were ready to ride hard, whipping and getting as soon as any steers were located. I have often inquired whether the two Amos brothers are still living and think about the hardships they and their horses endured that fall gathering OH beef.

The water continues to tumble down Ings Creek past the OH Ranch buildings and empties into the mighty Highwood River. The old ranch has changed ownership several times since and a multitude of different cowhands have helped with the beef gather during the years gone by. The native families from either the Eden Valley or Morley Indian reserves do not help with the fencing, or the winter feed supply the way they used to, as new technology has changed the ranching industry a great deal since the Second World War.

During 1948 the federal government purchased the Eden Valley Ranch west of Longview as a second reservation for the native people of the Stoney Indian Nation. Prior to this time many native families who had been residing on the Morley Reserve camped out continually throughout the ranching country that is situated south of the Bow River. These families usually found employment with the larger ranches along the foothills during the summer, cutting and burning brush, cutting firewood, repairing or building new fences, also stooking and stacking green feed.

During the winter months when there was little work available they would locate themselves at a favorite camping location where there was good shelter from the wind, plenty of dry firewood, with a sufficient supply of fresh open water. Their horses were turned loose to care for themselves and their single wall canvas tents were made as comfortable as possible for the women and children. They would travel to the nearest town as little as possible during the winter months by either horseback or team and democrat to purchase the basic needs of a simple life-style with their major food and clothing obtained mostly from them hunting wild game. The majority of them were self-motivated people in their own way who lived and cared for their families, often under some difficult circumstances.

If the truth could be revealed, it was doubtful whether the people of the Stoney Nation fully understood the terms of Treaty Seven when it was signed during 1877. There is evidence that their people signed the treaty with reluctance, and although they were allowed to choose the site of their own reservation, its people soon found they were given far less land than was promised.

Many of the changes that have happened over the years have allowed the cow business to survive to where modern day ranching is an entirely different lifestyle than it was 50 years ago. Without a doubt, some of the people currently ranching under modern practices would be willing to revert back to some of the old styles methods of ranching, if they had the opportunity.

# Northwest Stampede

During the summer of 1947, movie producers from Hollywood, California, came to the Longview area to do a western film called "Northwest Stampede." The location selected to make the movie was the Stampede Ranch, situated about fifteen miles upstream from Longview along the Highwood River. The ranch owners at that time were Joe Caldwell and Dick Machin, who had recently purchased the ranch from Guy Weadick. Other portions of this movie shoot were taken at Banff and the Calgary Stampede.

The main actors were James Craig, Jack Oakie, and Chill Wills, with Joan Leslie as the supporting actress. James Craig was filmed as a rodeo performer whose late father bequeathed him a ranch near Calgary, Canada. Joan Leslie, who was responsible for the daily operation of the ranch, figured Craig was shirking his duties as a ranch owner and should forget about the rodeos. Meanwhile a wild stallion showed up in the hills, which became a problem with their horse herd. Craig's determination to capture the wild stallion was successful, but he was injured when he tried to tame the horse for riding. I cannot remember if the stallion became accustomed to being handled, or whether he was turned loose again. The white stallion was the star in the movie, had been trucked in from the United States. It was the same animal used in the television series, "The Lone Ranger." I do not recall either, how the story ended and what romance transpired between the leading actor and the actress.

The cast and crew that consisted of well over one hundred people stayed at the Palliser Hotel in Calgary, while in Canada. The Canadian Pacific Railway ran a special train daily to transport the movie crew to High River, where Greyhound buses would haul them to the Stampede Ranch. Every morning for several weeks about eight in the morning, seven or eight big buses would roar up the gravel trail passed the OH Ranch, filling the Highwood valley with road dust, and returning back to High River late in the afternoon.

The movie story required a large herd of loose horses. Burns Ranches at the Bar U; were the only outfit raising large numbers of horses during those years, so they supplied approximately 500 head for the movie. They gathered all their horses at the Bar U Ranch and the 44 Ranch, both owned by Pat Burns; with exception of the work teams that were being used by their haying crews. These were assembled at the Buffalo Head Ranch, that was also part of the Bar U Ranch at that time. Raymond Clifford, Superintendent for Burns Ranches, stipulated that if Burns horses were being used; he would hire the wranglers, recognizing the fact that there were no Hollywood cowboys with sufficient experience to move and handle their horses properly.

Local ranchers that Clifford hired were: Allan Baker, Allen Christenson, Hal Caton, Dave Deibel, Dunc Fraser, Floyd Haynes, Glen and Walt Jackson, Bob and Jack Miller, Wally McIntyre, Henry Sorkilmo, Jimmy Troute, Glen Wooden, and Lawrence Watrin, plus Floyd Erickson and Ed Peters who were Bar U cowhands. The wranglers were paid ten dollars a day by the movie producers, plus all the grub they could eat and a place to sleep. The wages paid to ordinary ranch hands during those years was seventy dollars a month.

When filming the movie on the Highwood finished, and before the Bar U Ranch turned all their horses loose again, Raymond Clifford saw an opportunity to cut back any crippled horses or pensioners, that were no longer of any use to them. There were approximately ninety horses they wished to dispose of, which were to be trailed to Calgary to be sold for fox-meat. The Bar U cowhands trailed the ninety head down the river, and stopped overnight at the OH Ranch. The OH Ranch also had several horses they wished to be rid of, so the following morning the two

Bar U cowhands and myself, left the OH Ranch about 7:00 AM, each of us riding fox-meat horses. We headed north through Fireguard Coulee, and crossed the Sheep River upstream from the traffic bridge at Black Diamond. Continuing north for another four miles, the North Fork of Sheep Creek was forded just below the old Millarville Church. Several miles after passing the old church, we headed north again through the Red Deer Lake country, then turned east to cross Highway #2, two miles south of what is now Highway 22X. By time we reached the Bow River, the afternoon shadows were beginning to lengthen, so we headed north up the west side of the Bow, 'pushing' some tired horses! We reached Burns Ranches feedlot, a bit late for supper. Their feedlot was situated where 82nd Avenue S.E. meets the Deerfoot trail; near the location of the new Costco store.

The ranch foreman at the OH was at the feedlot before breakfast the next morning, anxious to get me back on a horse mower at the OH Ranch. The feedlot foreman helped the Bar U cowhands move the horse herd across the Bow River to the Red Top slaughter plant, which was situated on Nose Creek in northeast Calgary. The Bar U men were sent back to High River with their saddles; on the Greyhound bus.

Trailing range horses fifty miles in a short twelve hours was just another day's work! A lot of water has tumbled down the Highwood River since, and yet the incident remains as vivid as if it happened last week. If the calendar could be turned back fifty-six years, there is little doubt we would do it again.

# Opening Ceremonies at the Bar U Ranch National Historic Site

When Parks Canada purchased the headquarters area of the famous Bar U Ranch in December 1991; it was announced at that time, that the Historic Ranch Site would not be ready for public use for at least five years. This ranch, which is situated about ten miles south of Longview along Highway 22 was established in 1882, making it one of the oldest cattle ranches operating in Alberta. Due to the involvement of local ranchers in the development of this historic site; the partial operation of the ranch, become a reality much quicker than expected.

The Bar U National Historic Ranch was opened for the public on Saturday, July 1st 1995, eighteen months ahead of schedule. Ceremonies which officially opened the Bar U Ranch site, took place on Sunday July 30th. Those who did not attend this function missed a great afternoon in the Alberta foothills, as well as a pageant that displayed a large portion of the early ranch history of southern Alberta.

Functions of this nature do not happen without a large amount of volunteer work from many capable people. The opening ceremonies along with the ranch history pageant was organized jointly by volunteers from Friends of The Bar U Historic Ranch Association and employees of Parks Canada, who are currently working at the historic ranch site. Friends of The Bar U, are an organization of volunteers governed by a thirteen member board, who have an agreement with Parks Canada to assist with the development and administration of the Bar U National Historic Ranch.

A large amount of credit to the success of the opening ceremonies pageant must be given to both Pamela Brown and John Scott. Pamela was Ceremonies Chairperson who coordinated the work done by the different committees; and wrote the pageant script along with much help from Julia Parsonage and Gaylle Geres. With John Scott's capable direction; the work done by each committee was staged into a grand finale performance. The pageant would have never been the success it was, without the support received from John Scott; who supplied the horses, buggies, and wagons that were necessary to carry out the major features of the pageant . Without John's equipment, it would have been nearly impossible to beg, borrow or steal the same kind, and such a large amount of equipment elsewhere.

The Roy McLean family contributed a great deal to the pageant parade also. Joe McLean acted as Fred Stimson; who rode to the headwaters of Pekisko Creek, leading a pack horse; depicting when the initial Bar U ranch site was selected in the spring of 1882. Lenore McLean represented Mrs. Stimson throughout the pageant, who was taking an afternoon drive with her single horse and buggy . Tim McLean acted as Guy Weadick, who was successful in finding sponsorship to promote the first Calgary Stampede in 1912. The McLean family also supplied the black Percheron team and wagon that transported visitors around the ranch headquarters all afternoon.

The cooperation and attendance of the native people from the Eden Valley Indian Reserve was very much appreciated. It was only fitting to have descendants of these same families take part and be recognized in the pageant activities, since families from this same native tribe made up a large part of the work force during the George Lane and Pat Burns eras of the Bar U Ranch.

Band councilor Rex Daniels supplied and set up the three teepees that were visible over near the creek. Rex also led the horse and travois to lead off the pageant; and his son Tom Daniels sang our National Anthem in the Stoney language. Long time Bar U Native cowboy, Webster Lefthand; along with Johnny Lefthand Junior, Taylor Bearspaw, and Ernie Rollingmud, were the four native cowboys representing the past participation of native cowhands on the Bar U Ranch. Many miles of wire fence on the Bar U Ranch were repaired by the Stoney people over the years, and to recognize this activity a fencing wagon was driven by native cowboy, Judy Dixon.

Organizers of the pageant extend their appreciation to the Bob Nelson family for supplying the cattle that were used to depict the first cattle trailed to the Bar U, from Idaho, for the North West Cattle Company during the summer of 1882.

Possibly the most rewarding thing about the pageant were those people who attended that were descendants of men who owned the Bar U Ranch in years gone by. George Lane was represented by at least two grandsons, and several great nephews of Pat Burns were also in attendance. Both Gordon and Ironside of the Gordon, Ironside and Fares Company were represented with descendants, but it was impossible to find descendants from the Fares family of that partnership. Fred Stimson was not represented with any descendants either, because it was not established whether he has any family living. It was gratifying to have Sandy Cross attend the function, who represented his father, A. E. Cross, founder of the Ranch and a member of the Big Four, sponsors of the first Calgary Stampede.

Modern day owners of the famous ranch were also in attendance; with

J. Allen Baker, his oldest daughter Judy, and his son Jim Baker, who was commentator for the pageant, supplied appropriate western music. This family owned the Bar U Ranch for twenty seven years, longer than any other owner since it's inception. The Wambeke family was well represented along with the Melvin Nelson family, who currently own the remains of the original grass land that lays north and west of the historic ranch site.

The idea of using three barbed wires to officially open this historic ranch, was certainly different than most ribbon cutting ceremonies! The first wire was cut by Bert Sheppard, who represented the oldtime cowmen of the Bar U; and Webster Lefthand cut the second wire representing the native involvement in the ranch over the years. Stan Wilson, cutting the third wire; represented both Parks Canada and Friends of the Bar U, who are currently maintaining the Bar U as a Historical Ranch Site for visitors from around the world to enjoy .

Neil McKinnon from the pioneer McKinnon ranching family, and whose Great Uncle Charlie McKinnon, was wagon boss for the early Bar U ranch; drove the old Bar U chuckwagon through the pageant. Neil was also responsible for the authentic round-up camp that was set up on the flat east of the ranch buildings. The makeup of this round up outfit was as real as any round up outfit that operated on the open range a hundred years ago. Cow camp coffee, which was brewed over an open fire pit, the same way it was done on the round ups during the years gone by, was available for guests to enjoy.

The open fire pit, burning diamond willow firewood that had cured with time, was used to heat the branding irons for the boardwalk branding. This was typical of the way branding irons were heated on the old time round ups and early ranches. The interest shown on the branding idea was somewhat of a surprise, when over seventy ranchers donated one hundred dollars each to have their brand burned twice on a two by ten wooden plank. These planks have since been hung from the railing on the west veranda of the new Visitor's Centre at the Bar U Ranch. These brands will be done again on smaller pieces of board, which will be displayed along the lower beams inside the Visitor's Center. The registered position of each brand will be shown along with the owner's name and the year it was first registered. With the cooperation of brand owners, a short history of each brand could be displayed in a special book for the purpose of retaining the heritage for future ranching generations.

Displaying brands inside the Visitor's Centre at the Bar U Ranch will continue as long as there is room available to do so. Brands can also be exhibited as memorial brands in recognition of people who owned the brand in the past. Those who would like to have their brands displayed, can donate one hundred dollars to Friends of The Bar U Historic Ranch Association, by contacting any director of this Association, or an employee of Parks Canada at the Bar U Vistor's Centre.

There were other people who were part of organizing this special day at the Bar U Ranch and more who were involved in the pageant, whose names have not been mentioned. Some of these were the four lady flag bearers, members of the polo team, and those who represented the North West Mounted Police. Friends of The Bar U, want each of them to realize their participation was greatly appreciated and omission of names has been necessary because of space available in this article.

Most everyone involved, felt the Official Opening Ceremonies for the Bar U National Historic Ranch were a tremendous success! If the cooperation of the people who were part of this success is any indication for the future of this ranch; it's destiny can only increase in magnitude and recognition!

# Wolves at the Bar U Ranch

Raising livestock throughout Western Canada has not been an easy business during the past century, and will become more difficult if the Federal Government is allowed to enact new legislation referred to as the Canadian Endangered Species Protection Act.

Raising cows a hundred years ago must have been a much simpler lifestyle, when there was no interference from government organizations, environmentalists, and animal rights groups. All species of wildlife were allowed to exist and multiply in their own habitat unless they became a menace to the livelihood of ranchers. The timber wolf has been one of those species, since the great buffalo herds disappeared. During the days of the open range in southern Alberta, the ranchers joined forces to manage the wolf population themselves; but now it seems a common practice for government environmentalists to interfere and protect any wildlife that may hinder annual livestock production.

Before the mighty buffalo herds completely vanished by 1880, men who were called 'wolfers' kept the wolf population in the Canadian Northwest under control. These men usually worked in pairs and would shoot down a buffalo in such a manner that it would not die immediately. About an ounce of strychnine would then be injected into the animal's blood stream, carrying the poison throughout the complete carcass. This technique usually left a large number of dead wolves as they fed on the carcasses, whose pelts were sold to the traders at the whiskey forts. After the buffalo herds became extinct, the 'wolfers' disappeared also.

With the disappearance of the buffalo, the North West Mounted Police were encouraging the Canadian Government to have cattle ranches established in Western Canada, or bring in cattle from south of the border, to help feed the starving native population. During the early years of the 1880s, ranching companies began trailing large herds of cattle and horses into the Northwest Territories; which became immediate prey for the persistent timber wolf. The early ranchers were forced to take over where the 'wolfers' left off; and started assessing each livestock owner a fee of two cents a head for cattle and four cents for horses. The money collected was paid into a wolf bounty fund that did help to control the wolf population to a large degree.

The Stoney Indians who camped along the foothills, were good hunters, and would find the wolf dens and dig out the pups. The cowhands who worked on the ranches were also continually on the lookout for wolves and their dens. By 1900 the bounty on grown wolves was fifty dollars and twenty five dollars for each pup. As the Stoney Indians had already received a large amount of bounty money, it was realized that the Indians were not killing the female wolves; because they knew it was a paying proposition for her to have another litter of pups the following year. For this reason the bounty for grown wolves was increased to sixty dollars, and decreased to fifteen dollars for each pup. The Alberta Government paid ten dollars also, for grown wolves and one dollar for each pup. Pat Burns Ranches had their own wolf bounty, that was the same price regardless of size or age for all wolves killed on any of their ranches in Southern Alberta.

After many years when no bounty was paid, and it seemed the 'Big Bad Wolf' had completely disappeared. The ranchers in the Pekisko district southwest of High River, were alerted in the fall of 1940, when a big black wolf had been seen along the north fork of the Highwood River.

Mike Burke confirmed the report while returning one afternoon from the 7U Brown Ranch to his own ranch further back in the hills, when he saw an enormous size black wolf running swiftly across the range. More stories quickly surfaced when Guy Weadick, Frasier Hunt, and Ed Marston reported losses of colts and cattle; and soon it was discovered that the wolf was ranging further to the south, after the Bar U Ranch on Pekisko Creek reported some heavy losses.

The wolf bounty fund that laid dormant for so many years, with the residue held in an account of the late 7U Brown; quickly came to life with the appearance of the cunning black wolf. The bounty fund under the authority of Miss Sarah Brown, was brought into immediate operation when King Bearspaw, a Stoney Indian was "staked" to a grub supply to chase down and kill the big wolf.

Bearspaw rode and searched the district for three consecutive weeks, and was finally rewarded with sight of the wolf within rifle range. He fired and severely wounded the predator, who made off through the underbrush. After patient trailing by Bearspaw, he was finally able to kill the wolf. The Indian proudly brought his prize to be viewed by the ranchers of the district and collected the sixty dollars bounty. Although not fully mature, the wolf was the largest ever seen in that district, measuring seven feet six inches from the nose to the tip of the tail.

Three years later during the fall of 1943, another black wolf made a terrible mistake by making the Bar U Ranch his main hunting ground. Several people reported seeing the new intruder and with several cases of frightened livestock, fingers of suspicion were pointed at 'Mr. Wolf'. No effort to hunt down this unwanted visitor happened until mid-December, when Bill Elliot from the E. P. Ranch, spotted the wolf one afternoon. It was heading north from the Bar U buildings, along the trail leading to Longview. Mr. Elliot immediately reported the wolf's whereabouts to the Bar U's general manager Raymond Clifford. Mr. Clifford quickly grabbed a rifle and in his truck, easily caught up to his cow foreman, Oscar Brandham, who had just left the ranch on horseback, to investigate a disturbance of livestock the previous night. Cow foreman Brandham armed with Clifford's rifle took up the chase from there.

Brandham trailed the wolf for five or six miles without getting within rifle range, but some luck happened when two of his riders, Jack Crowe and Bill Windiate, appeared over the hill. Jack Crowe was riding a big half thoroughbred gelding, and with a long rope, he had the wolf in his loop in no time. That was not the end of Mr. Wolf, because he quickly reached around, and cut the rope with one snap of his jaws. By this time Bill Windiate was the only one who had not shared in the chase, so he took the rifle from Oscar, in time to plant a bullet in the wolf's hind quarters as he was escaping away from them. Oscar finished the tired animal with a well placed shoulder shot; which ended a fun afternoon for the Bar U cowhands! Nothing remained to be done but for them to take the pelt and ride triumphantly back to the ranch to collect the various bounties, which amounted to ninety five dollars.

More than fifty years have passed since the last wolf was killed on the Bar U Ranch; when suddenly wolf matters at the Bar U continued in a somewhat unusual situation. The current issue of wolves indirectly involved the painting done by cowboy artist Charlie Russell, of George Lane being attacked by wolves, while riding home to the Bar U Ranch during the winter of 1886.

Veteran rancher Bert Sheppard, along with two of his late brothers worked at the Bar U Ranch during the George Lane era. He appreciated having the opportunity of being directly involved with the history of the old ranch and the knowledge he obtained from the experienced cowmen he worked with there. Mr. Sheppard chose to contribute a life sized bronze sculpture of George Lane and the Wolves, as depicted in the Russell painting; as a lasting legacy to commemorate Alberta's ranching past. The life size sculpture costing $150,000 was to be situated near the Visitor's Centre at the Bar U Ranch National Historic Ranch Site when it became completed.

Friends of the Bar U National Historic Ranch Association, which is an organization of volunteers who have assisted Parks Canada in the development and administration of the ranch site since it's inception; initially agreed to accept Mr. Sheppard's offer. At a monthly meeting of this organization during April 1995, the matter of the bronze sculpture was proposed in a resolution to reject the initial idea of having the bronze erected at the historic ranch site. The motion was carried by the majority of the directors who were in attendance at that meeting. Mr. Sheppard was advised accordingly, but did not fully accept any reasons given for his offer being rejected.

Bert Sheppard contracted cowboy artist Rich Roenisch to do a life sized bronze sculpture of George Lane and the wolves; regardless of his generous offer not being accepted. The life size sculpture was to be completed and ready to be erected within two years after work had started on the enormous size project. After Sheppard's offer was rejected, he approached the town of High River, who gladly accepted the bronze sculpture to be situated in the George Lane Memorial Park in High River. The Western Heritage Centre at Cochrane, also indicated they would be happy to have the life size bronze sculpture set up at their location. Bert Sheppard became somewhat confused over the situation, with all the bickering that was happening with his life size bronze, but continued to believe the large sculpture belonged at the Bar U National Historic Site, because that was where the incident initially took place.

Meanwhile, as the months passed, the large size bronze was taking shape, piece by piece. Friends of the Bar U Association were keeping the matter as quiet as possible, and even had the Calgary office of Parks Canada convinced that the Bar U site was not the proper location for Sheppard's life size bronze. Those Directors of the thirteen-member board of the Friends of the Bar U, who had rejected the proposal of the bronze sculpture going to the Bar U, each had personal reasons why the bronze was not suitable for that location. None of the reasons given were valid for the occasion, and seemed to be more personal issues, rather than being accurate facts.

Several reasons given for not accepting the bronze sculpture at the Bar U. One was that the animal rights people would not be in favor of displaying a life size bronze showing wolves being shot. Other reasons were that some directors doubted whether the incident actually happened on Bar U land during 1886, along with the excuse as to why should a sculpture of George Lane be displayed, without having one also of the other two early ranch owners who were Fred Stimson and Pat Burns. Shooting wolves was a matter of survival with the early ranchers a century ago, and represented a part of Alberta's ranching history; similar to the native people who had to kill buffalo, as currently displayed at the Head-Smashed In Buffalo Jump World Heritage Site, west of Fort Macleod.

The life size bronze sculpture was near completion in the late months of 1996, but Parks Canada or the Friends of the Bar U Ranch Association had not changed their decision on the bronze sculpture being situated at the Bar U Historic Ranch. A group of enthusiastic members of the Friends of the Bar U organization began a partition, requesting Parks Canada to allow the bronze to be placed at the Bar U location. More than seven hundred rural and urban people of southern Alberta were in favor of the petition that was forwarded to the Minister responsible for Canadian Heritage in the Federal Government. Several months later the same group of people proposed and passed a resolution at the Friends Annual General Meeting identifying the same request with reference to the bronze sculpture. The results of this meeting were forwarded also to the Minister's office in Ottawa.

On March 21st 1997, Heritage Minister Sheila Copps, announced to the Canadian people that the bronze sculpture will find a home at the Bar U Ranch. In the same news release she indicated, "I am pleased to accept this generous contribution to the Bar U Ranch on behalf of Parks Canada. The sculpture represents a significant incident in the life of one of the Bar U's important historical figures and will make an excellent addition to the Bar U Ranch experience".

Although all obstacles had been cleared for the large bronze to be set up permanently at the Bar U Ranch, the sculpture did not get erected there on a solid foundation for another three months. There continued to be some argument as to exactly where it should be situated at the Bar U site, and who was going to stand the cost of a foundation base and future maintenance of the man size sculpture.

Finally, on June 27th, after two years of contentious arguments Sheppard's donation of 'George Lane and the Wolves' can be seen towering high above the skyline at the Bar U National Historic Ranch Site. A small and short ceremony took place in the unveiling of the bronze sculpture that day, with about 100 people in attendance; mostly local ranchers and old friends of Mr. Sheppard's. Sculptor Rich Roenisch had already christened his masterpiece "A Question of Survival." At ninety-six years of age Bert Sheppard was unable to see the bronze because of his failing eye sight, but was happier than an old cowboy heading for town; knowing that his controversial bronze had finally arrived at the famous Bar U Ranch. Sheppard commented on the fact that the sculpture is a living memory of early ranching in Alberta, and should remind future generations of some hardships that were encountered during that ranching era and the action necessary at times, in order to survive.

# Cayley Stockyards

As recently as March 17th, 2001 the small village of Cayley turned the calendar back more than one hundred years to commemorate the Cayley Stockyards; recognizing that the old stockyards was the reason the little village was first established. The stockyards, built by the Calgary / Edmonton railroad company during 1894, remained an integral aspect of Southern Alberta's cattle industry, until more modern methods of marketing livestock became a reality during the early 1950s

The idea of remembering a piece of Alberta's ranching history in having the old stockyards commemorated with a proper Alberta Highway Sign, was started several years ago by Bill Dunn who lives near Cayley and Oliver Christenson from Strathmore. Dunn who is a community minded enthusiast, came to Alberta from a farming area of Southern Manitoba about ten years ago. Christenson, a native Albertan had worked as a cowhand on the famous Bar U Ranch during the 1940s.

Together they quickly put together a small steering committee of interested individuals from Cayley, High River, the Alberta Government, the Museum of the Highwood, and along with the M.D. of Foothills the project was off and running. The result of many committee meetings at the Museum, saw the project quickly come together. When the highway sign was installed along Highway 2A at Cayley on January 10; a day of recognition was organized for the Cayley community. The unveiling of the sign along the highway took place at 1:00 PM, followed by a special program at the Cayley school, where nearly 250 people were reminded of a ranching legacy not forgotten.

The early ranchers and old time cowmen who settled the area during the 1880s and 1890s were the real reason the stockyards became a part of Alberta's ranching heritage. A few of the more frequent shippers of both cattle and horses to the Cayley stockyards were: George Emerson, Charlie Knox, the Northwest Cattle Company, Dan Riley, George Lane, Rod MacLeay, A. E. Cross, Pat Burns, the Oxley Ranch, the Circle Ranch, Cartwright and Thorpe, Dick and Percy Gardner, and Gordon, Ironside and Fares. There were another thousand shippers that could be mentioned and if an attempt was made to do so, there would be some still missed.

There was also a multitude of trail hands that were true to the brand they rode for; but the majority of them have since saddled their last horse, and rode across the Great Divide. They were part of the large cattle drives that were trailed to the Cayley stockyards under every kind of weather possible, who made sure the big herds arrived on time to be loaded for shipment to eastern and export markets. The old stockyards have not been active for at least fifty years but in planning the commemorative afternoon, twenty-five living trail hands were located who were mailed an invitation to attend the program activities.

Those invited were Allen Baker, John Ballachey, Bill Burles, Dallas Campbell, Oliver Christenson, Jim Drumheller, Rudy Everson, Floyd Erickson, Tom Fiest, Dick Gardner, Charlie Hale, Allen Hornecker, Tom Irwin, Jim Kewley, Webster Lefthand, Dale Miller, Blair McPherson, Swede Nelson, Ed Peters, Alfred Sawley, George Sorkilmo, Bill Stephenson, Alan Waddell, Jack Waddell, and Jake Wambeke. There were twelve who attended the function recognizing that some had a long distance to travel and others were not able to be present because of health reasons. The writer personally knows more than half of these trail hands and has spoken to several to find out what they remembered best about the trail drives to Cayley.

Floyd Erickson was cow foreman at the Bar U Ranch during the late 1940s and remembers many drives to the old stockyards with Bar U cattle. Each drive was made in one day, leaving the cattle in the same field each time overnight, a short distance west of Cayley. A lady named Edith Farrell had a boarding house and stable in the village where the cowhands always got overnight accommodation. It always depended on what time the train was scheduled through the village the next morning, as to when the cattle were gathered again to be corralled and loaded for shipment the second day.

Rudy Everson rode for the Bar U Ranch during some of the same years that Erickson was there. He told about one drive they made to Cayley during the spring of 1948 with a herd of dry cows and heifers that were being shipped to Burns' Lazy H Ranch at Armada. The weather was cold and wet, which left the pens in the stockyards a mess from all the moisture, and cattle worked the corral dirt into a foot or more of muddy slop. One cow got down and could not get herself up out of the mud. Erickson threw his rope on the cow to pull to where the mud was not so deep when his horse bucked him off into the wet slop; which he remembers very well because of the long cold ride back to the Bar U Ranch.

Webster Lefthand, a native cowhand now living on the Eden Valley Reservation, enjoyed talking about the many cattle drives to Cayley that he helped with between the years of 1939 to1950. He indicated he always liked getting up early in the morning; remembering how peaceful and quiet it seemed when only a few others were up and moving about. He remembered also how well the cattle handled early in the day compared to later when the flies came out and before the sun got hot. He always enjoyed being a part of the trail drives, because it was a break from the routine of regular ranch work. He mentioned that it was a treat trailing to Cayley, because of it being a small quiet place, where the people of the village were friendly and would stop and talk with him as a native person.

Tom Fiest remembered the twenty five mile trail drive from the Bar U, always being a challenge. Every rider had to be continually aware of the possibility of other cattle along the way getting in with their herd, or losing some of the herd with other cattle along the trail. Tom recalls the stockyards being full of sheep one time when a drive of Bar U cattle arrived there, making them wait until the men from the Cayley Colony got the sheep loaded before they could corral the cattle. He remembered also that they always borrowed a milk cow from a family that lived near Cayley to help lead the big herds across the highway and into the corrals.

Charlie Hale, who was only eighteen years old when he rode for the Bar U Ranch during 1940 - 1941 remembers the most difficult part of trailing cattle to Cayley, was getting them across old

Highway #2, across the railroad tracks and into the stockyards. Most everyone mentioned that seldom did all the cowhands have to ride back to the ranch. They would pull off their saddles and turn their horses loose, since they knew the route home themselves. The cowhands would draw straws, and whoever was unlucky had to follow the loose horses by horseback the twenty five miles back to the ranch. The remaining riders were taken back by the ranch manager with their saddles in the back of a small truck used at the ranch.

Kathleen Caspell, at the age of 91 years, now living in Calgary did not attend the afternoon function in Cayley but can clearly remember the large cattle and sheep herds that were trailed past their farm, which was situated a short distance west of Cayley. Her father Frank Shier, homesteaded the area during 1902 and the years she spoke of during the 1920s, when she was going to school in Cayley. The big herds would pass by their farm about school time, and the cowhands would always make sure the children got by the cattle safely.

The Village of Cayley can now be proud of an attractive Provincial Historic Marker that will bring worthy recognition of the Stockyards that once stood there in the successful development of Southern Alberta's ranching industry. The Cayley Stockyards may be long gone, but the Historical Marker will ensure that the heritage it represents, will live on.

# Thirty-Mile Horse Race

An ocean of water has tumbled down Fish Creek past Midnapore since the marathon 30-mile horse race was run near that location, more than fifty years ago. Midnapore during that era, was a small hamlet along Highway #2, where very few people who were traveling to or from Calgary had reason to stop. It was located about seven miles south of the city limits. Hidden from view of the highway, by the large cottonwood trees, was a camping area along Fish Creek, named Paradise Grove. Here there was a large meadow that staged the start and finish of a grueling horse race on May 24, 1946.

This event was organized and sponsored by the Calgary Western Riding Club, a group of enthusiastic people who separated from the Alberta Light Horse Association; and were interested in the western style of riding. This new club was organized during the fall and winter months of 1945 and the club directors; wanting to launch something big to start the 1946 season, staged Calgary's first and only thirty-mile horse race. How and where the race was advertised is not recorded, but it created a large interest with people throughout Western Canada and the Southwestern American States. The official program for the big race identified it as being the first running of "Canada's Greatest 30 Mile Stock Saddle Stake."

Forty-six eager horse owners registered for the race, with an entry fee of twenty-five dollars for each horse entered; each being optimistic of getting the winning purse of one thousand dollars cash money. Only forty-two horses started. Thirty-three of the horse owners rode their own horses and the remaining entries had riders other than the owners themselves. A few rules governed the race that specified that western tack was mandatory and each rider must be dressed in western attire. A weight condition was another factor, stating that each rider and his tack had to weigh no less than two hundred pounds. Those who did not meet weight specifications had to carry extra weight of some kind.

The event was an outstanding success from the standpoint of attendance. It was estimated that thirty thousand people watched the triumphant runners return to the same location they had left seemingly a short time earlier. The minute hand of the time watches had circled once and had only passed the 41st minute of the second hour when the front runners were seen riding hard for the finish line. The organizers of the race later realized that only about one third of those in attendance had paid admission since the entrances to Paradise Grove were altogether inadequate to handle a crowd of that magnitude, causing a financial loss for the riding club. Automobiles were crowded into the Stampede Grounds at Midnapore, while the hills within the area were covered with people as far as the eye could see. Cars lined the highway as far back as Calgary, and thousands of interested country folk had to be turned away.

The large attendance at this unusual function could have been related to several factors. Southern Alberta had successfully recovered from a most difficult previous fall and winter. No grain crops were harvested during 1945 and because of an unusual early spring in 1946 the previous crop had been threshed and a new one planted well before the middle of May. The Second World War had finished about nine months earlier and the people of Western Canada were beginning to feel some freedom from the wartime rationing of food and gasoline. Many of the service men and women had already returned home and it was time to go places and do things that many families were deprived of during the wartime years.

The course for the scheduled race went straight west from Midnapore before entering the Sarcee Reserve. On the reserve it followed a selected route, and left that area again at the same point where it entered; then returned along the same trail to where the race began. It had been carefully planned with strategic points set up along the thirty-mile course, which were controlled by veterinarians and officials of the riding club. Every horse was carefully examined prior to the race, and any animal that showed any evidence of unsoundness was not allowed to start. What had been originally planned as a fitness and endurance test for horses, developed without warning into a speed test that race officials had no control over after the race began. A number of the horses had been saved from fatal injury by officials at the final control point, advising riders that it was useless to push their horses any further after the first fifteen horses had already passed.

The day of the big race dawned as a pleasant spring time morning. Many of the horses had been stabled at the old Chinook Race Track and were either rode or trailed the short distance south to where the race was to begin. The late Eddie Bowlen was selected as the official starter, and he got the large field of horses away in perfect fashion. When the gun was fired the forty-two fresh horses eager to run and charged off across the big grassy meadow in a great and colorful stampede. The veteran cowboy and rancher Clem Gardner from west of Calgary was the favorite to win the race prior to the beginning, not overlooking the fact that he was then sixty years of age. The strategy being considered by other contestants who were the real contenders, was to stick close to Gardner and match strides with him in the final run to the wire.

Bill Renard, riding a half thoroughbred gelding, was in the lead at the top of the first hill, that was about three quarters of a mile from the starting post. By time the lead horses reached the gate into the Sarcee Reserve, three and a half miles into the race, Floyd Haynes from High River and Slim Riddell of Big Valley had taken the lead and were running neck and neck. For the first fourteen miles, the Big Valley horse set the pace for the whole field and for twenty-five grueling miles never dropped below second place. Race officials attempted to flag the horse out of the race at the twenty-mile post but the horse could not be stopped. The eager horse from Big Valley thundered on for another seven miles, before he collapsed and died along the course. After the leaders had covered more than a third of the distance, Bridge Hartley riding a thoroughbred mare took over the lead and held it for several miles. Floyd Haynes was content at this stage of the terrific pace to allow his small half-bred gelding to have a bit of a breather while three or four others were fighting it out for the lead.

Gardner's plan was to out figure the more experienced riders, by deliberately leaving the starting post last and gallop along behind the field at a leisurely lope. His strategy nearly worked and fooled everyone except the ultimate winner Haynes, a nineteen-year old cowboy from High River. At the eleven-mile post Gardner caught up to his daughter Joan who was riding in fifteenth position of a scattered field of tiring horses. The two rode along beside each other for several miles, at which time Gardner said to her, "They have got to break this pace, they have got to slow up." The horses pounded on for another four miles but none of the riders were prepared to slacken their speed. At the fifteen mile point Gardner saw how the big gelding that was being ridden by his daughter was tiring; so at an appropriate time she pulled out, and Gardner rode on in an attempt to win.

As the front running horses passed through the gate out of the reserve where they had entered only a short hour and one half earlier, Gardner and Haynes had taken a big lead ahead of the next horses. With two miles to go Haynes had prepared for a battle to the finish of the most torrid and talked about horse race that had ever been scheduled for the North American Continent. Within the last three-mile stretch of the course, both Bridge Hartley and Floyd Woodward passed Happy Campbell, leaving him running fifth.

For the last mile it was only Haynes and Gardner and as both horses galloped down the last hill with a half-mile to go, Gardner had cut Haynes' lead to about thirty feet; the distance that separated the two horses at the finish. Floyd Haynes, who no one thought had any chance of winning, finished the endurance race in one hour, forty-one minutes and eighteen seconds. This unexpected fast time calculated the lead horses at a speed of about eighteen miles an hour; which broke all known records for a distance of thirty miles. After the race had finished Gardner complained to the race officials that Haynes had bumped him coming through the gate off the reserve, and felt the winner should be penalized. Haynes denied touching the Gardner horse in any way, and the protest was rejected.

Out of a field of forty-two contestants who started the race, only the first fifteen horses and riders were recorded as finishing in the following order. 1.Floyd Haynes, High River on Skipper, 2.Clem Gardner, Pirmez Creek on Cavalier, 3.Bridge Hartley, Bassano on Miss Dividend, 4.Floyd Woodward, Burmis on Sultan, 5.Happy Campbell, Jenner on Mouse, 6.Garth Harker, Raymond on Humpy, 7.Lane Berry, Cochrane on Spider, 8.Bill Renard, Calgary on Playboy, 9.Dick McLellan, Washington U.S.A. on Kiska, 10.Albert Skelding, no address on Ronnie, 11.Ike Zeer, Wardlow on No Name, 12.Tom Peake, Dorothy on Rock, 13.Jappy Rodgers, Bottrel on Red Bird, 14.W.C. Fulton Jr., Wardlow on Breeze, 15.Alex Baptie, Cochrane on Rocket.

One surprise of the race was why the half-bred Arabian horse from Washington did not place in the money, after winning the Spokane Thirty-Mile Race the previous year. The only other American horse in the race, also a part-bred Arabian, was a strong contender, but only finished in ninth position. The American riders offered no excuses for not finishing closer to the front end, other than the fact the pace was just too fast.

Floyd Haynes was raised and educated in the town of High River. His ambition was to be a cowboy and to fulfill his dream he worked for different ranches in that area. He became involved with the sport of rodeo for a short while during the early 1950s and then began training horses on the Western Canada Racing Circuit. The races took him to Winnipeg where he married and raised a family. As a result of heart failure, he passed away during March 1991, at the age of sixty-four years.

Clem Gardner was also a native Albertan and a veteran cowboy who competed at the first Calgary Stampede in 1912. He ranched for a lifetime along the Elbow River west of Calgary, and was possibly a man who traveled more miles and did more things on horseback than anyone else on record. His successful ranching career ended during April 1962, when he also passed away from heart failure. The Gardner ranch property has continued to operate since, under the name of the Gardner Cattle Company, which has been managed by his grandson Michael Hawes.

The big race caused much controversy and was debated and talked about throughout the countryside for weeks and months afterwards. The news media reported that only five horses died or had been humanly destroyed, but according to public opinion more horses had died that were never reported. The race was condemned and the race officials were strongly criticized for sponsoring an event of that kind. A bitter feeling of indignation had risen over the death of the horses, but yet where did the blame belong? Some people thought the race was a good contest for horseflesh, but expressed the opinion that the horses had been pushed beyond their ability. They identified the race as a contest of speed and the sponsors of the race argued the point that any race that had to be run at a pace that was mandatory, would become nothing more than a parade.

The veterinarians who examined the horses that finished, concluded that if more of the race attendants would have had additional post-race experience, most of the casualties could have been eliminated. Many of those who saw the race, felt the responsibility should have rested with the owners and riders, and not with the people who organized the event. The horse that finished first handled the race in fine shape and to support this fact the same horse was entered and won a twenty-mile race ninety days later at Maple Creek. Gardner also had a horse entered in the Saskatchewan race, and there was considerable controversy whether it was the same horse that he raced at Midnapore.

Of the forty-two riders who experienced this marathon horse race, I have known twenty-two of them during the years, but was only able to find ten still living. Of the remaining twenty riders, there may be others alive whom this writer never had any acquaintance with. Several of those still living were contacted for their opinion on the big horse race and their comments are quoted:

Happy Campbell who ranches at Bindloss said, "They were traveling too dam fast. He was riding an in-bred cayuse that had been raised on the V-V Ranch, which had been trained by another fellow. My horse played out and if I had a chance to do it again, I would condition the horse myself."

Fred Crawford who ranched at Caroline, remembered having to carry some rocks for extra weight and said, "It was ridiculous the way some pushed their horses to the point of death."

Tom Peake, now residing in Drumheller, who rode a horse owned by Ed Hodgkin, indicated, "The whole affair was a crazy idea."

Chet Baldwin from Cochrane said, "It happened so long ago that I had nearly forgot about it. The horse I rode was owned by Lane Berry and it went gimpy in one hind quarter so I pulled out part way through the race."

Warren Fulton at Duchess recalled, "There were quite a few horses there from the prairie country and the higher altitude of the foothills had a big effect on the horses' breathing." He mentioned that he was a small man and had to carry pieces of lead on both sides of his saddle fork for extra weight.

Ted Glacier, the veteran rodeo cowboy from Coronation indicated, "The race was too tough on horses. I could see no reason for killing my horse so I pulled him out early in the race."

Ike Zeer who ranches at Wardlow could remember the race very well. He said, "The majority of the riders made a big mistake at the start by running their horses up the first hill, and that finished a bunch of them because only about half the horses were in condition to run that distance."

Every rider spoken to with the exception of Crawford and Glacier implied that if it were possible to turn back the calendar about thirty years, they would like to run the race again. John D. Munn from Montana must have visited Alberta that day and wrote a poem about the race. The poem is too lengthy to include with this article, but I have taken the liberty to use his last verse with some modifications, to conclude my story of a horse race that will remain recorded in the annals of racing history:

"That was a day of uncommon sport, a day most won't forget.

It was in the foothills of Alberta where a race record was set.

The winning horses were Alberta raised, and a victory they unfurled.

So let them come from where they may, it was a challenge to the world!"

# Home Grown Beef

People who have had the opportunity of growing up a cow ranch or a farm where cattle were raised, have had the chance of enjoying some home grown beef. Seniors will no doubt remember the era when beef animals were always butchered where they were raised, in order to keep the cookhouse or kitchen supplied with fresh meat. I would be surprised if any farms or ranches these days bother to butcher their own beef animals. Instead, the majority of them are taken to a meat processing plant and for an established fee; they are slaughtered, hung to age and then cut and wrapped with directions to suit the owners.

I was fortunate enough to be raised on a cow ranch and eating good grass raised beef is something I will always remember. During this period I had the opportunity to watch as a youngster and later became involved with the actual butchering of many beef carcasses, which required some experience for it to be done properly. Butchering a beef animal was always a kind of a special occasion on a cow ranch and was always scheduled when the cookhouse or kitchen needed more fresh meat.

During the cooler seasons of the year, when there were no flies, the butchering was usually done during mid-afternoon. The animal being butchered would have already been in a dry pen, located in area that was secluded from any noise or activity that would cause excitement of any kind, and was without feed or water for at least twenty-four hours . At least two ranch hands were always involved with this responsibility; and they would kill the critter by shooting it in the forehead, and quickly cut the juggler vein to expel all the blood from the dying animal.

Most animals were butchered under a rail gate that had a gate cap strong enough to hang a heavy beef carcass or sometimes a three-legged tripod would be erected especially for that purpose. A block and tackle, which was also referred to as an endless chain, would be fastened to the gate cap or the top of the tripod in order to lift the carcass off the ground as the butchering progressed. Some of the larger ranches maintained a special building that was used solely for the purpose of slaughtering beef animals. Other outfits used a windlass, which was a contraption built outside to lift and hang carcasses of beef. If fresh meat was needed during the summer months, a beef animal would be slaughtered in the evening after supper, when the blowflies had disappeared.

The hide would be removed as the animal was being lifted, with the offals taken out when the carcass was about halfway off the ground. The first thing removed was always the liver, which would be placed in a large basin or pan and taken to the cook immediately, to be placed in cold salt water to help remove the blood. If the animal was butchered during the afternoon there was always fresh fried liver for supper. I remember there would be fresh liver for breakfast the following morning, along with the brains that were fried for anyone who enjoyed them. The heart, tongue, and kidneys of a beef animal were always cooked in boiling water and eaten cold several days later.

The dressed carcass was left hanging overnight to cool off, and was then quartered and taken down early the next morning to prevent it from being exposed to the flies and magpies. The quarters were hung in a clean building with a strong table where each quarter could be lowered onto the table in order to cut off roasts, steaks or stew meat as they were required by the cook. The 'green' hide was always taken to the back side of the corrals, somewhere out of sight, and thrown over the top rail to cure in the sun. The entrails would be taken to a remote area of the ranch where the coyotes and magpies were happy to take care of them. Whenever there were any native people camped nearby, they were always invited to the butchering and they were happy to take all the entrails to their camp for a special feast.

When farm and ranches slaughtered their own beef animals during the summer months; before any rural refrigeration was available, all the meat from a carcass had to be boned, rolled and tied into different size bundles and placed in a salt water brine. Otherwise the fresh meat would quickly spoil. The meat was placed in a coarse salt-water brine using a wooden barrel, and after about five days it was ready to be eaten as corned beef. By the time a large beef carcass was consumed in this manner the meat at the bottom of the barrel would become mighty salty.

The early roundup wagons would have butchered one beef animal weekly in order to feed a crew of fifteen to twenty cowhands. To keep the meat from spoiling during the hot summer weather, a pole thirty feet long was strapped the right hind wheel of the chuckwagon, with a small pulley fastened to the top of the pole. The fresh meat was wrapped in burlap and hoisted to the top of the pole by a rope and keeping it out of range from the flies. This system allowed it to be raised and lowered, as the meat was needed.

Some farming communities used the idea of 'beef rings', where a different farmer slaughtered a beef animal each week. The fresh meat was then distributed amongst enough of the other farm homes and consumed within a short enough period so that none of the meat spoiled.

The feedlot industry in Alberta has become big business during the past forty years in the fattening and finishing of beef cattle. A lot of dollars have been spent on the promotion of Alberta beef, and now the beef industry throughout Canada is facing troubled times. Most Canadians have only tasted grain fed feedlot beef within this forty-year period. In my opinion, no one will taste better flavored, tender, meat than a steer or heifer that has grown to a mature age of at least twenty four months, and has been raised and allowed to fatten on some of Alberta's prairie wool grass!

# Horses I've Ridden

Anyone that worked on large cow ranches before cattle liners and horse trailers became a major part of the livestock industry, would have rode a good number of different horses. Those who had a chance of this kind will no doubt remember several horses that were much better than others, recognizing the different qualities that each person appreciates in a good horse. I am grateful I had this opportunity and can recall several horses that excelled above many others that I have ridden. Horses are somewhat like people; with different personalities, the ability to learn quickly or otherwise, and those that could perform physically where others were not so inclined.

The horse I enjoyed riding the most was a bay gelding I rode at the Y Cross Ranch west of Longview, while I worked for the late Joe Bews during the latter years of the 1940s. The horse was blood bay in color, stood about fifteen-two hands, and had the size and conformation of a model cow horse. This gelding was raised by Guy Weadick at his Stampede Ranch and was sired by a thoroughbred horse named Billy D. Guy Weadick gave the horse to Joe as a three year old, after which Joe broke and schooled the gelding to the point of being perfect in many ways. He had been named "Dandy", a name I felt suited the horse to perfection.

Dandy was amongst the string of horses given me to ride when I began working at the Y Cross in the spring of 1948. He had somewhat of a nervous disposition until he became accustomed to having only one person handling him. He was always difficult to catch in a cavvy of horses and for some reason during his lifetime, remained deathly afraid of any type of automobile. Dandy was the type of a horse that made a person conscious of the places and predicaments you would sometimes have to put a horse into, and the possibilities of having the horse injured or crippled. The days I was aware of having to ride country with a lot of bog or fallen timber, this would give me reason to ride a different horse, even if it disrupted my horse rotation.

Joe Bews kept a few sheep on the ranch, mostly for the purpose of keeping the weeds and tall grass eaten off around the buildings. To protect the sheep from the coyotes, there were two male billy goats that always stayed with the sheep. They would graze close to the ranch buildings and would seldom go beyond the 'jingle' pasture where the buildings were situated. One of the goats was a big tan colored fellow that could really run and turn. If the footing was good on the days I returned to the ranch riding Dandy, I would often cut the big goat away from the sheep and attempt to keep him separated for several minutes. The big goat kind of liked this exercise, and every time I approached the sheep on horseback, he would lift his head and dare me to separate him from the other sheep. He would run out about fifty feet from where the sheep were grazing and then the action would begin. From all the times we had our own little cutting contest, it was possibly an even draw, because the goat won as many times as the horse did.

I discontinued ranch employment and left the Y Cross during the fall of 1949. In the summer of 1953, I spent my summer vacation back at the Y Cross helping Joe cut and stack that year's hay crop, using horse mowers and an overshot stacker. The bay gelding was turned out and had not been ridden much since I left the ranch four years earlier. In the meantime Joe had started raising a few horses himself, and had some already schooled enough for them to be useful cow ponies. When haying was completed, Joe offered me the bay gelding, a gift I certainly did not refuse. We gathered the horses from their summer range and I trucked the horse to the Calgary Stockyards. The bay gelding was now eleven years old, but was as sound and useful as he had been during his younger years.

The stockyards company did not own any saddle horses, and allowed some of the brand inspectors to keep horses there free of charge so there would be horses available to recover any animals that escaped. During the fourteen years I inspected at the stockyards I always had at least one horse there, and sometimes two or three. The horses were kept in open shed pens on the west side of Portland Street that ran through the stockyards. Enough prairie wool hay not eaten by the cattle could usually be found in other pens nearby, and grain was fed if my horses were working or being conditioned for a show. The fact the horses were on dry feed for lengthy periods, I always fed a sweet beet pulp mix to supplement the dry feed.

The bay gelding was rode continually at the stockyards for two years, where he was kept grain fed and shod. During those years, Calgary Packers operated the packing plant near the stockyards, and had leased a feedlot that was located on the flat about a mile south. The feed lot was used as overflow pens for the slaughter plant and some cattle were moved at least two or three days weekly, depending on what class of cattle were being slaughtered. Clarence Gingrich and myself had an agreement with the packing plant to move their cattle as required. This was usually done very early in the morning before the city traffic began, or late in the afternoon. I remember trailing a lot more cattle back and forth in the dark than when it was daylight.

During the summer months I entered the gelding in as many horse shows in and around Calgary as was convenient. In 1954, the horse won the

Stock Horse Class at both the Calgary spring show and summer show of the Alberta Light Horse Association. At Stampede time in 1955, I was recruited to find suitable horses for the Stampede queens and rode the bay gelding myself escorting the queens riding horseback to their scheduled appointments downtown.

When the Stampede finished I turned the gelding out for a short time at a friend's place near where the CFCN radio tower is located. I kept riding the horse enough to keep him ready for the summer horse show that was happening within several weeks at the old Chinook race track. When the show arrived, I intended to haul him by trailer to the show location along with another horse, which was loaded first. The bay gelding ran in beside the first horse loaded and quickly backed out again before the safety chain could be fastened. As soon as his hind feet touched the ground off the trailer ramp, he reared up, lost his balance and fell over backwards. He was stunned when his body hit the ground because the top of his head took the shock of the fall. His head was split open at the pole, and within five minutes every ounce of blood in his body had ran out onto the ground. My friend owned a small tractor with a front-end loader and rest of that day was spent burying my companion Dandy in a shallow grave that overlooked the Bow River.

My second choice of good horses I have rode, would be a brown gelding that carried the Bar U brand on the left shoulder. The horse was raised at the Bar U but was used at the OH Ranch during the 1940s. The brown gelding was seven years old when I first saw him in 1943, making him a 1936 foal that had been sired by a thoroughbred horse called "Burdock" that Burns Ranches used at the Bar U. The brown gelding had been named "Peanuts," which suited his common appearance, but some good qualities were his deep girth and ribs, with a shoulder and wither that positioned a saddle properly. He would have never won any conformation classes because of his peaked rump and U neck, but he was a cow horse through and through.

Most ranch horses that were broke during those years were rode without being given any additional schooling in lead changes, or using their hindquarters to stop properly. This gelding was a natural in that regard and learned those qualities himself, chasing cows. If any animal had to be caught outside, or separated from the herd, his rider only needed to show him the animal wanted, and then hang on and ride. Peanuts was well cared for during his life at the OH Ranch, but when the owners sold the ranch in 1950, he along with other old horses that had served so faithfully for years were taken to the place where old horses go when they are no longer needed.

The next choice of horses I have ridden was another bay gelding I bought from a good fellow named Eddie Rowe who lived at Cochrane. Eddie always kept a few trading horses around, and had them pasturing along the trail off Highway 2A near Spencer Creek west of Cochrane. I often saw this horse from a distance while on my way to the Mount Royal Ranch to help Ed Bowlen with some cow work, so I arranged with Rowe one day to have a closer look at the horse. The day I arrived at the Spencer Creek Ranch, Rowe had the horses already corralled. He kept grinning all the while I was looking the horse over and I asked him what his price was on the bay gelding. He replied, "two and a half." I said, "I would match him to see whether I would pay two hundred or three hundred dollars for the horse." He agreed to match on the price, which I won, so I wrote him a cheque for two hundred dollars. Rowe laughed about the match and made a comment about how things sometimes happen that way. During that same time, country singer Johnny Cash had a song on the western hit parade called "Things Just Happen That Way" which enticed me to name the gelding "Johnny Cash!"

After I got the horse back to Calgary and trimmed him up a bit, he reminded me of the Bews gelding that was killed. The two horses had much the same conformation, except this horse was slightly smaller in size and a bit lighter in color. Johnny Cash was also a pleasure to ride and I enjoyed participating with him in horse shows and gymkhana events. He was not as capable as Dandy, but always won more than his share of show ribbons. After owning him for five years, I was offered a good price for the horse and sold him to play polo in Minnesota, U.S.A.

I knew another old cowboy that was also trading a few horses and who sold a lady rancher a gentle saddle horse. The lady met the old cowboy one day unexpectedly and confronted him about her saddle horse having one bad fault. The cowboy knew he had sold the lady a canner type, but inquired anyhow as to what the problem was. The lady said that her horse would often stumble and fall down. The cowboy was quick to reply and said, "Well now, your horse will also have one good fault." The lady rancher sarcastically asked him, "What might that be?" The old cowboy replied, "I bet he gets right up again."

# The Village of Longview

Longview is a village nestled in Alberta's foothills, located on the north bank of the Highwood River; about twenty five miles upstream from the town of High River. The small village supports not more than ten businesses, which are situated along both sides of Highway #22 just prior to its route southward over the water and through the beautiful river valley. Of the thousands of people who travel the busy highway through the village annually, some stop for gasoline, a meal, or just to have a smell of the fresh air and a good look of the attractive ranching country that is visible in all directions. Very few of those who stop would bother to inquire as to length of time the quiet little village has been there or why it was started initially.

Less that seventy-five years have passed since the land where the village is situated was virgin grassland, and owned by several different ranchers who were struggling to survive the depression years of the 1930s. The waters of the mighty Highwood River have tumbled eastward past the village every year since, seldom noticed by anyone except those ranchers who owned land adjacent to the water, or had to ford it from time to time for various reasons.

During the dry hot summer days of July 1936 while a major forest fire back on the Castle River was threatening the whole area of the Highwood watershed, a discovery oil well blew in, that was drilled by a company named Brown, Moyer & Brown. The location of this large oil find was on section 28 of township19, lying on the east side of Highway 22 about one and one half miles north of where Longview is currently situated. This caused a major oil field to happen very quickly within the surrounding area, with tar-paper shacks, restaurants and boarding houses springing up like mushrooms overnight. Live leaky gas lines were laid everywhere above the ground for inside heat, with an outdoor toilet in every yard and a small flare to burn garbage.

This settlement of people was first called 'Little New York', because the village up the hill was called 'Little Chicago'; because of the habits of a man the locals called 'Al Capone'. The reason for the unusual name was because this storekeeper had a habit of threatening customers if they allowed their grocery bill to become too large. It was soon given a legal name of 'Royalties' in recognition of all the tax money the government was making on the crude oil that was being produced. Royalties supported at least twenty active businesses including a post office, a movie theatre and a high school. By December

1970, any evidence of a village ever being located there had completely disappeared.

The village of Longview was first started during the winter of 1936, when a tall Chinaman from High River named Tom Kee, had a small restaurant built in the northwest corner of section 16, across the road and slightly east of where the feed store is now located. In the spring of 1937, a bank clerk from High River, named Neil Webster, along with Alfred Baines from Pekisko, built the first grocery store west of Tom's cafe. The third business established was a boarding house, built in that same area which was started by Vera Curtis, a widow lady from Saskatchewan. These people first named the location 'Little New York', because it was going to be bigger and better than the village that had already been started north of them on the hill. The little settlement quickly grew because of the men and families that hurried to the area looking for work. The dwellings and businesses that followed were similar in type and number to those that were being built up the hill in Royalties.

The original Longview post office that was situated where the East Longview Community Hall is currently located, was moved to the new village site during March 1938; with the official name of the village being called Longview thereafter. The Twin Cities Hotel that opened for business in September 1938, would have been a big addition to a village of that size. A general store that first started during 1937 and later owned by Gallup & Sons, became widely known as the most unique country store in the area. The Barber Machine Shop employed a large number of men who lived in the village and when they moved their business to Calgary during 1946, it signified the end of the oil boom in what was called the 'south end' of the Turner Valley oilfield.

It was surprising to learn that the village did not obtain the proper status of a village until January 1, 1963. This is when the official surveying and division of lots was accomplished along with the installation of a water and sewer system, which greatly improved the appearance of the small village, and no doubt made it a more comfortable place to reside.

Those who have traveled through Longview may have seen an older gentleman traveling along main street on a small garden tractor. His name is Homer Hayden, and he has been a businessman and resident there since the village started more than seventy years ago. If anyone is interested, Homer would enjoy visiting with them and telling the 'rest of the story'as to how the village began and also the important things that have happened there since.

# Christmas Memories:
# Son-of-a-Gun in a Sack

Christmas should be the time of year when most people think of other family members, decorated Christmas trees, turkey dinners, gaily wrapped presents, and the age old hymns that are featured every year at Christmas, describing the events and birth of our "Lord Jesus Christ." It often is a season for happiness or loneliness, a time for memories of life's events . It is the season for nostalgia as we reflect upon the years that have passed, when life was much simpler and people celebrated the holy day without having to experience all the commercialism of our current day life-style.

If someone were able to consult a good number of older Canadians on what each person remembered best about Christmas, their answers would be somewhat similar. The majority would remember the years they were in grade school with the excitement of being involved with the different Christmas programs produced. Some would also mention their families at home and how the meaning of Christmas seemed to be more sincere years ago, than the customs accepted during more recent times in celebrating this holy day .

It is not difficult for me to remember Christmas of the 1930s and 40s, reminded of the fact that the Second World War happened during this era, which made Christmas time much different for most families, including ours; since brother Joe was killed in action. By time the 1950s and 1960s arrived the economy of our country had changed and every business large or small was trying to impress their employees with large parties at Christmas time; that contradicted the true meaning of Christmas.

I belonged to a large family; we were raised on a cow ranch where Christmas had a definite purpose and was recognized as a special time of the year. Plans for Christmas day always started months ahead of when it would arrive. My mother would never relax until she had a large Christmas pudding prepared which was to be eaten as dessert for Christmas dinner. I remember it being a large project with the preparation of all the different kinds of dried fruit, sifted flour and the proper amount of suet from a beef animal. After all the proper ingredients were mixed together, the dough was wrapped and tied in a hundred pound flour sack. It would then placed in boiling water to be cooked for several hours on top of the cook stove in a double size wash boiler. After cooking, the large sack of pudding was hung from kitchen ceiling and not touched until Christmas morning. Several hours before the Christmas feast, the pudding was taken down and placed back in boiling water for it to be eaten hot with a sauce made with cornstarch .

After everyone had eaten their share of turkey, dressing, sweet potatoes, other vegetables and mince meat pie, not many were anxious to eat much of the rich Christmas pudding. The largest portion of the pudding was allowed to become cold and eaten later at another meal. I always enjoyed mother's Christmas pudding better the following day, when it was cut in half inch slices; heated in a frying pan and eaten with some fresh cream. This delicious Christmas pudding was a super model of a similar pudding that we were often treated to at other times of the year. The other pudding had somewhat the same ingredients without all the special dried fruits, which was always made, cooked and eaten the same day. The recipe for the pudding would have come from my father, who had eaten it often while working with the old time round-up outfits. Every cook on the round-up wagons had the recipe and would treat the cowhands on special occasions, if an outfit remained camped at one location for several days or more. I remember a number of different names for this special pudding, which I have not seen or tasted for more than fifty years. Some used to call it plum duff; others referred to it as a suet pudding, and the old round-up cooks called it "son-of-a-gun-in-a-sack."

More memories about Christmas were the concerts and programs organized at the country schools houses that existed throughout southern Alberta, before the Province centralized our education system to the larger urban centers . The country schools were different sizes, which depended on whether they were located in a farming or ranching area. All would have presented some kind of a program at Christmas time for their community, regardless of the number of children attending the school. My grade school years were spent at Lineham school, which was located south-west of Turner Valley, and was closed in June 1940.

It was always an exiting time preparing for a school concert at Christmas time. There were not more than a dozen students attending this school during the latter years it operated, but they always mustered up a Christmas program. The program would consist of several plays, comedy recitations, and singing of Christmas carols. The older students were always given the more major parts in the dramas that were selected, and I recall having to be the school teacher in the last Christmas production presented at that old school. The unheated wood shed at the back of the school had to be used as a place for the players to change costumes. The school had no benches or chairs to seat an audience; so big heavy wooden planks set on blocks of stove wood provided the comfort of a theatre atmosphere! I am not aware whether there were any John Wayne's or Ginger Roger's discovered from the many country school plays produced, realizing that possibility may have been feasible, had there been video cameras available during those years.

In spite of today's computer age, the philosophy of family and prayer have not entirely disappeared; nor has the feeling that people want to be with their loved ones at Christmas, and are lonely and dejected, if this is not the case. Those who are inspired to read old newspapers and magazines will be impressed by how much Western Canadian history has been revealed through recollections of the Christmas season.

Anyone who finds time to read this article, I hope it helps them to remember some of the better Christmases they have experienced. I do wish everyone a "Merry Christmas" and especially those who have never found the true meaning of Christmas. I do hope also, that you have enjoyed some good Christmas pudding!

### Son-of-a-Gun in a Sack

This recipe was made by Mrs. Pallister for thirteen children every Christmas, it was special due to the cost of ingredients; which was the reason it was reserved for family only at Christmas!

1¼ cups flour 4 eggs well beaten

½ to 2/3 cup milk ½ tsp cinnamon

2 cups raisins ½ tsp nutmeg

2 cups currants ¼ tsp. ground mace

1 ½ cups chopped fruit peel ¼ tsp cloves

¾ cup almonds (cut and blanched) ½ tsp salt

1 cup halved glace cherries 1½ cups stale breadcrumbs

½ cup honey 1½ cups shredded suet

½ cup fruit juice, wine, or brandy 1½ cups brown sugar

½ teaspoon baking soda dissolved in warm water

Mix ingredients together, The amount of milk will depend on the staleness of the crumbs. Fill well buttered molds or bowls 2/3 full. Cover with strong paper and steam for five hours. Steam for a half hour before using. Serve with Brown Sugar Sauce (1 tbsp corn starch, 1 cup brown sugar, 1 cup water, Vanilla or rum extract; Cook over medium heat, stirring constantly, add butter and vanilla after cooking). Enjoy!

# A CHRISTMAS STORY

By H.G. Pallister

It was the night before Christmas, and back at the ranch,
The owner was somewhere, and now was the chance;
The cattle were gathered and corralled in the dark,
But their tracks in the snow, made a rustler's mark!

The cows were odd colors, but branded the same,
Some had burrs on their tails, and several were lame.
They were cropped on both ears, with a pop on the jaw,
And the crust on the snow had their legs a bit raw.

The truck was left handy, but kept out of sight,
And the moon on the snow gave them plenty of light.
So the cattle were loaded from a gate on the side,
In the back of the truck, the horses were tied.

They traveled all night with their radios on,
The road was all clear, and the speed traps were gone.
The lawmen must have been out with the boys,
Or escorting Santa Claus, who delivered the toys.

By daylight next morning, they were way down the line,
And the buyer at the feedlot, said they were nearly on time.
To the shack he straight went, and grabbed up the phone,
And caught the Brand Inspector, who was just leaving home.

A short time had passed, when a pick-up appeared,
That was blowing black smoke from two stacks in the rear.
A lanky cowboy stepped out, all dressed up in style,
Who carried a rope, not used for a while.

He was half walking sideways, and appeared a bit lame,
From the look of his boots, he was new at the game.
He was slack through the middle where his jacket hung loose,
And from his pocket inside, he took a mouthful of snoose!

He went straight to the corral, where the cattle were penned,
And took a good look, before he walked in.
The cows were rear spooky, and were milling about,
So he closed the gate careful; so they wouldn't get out!

He called for the paper that showed not a brand.
And then swallowed his snooze, and said "I'll be damned,"
But he looked at the cattle and said "Everything's fine,
Then left in a hurry, mumbling about overtime!

The rustlers went clear, with no questions asked,
So they loaded their horses, and left with the cash.
Several months passed, with no evidence found,
Because the brands were not clear, when the cows turned around.

A missing report was made out, just in case,
The cows would be returned to the rancher's place.
Now the reason that they were never found,
Is because they had a new brand, when this bunch went to town!

Now if this story has a message to tell,
It's that everyone should know very well,
For missing cattle to be found by the brand,
You must keep your ear to the wind, and know the laws of the land.

This story may be read as fiction or as fact,
But for the time being it doesn't matter at that.
For we want to wish everyone at Christmas some "Good Cheer!"
In hopes that the brands will be better Next Year!

Christmas card sent to the Alberta Brand Inspectors from the Stettler Brand
Office Staff in1985

# Smoke from the Branding Fire Goes out

Biography of H.G. (Hank) Pallister
October 13, 1925 - April 27, 2005

The heart is like a treasure chest that's filled with souvenirs
It's where we keep the memories we've gathered through the years.

Hank was the son of Guy and Evelyn Pallister, and was raised on the Lineham Ranch near Turner Valley, with nine brothers and three sisters. He was the only child who followed in his father's footsteps to make life's occupation in the cattle business. His father Guy Pallister came to the ranching frontier in 1888 from Sheffield, England, and this family was recognized by Friends of the Bar U Historic Ranch Association as a Pioneer Family, in January, 2005.

Hank walked daily to a country school, which consisted of two large families, the Denning children and the Pallister children. After finishing high school he started working for various ranches in the area. He worked for the late Joe Bews, owner of the Y Cross Ranch in the spring of 1948 until the fall of 1949. Joe Bews gave him a horse named "Dandy", that was raised by Guy Weadick at the Stampede Ranch. This was the beginning of his love for schooling horses.

Many young men were drafted to war in those years, and he had four brothers who joined the armed forces. He was exempted from military service, due to the fact he was employed in agriculture, working in the spring of 1945 at the OH Ranch at Longview. He loved riding the hills and the open spaces, but soon realized that he had to make a major change that paid him more money. He left the ranch life early in 1950 when he was accepted for a position as a Brand Inspector, working at Edmonton stockyards and then moving to the Calgary Stockyards.

He took his holidays in September so he could help Eddie Bowlen gather cattle for his sister, Helen MacDonald at the Mount Royal Ranch at Cochrane; just another way he could enjoy the ranch life, and be with good friends at the same time. He loved ranch life, and made it a priority to renew friendships and attend brandings at various ranches every spring.

In 1964, he was promoted to Supervisor of Brand Inspection for Southern Alberta, and he covered many miles to Stockyards and Auction markets, from Red Deer to the American border. In 1968 he was promoted to Co-ordinator of Regulatory Services in Edmonton to supervise the Brand Inspection Service for the Province of Alberta. As Co-ordinator, he played a vital role in establishing a brand inspection computer system that provided a more efficient service, assuring the protection of cattle for Alberta producers. He worked closely with K. Division of the Royal Canadian Mounted Police on livestock investigations and was called to court many times to testify on stolen cattle cases.

During the early years of the Provincial Progressive Conservative Government, it's platform was to decentralize government departments. Hank was responsible for moving the Alberta Brand Office out of Edmonton to Stettler during February 1975. He supervised an office staff of thirteen and field staff of approximately ninety inspectors. Hank retired in November 1992 after 42 years of dedicated service to the Province of Alberta. The Western Stock Growers presented him with an honorary lifetime membership on his retirement.

Nearing the end of his employment, he started writing stories of early ranch history from memories of the early range men that his father had talked about; backed by information gleaned from the Brand Office files The secretaries tired of typing his stories for him, so they purchased a computer as a retirement gift. This opened many hours of enjoyment as he wrote; recalling many of the early rangemen his father knew, and incidences of events that he chronicled about many of the early ranches in Alberta. He had an incredible ability to remember dates and events, and his column "A History to Remember" in the Regional or "Smoke From the Branding Fire" in the Alberta Beef Magazine was always a favorite with readers. The last article he wrote was entitled "Alberta's Centennial", and was published in the Alberta Centennial Brand Book, and in the September/05 issue of Alberta Beef Magazine.

His years at the Calgary Stockyards allowed him to keep his horses there so he could participate in many horse shows, gymkhanas and cowboy polo. He became a recognized Horse Show Judge for the Alberta Light Horse Association and a Registered Cutting Horse Judge. He eye for 'good confirmation' showed very clearly, when he chose a wife in Joyce Haberer, who worked at the stockyards in Paul and MacDonald's office across the hall. They were married on August 29th, 1964 and had two children Guy in 1967, and Wade in 1971.

One of the highlights of Hank's life was attending the Rangemen's Dinner every Stampede week. The first one he attended was in 1956 with his father Guy, who was a guest at the first dinner in 1929. The last Rangemen's Dinner he attended was in July, 2004 ,which he attended with his son Guy.

He counted it a privilege to be recognized as a native son. This gave him many hours of volunteer service as past president of the High River Old Timers, and as a member of the Southern Alberta Old Timers. He organized the Old Timers section of the Stampede Parade for 25 years, came home from that parade and 'hung up his saddle' saying, "25 years is long enough for that job!"

His love for ranch history became evident in another way, after his retirement when he saw an ad in the Alberta Beef magazine, for help making movies. He was given the job because he could drive the mule team, but I'm sure his weathered appearance as a genuine cowboy helped in the selection. He enjoyed participating in the "Hooves of History" cattle drive in 1990, and the Western Stock Growers Cattle drive in 1996 when he teamed with Larry Boyd and drove the OH bedwagon over the trails at the age of 70!

When he married, he announced to Joyce that he intended to retire in High River, so that goal became a reality in July of 1999 when they moved from Stettler to High River.

Hank felt like he was home at last. He had traveled many miles from Stettler to attend board meetings with Parks Canada and Friends of the Bar U, for the selection and establishment of the Bar U Ranch National Historic Site at Longview. The spring of 2000, he took over as Manager for Friends of the Bar U. During that time he worked with Bill Dunn, Oliver Christianson and the Museum of the Highwood to commemorate Alberta's ranching history by having the Province of Alberta establish a sign on Highway 2A, at Cayley, the site of the original stockyards in Southern Alberta; where cattle were driven from points south of the border to be shipped by rail to eastern and export markets. The next project in his mind was to have a sign placed at the site of the old Calgary Stockyards, but that dream will have to be picked up by a younger man who worked there who has the same love for history that Hank did.

The Brand Inspectors at the Stockyards will remember how he enjoyed playing crib, a talent he passed on to his sons, who organized crib tournaments at family gatherings, "the old boys against the young bucks!" Needless to say, he hated to concede the win, and will be missed at the card table!

May our memories of Hank never fade. He was a genuine cowboy, a true friend, a good boss, a talented author, and a loving husband and father.

# A Cowboy's Heart

Joyce Pallister

When God created cowboys,
He used a different sort of mold,
They are a very special bunch
Who stick together, I am told.

You'll never see a cowboy,
Without looking at his horse,
The two came together.
They're made like that; of course.

And most of them are long and lean,
But some are short and fat,
Some have been known to be slightly mean
But they're all known by the hat!!

His hat has got that special shape,
It's really quite specific;
To see him through sun, rain and snow,
And weather that's terrific!

And some of them have got a dog,
And others took a wife,
Regardless of which they chose,
It lasted them for life.

Another part of the cowboy's gear
Is his saddle tried and true,
It had to be custom fit;
Or you know what was blue!

Now every cowboy can throw a rope
To get the heel of that little calf,
And others, why they used that rope
To catch their "better half."

And then he's got a slicker
To use on a rainy day,
It's rolled up behind the saddle seat,
In a tidy sort of way.

He keeps his bridle in the barn
A hangin' on a hook.
And every now and then,
He takes a better look

To be sure that bridle gives some comfort
As he jerks upon the rein
Nothins' worse than a sore-mouthed horse.
As he pats him on the mane.

He's got a pair of leather chaps,
To put on when really needed.
Makin' the gather in the fall
Through trees, and brush, and territory deeded.

And then, of course, there's them thar' boots,
He wore them as a lad.
He started wearin' boots when he was small,
To be just like his dad.

He loves the open range, you see,
He'll ride and do his part,
But the love that shows the very most,
Is the love God placed in his heart!

# WHOOP-EE-E!   IT'S OUR NIGHT TO HOWL!

## OLD TIME OPEN RANGE MEN'S

# .:. Dinner .:.

## PALLISER HOTEL
### CANADIAN PACIFIC HOTEL
#### JULY NINTH   -   NINETEEN TWENTY-NINE

# THE NORTHWEST TERRITORIES POOL WAGON

Will Camp on the Palliser Flats, at the Junction of the Bow
and Elbow Rivers

TUESDAY, JULY 9th, 1929

*Chuck will be ready at 6.30 p.m.*

Andy Halkett of the C.P.R. Outfit will be Captain of the Round-Up

All reps must be at the "wagon" by 6 p.m.   Be There!

---

The C.P.R. Outfit covers a lot o' range.
You boys have worked over lots of it, and we are sure glad to have you
camp with our "wagon" tonight.
We told the cooks to do it good.
All ranches have told cooks many things.   Sometimes they do it.
Put your name on the list and try an' live over the old days.
They were good ones.
The results of the old time range men's hard work are to be seen all over
this Northwestern range.
Their efforts have done much to produce the present prosperity.
We're glad you are here, and hope you are.

CANADIAN PACIFIC

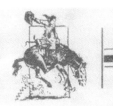

## TROUBLE FOR THE RANGE COOK.

*By E. A. Brininstool.*

Come, wrangle yer bronco an' saddle him, quick,
The cook is in trouble down there by the creek!
Oh, cinch up yer latigoes, all O' you runts,
An' pull 'em so tight that yer ol' bronco grunts!
'Twill need all you punchers the foreman kin send,
'Cuz the chuckwagon's mired down there at the bend!

The cattle are scatterin' over the plain,
While punchers are yellin' in language profane!
But let 'em jest go—for the cook's in a muss,
An' quicksands are causin' the feller to cuss!
Oh, this is the time ev'ry puncher's his friend,
'Cuz the chuckwagon's mired down there by the bend!

Come on with yer ropes that are heavy an' stout!
No grub for the bunch till the wagon's pulled out!
It's in to the hubs, an' a-sinkin' down slow,
An' cookie is cussin' an' watchin' it go!
Come! hustle, you punchers, an' haul him to land,
Before he is flooded by water and sand!

A-strainin' of ropes an' a gruntin' of nags,
An' woe to the puncher whose lariat sags!
It's spur 'em an' quirt 'em, an' make 'em lay to!
An'——now she is movin'! An'——hooray! she is through
It's worth all the time that the effort required,
'Cuz it's nothin' to eat when the chuckwagon's mired!

# GRUB PILE

*"Come an' Git It, or We'll Throw It Out!"*

---

ALBERTA CELERY AND ITALIAN OLIVES

—◇—

OPEN RANGE BEEF BOUILLON WITH WEDDING RICE

—◇—

DUTCH OVEN NESTER CHICKEN WITH SHAMROCK BACON

AND

COW CAMP CORN FRITTERS

—◇—

CANUCK PEAS WITH MINT AND CAMPFIRE FRIED POTATOES

—◇—

LEAF LETTUCE AND DANDELION SALAD WITH SAGE HEN EGG
DRESSING

—◇—

FRONTIER CORN CAKE WITH GOLDEN SYRUP

—◇—

WATER FROM THE SPRING IN THE BANK
*If you can beat it, produce*

---

After the usual gab during the meal, everybody go up to the bedwagon on the cut bank where augerin' and irregatin' plans will be discussed
an' gone into in detail.

## LET'S FORM A RANGE MEN'S ASSOCIATION AND FEED
## ON THIS CAMP GROUND EVERY STAMPEDE WEEK

# COPIES OF ORIGINAL LETTERS
# FROM OLD-TIMERS

□□□

Dear Sir:

Will you be so kind as to put my name down for the C.P.R. dinner on July 9th.

I started cowpunching in 1883 for the JR outfit at Deer Lodge Valley, Montana. Trailed in cattle with Tom Lynch in 1884 bringing in the "Z" the House ( ⊡ ) cattle, the "O2" cattle, and the " ᴚ " and joined with the Scouts in the Rebellion of 1885 for General T. B. Strange, manager of the House Ranch, and since that time have been running my own outfit, the "DIO".

Yours truly,

BOB NEWBOLT.

---

Dear Sir:

Will you please put my name down for the C.P.R. dinner on July 9th.

My qualifications are, I wrangled horses for the WR under John Lamar 1892, and from then on as cowpuncher for the Oxley Ranch until 1902, under A. Chadwick and J. Johnston.

Yours truly,

R. O. SYKES.

Address—906 18th Ave. W.
Calgary.

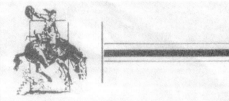

Dear Sir:

I understand that the C.P.R. desires to get in touch with the Old Timers for the purpose of a re-union July 9th.

I came into the country in 1885 ranching in the Pincher Creek district.

Wishing you and the Stampede all success.

Yours faithfully,

EDMUND A. ELTON.

Address—1006 13th Ave. W.
Calgary.

---

Dear Sir:

Having been on my ranch your letter of the 21st instant was only received on returning here last night, and thinking that I am eligible to be a guest at the dinner to be tendered to Old Time Cowmen by the C.P.R. Railway Co., I hasten to give you my qualifications.

I started in the Pincher Creek country in July 1883 with F. W. Godsell on the south fork of the Old Man River ⌒ brand, then with Garnett Bros. ⌐o⌐ on the same range, then on the Old Alberta Ranch on Pincher Creek, Dick Duthie was then the manager, and then with the old '76 on the east end of the Cypress Hills, D. H. Andrews was then manager, and Tom Henderson, wagon boss. Working as a cowpuncher until 1895 when I started for myself at Rush Lake, Sask., and am still in the business on the north side of the Saskatchewan River, north of Rush Lake.

Thanking you for your letter giving me the opportunity to participate in the entertainment.

I am

Yours very truly,

ROBERT CRUIKSHANK

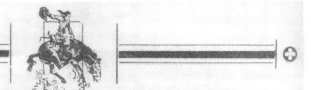

Dear Sir:

I would be very pleased to attend the dinner given to the Old Time Ranch hands at the Palliser Hotel, July 9th, 1929.

Am enclosing my qualifications which I hope will be satisfactory.

I am

Yours respectfully,

L. McKINNON.

Address—822 14th Ave. W.

Landed in Calgary in the spring of 1886. Soon after went as chore boy for General Strange's family. He being manager of the Military Colonization Co's. ranch about 45 miles southeast of Calgary on the Bow River. After 17 days chore boy was promoted to a ranch hand with this company. Their brand being House ⌂ left shoulder on horses and left hip on cattle. Remained with that outfit until 1891 with the exception of one year with A. H. Goldfinch, a share holder of the M.C.C. and owner of the horse track ◡ Brand.

In 1891 started to work for the Canadian Coal and Colonization Co. known as the Sir John Lester Kay outfit, the stock end being under the management of D. H. Andrews, headquarters on the Bow River where the late Curtiss Cattle Co. operated. Their brand being "76" left thigh for horses, and left ribs for cattle. Worked for this outfit till 1894. Followed the Bow River round-ups, also the High River and Willow Creek round-ups with the ⊔ wagon in 1890 as representative for the House outfit occupying a tent with Ed. Johnson, foreman, and Herb Miller, righthand man

Went through the spring and fall round-ups as rep. for the "76" outfit, and from 1891 to 1893 with the Oxley Wagon, with Harry White foreman, and Archie Chadwick righthand man. Dawson later became foreman of the Circle Outfit.

In 1894 established the "L. K." brand with ranch on the Bow River, joining round-ups with neighbors including old timers as, Moorehouse Brothers with the "Turtle" brand; W. R. Newbolt, "DIO" brand; Frank Addeman of the Horsetrack Cattle Co., R. A. Begg with the "Scotch Thistle" brand, and W. W. Brown, "Z X." the late C. R. Brown, who had acquired the House outfit, Janes Bros. "J3" brand, Roy Cowen -X- and others.

The original "LK" outfit has now become a family company as the L. K. Ranching and Farming Co. Limited, with C. H. McKinnon General manager, and D. J. McKinnon, foreman.   Owners of brands "LK" $\frac{X}{L}$ "X4" $\underset{W\,\exists}{\smile}$ with holdings at Dalemead, Bassano, Calgary and Airdrie.

---

Dear Sir:

I have received your letter of June 21st, and note contents.

I worked for R. Urch at Old Kippon, the Old Man River before 1900 up to 1912. his brand was UL on the left ribs, and left hips.   In 1902 R. Urch, Robert Patterson of MacLeod, and myself formed the Little Bow Pool, Patterson's brand was ]| left hips, my brand was ƷⴑⰀ on right ribs.   I was Urch and Patterson foreman and ran the Little Bow Pool Cow Wagon.   We ran our cattle on the Little Bow River at the mouth of Snake Valley.

Yours respectfully,

O. H. O'TOTT.

Dear Sir:

I thank you for your kind invitation to attend the Old Time Range Mens' dinner at the Palliser Hotel, Calgary, at 6.30 p.m. Tuesday July 9th.

I should like very much to attend if my qualifications will permit. I rode for the Douglas Lake Cattle Co., Douglas Lake, B.C., for the years 1898-1899, I was then 23 years old. The cattle brands were at that time 111 right or left hip, 25 on the right ribs, the horses with the same on the shoulder left or right.

We did not run a grub wagon, but three small pack horses, which carried the whole outfit for as many as fourteen to twenty riders, our country at that time was too rough for a wagon, and not sufficient roads to allow us to take a wagon where we wanted to. Joe Coutlie was captain of the outfit, and old man Mr. J. B. Graves, manager of the ranch.

I have been ranching ever since those days, was 8 years at Mosquito Creek in partnership with Mr. Joe Pemberton, on the Two Dot Ranch.

I came back to B.C. in 1909 to Douglas Lake, was appointed manager in June, 1910, and am still holding that position today.

Joe Coutlie is still captain of the round-up, and now has a wagon, drives four horses in the orthodox style. Mr. Greaves when he visited me some years later, remarked when he saw the wagon, "Those boys will want spring beds next."

Lawrence Guichon, Joe Bulman, Willie Lauder and Jim Frisken are a few of the names I can remember who are all eligible.

Hoping to see you before long and join the Old Timers' Dinner.

Yours truly,

FRANCIS B. WARD.

Dear Sir:

I understand there is to be an Old Timers' Dinner given by the C.P.R. and I should like to be present.

I arrived in Canada March 17th, 1887, and came west to the Willow Creek Ranch.

Yours truly,

C. F. A. LEEDS

---

Dear Sir:

Yours of June 21st, received.

I will be pleased to attend your dinner of July 9th, at the Palliser Hotel.

I have taken charge of the Cypress Cattle Company ranch in the spring of 1887 and have been interested in the company to date. We branded C Y on left ribs. Our range was on the Belly River between the Little Bow and Big Bow Rivers.

Yours truly,

A. J. McLEAN.

---

Dear Sir:

I worked for ꓱC Ranch, Mosquito Creek in 1897. Len Sexsmith in 1899, ⊞ Ranch 1898, A7 Oxley Ranch I 1899-1917. LU have owned the -E- since 1911.

Yours truly,

STONE ROBERTS.

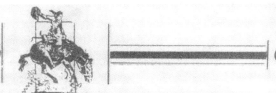

Dear Sir:

I accept with thanks your kind invitation to the Stampede.

I worked for the I. G. Barker Company, McLeod for six years, brand figure three on left soulder.

Also with the One Circle outfit, and owner of the $\overline{\wedge}$ ranch for twenty years, Cypress Hills, Medicine Hat

Yours truly,

JOHN READ.

---

Dear Sir:

In reply to your letter of recent date with reference to the Old Time Range men. I rode the range between the Little Bow, Mosquito Creek, the Livingstone Range and boundary line having a ranch between the north fork of the Old Man River and the foothills on what was called Todd Creek. I used 646 for my brand and also owned the |—| cattle which I sold to Geo. Lane. I worked with the **WR** and Pincher Creek and McLeod round-up wagons. I was boss in 1873 and riding that range from 1890 to 1903.

Every one I have spoken to in this district that is eligible has already received a letter from you.

Yours truly,

F. A. MEAD.

Dear Sir:

I herewith send you my qualifications to attend the Old Time Cowboy Dinner given by the C.P.R. at the Palliser Hotel.

I cooked on the wagon for six years from 1893 under Herb Miller.

Yours truly,

CHARLES LERHR.

---

Replying your letter re Old Time Range Men. The qualifications of Honorable James D. MacGregor are Sheep Creek Eighteen Eighty Eight and Bow and Saskatchewan Rivers Eighteen Ninety Eight.

J. H. MEANWELL (Secretary)

---

Dear Sir:

My attention has been drawn to an item in the Calgary Herald of May 18th re qualifications for Old Time Cowboy Banquet which is to take place at the Palliser Hotel, Calgary on July 9th, 1929.

I feel that I can qualify under the above, as I came to Lethbridge the spring of 1890, being then 22years old. Starting to work at that time for the Whitney Bros. "Hat Brand" ⌒ The cattle being branded on the left ribs, and the horses branded on the left thigh with the same brand Range North East of Lethbridge on the Little Bow River. I refer you to Mr. D. J. Whitney, 5661 Lime Ave., Long Beach, Cal., the other brother being deceased.

Hoping to get a reply at your earliest convenience, and oblige.

Yours truly,

ARCHIE HUTTON.

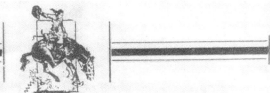

Dear Sir:

Your letter to hand in connection with the Canadian Pacific Railway Company giving a dinner to the Old Time Range Men of the Canadian North West at the Palliser Hotel, Calgary, on July 9th.

In 1892 I worked for the Kew Ranch, Kew, and in 1893 I worked for the High River Horse Ranch, and later for the Quorn Ranch.

Many thanks for drawing my attention to this matter, and hope that you will have a successful Stampede, and that the dinner given by the Canadian Pacific Railway Company will bring the Old Time Stock Men together.

With kindest regards

I remain

Yours very truly,

GEORGE HOADLEY.

Minister of Agriculture.

---

Dear Sir

The first outfit I worked for in Alberta was the H2-McHugh Bros. in 1893. ▲ 苏 and ⊟ Mosquito Creek Wagon in 1895 ⊽ wagon in 1896. NL wagon in 1897-8. ✚ Y T and ⊽ wagon in 1899-1902, 7 | Oxley wagon in 1903.

Sam Howe, Millicent, and Stone Roberts, Lathom, are the only others eligible for those dates who are here at present.

Yours truly,

W. S. PLAYFAIR.

Dear Sir

I wish to get a ticket to the Cowboy Dinner.

I came to Alberta in 1890.   I rode for the High River Horse Ranch in 1892, with Mr. Eckford manager, and Mr. Wm. Todd, foreman. In 1893 I rode for the Quorn Ranch with Mr. Swann, manager and Mr. Hill, foreman.   I was captain of the Sheep Creek Division of the General round-up in 1898.

Yours very truly,

R. McLAREN.

Address—City Cartage Co., 813 Centre St.
Calgary.

———

Dear Sir:

*Re Range Riders Previous to 1900*

I wish to advise you that I commenced working on round-ups in the fall of 1893.   I wrangled horses that round-up for the $\overline{U}$ wagon, Bert Wilder, foreman, and Hunter Powell, round-up captain.

I worked continuously on Round-ups from that time until the end of the year 1900.   When I left to go for myself I had been working for the Oxley Ranch under the foremanship of J. H. Johnston and W. L. Watt.

Yours truly,

HUGH M. SHAW.

Address—1008 Durham Ave.
Calgary.

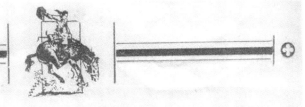

Dear Sir

    I intend being in Calgary for the Old Timers' Banquet.  Have been in the country since 1885.

Yours truly,

BEN McDONNELL.

---

Dear Sir:

    Seeing your piece in Calgary Herald about Round-Up Dinner, would say I think I was the first cook on a round-up in Southern Alberta, as I first cooked for Winder Ranch in 1878 for Captain Winder, foreman Charlie Shapels.  Next year with Walden Ranch, owner Mr. Walden, John Lamar, foreman; two years next with Oxley Ranch, Willow Creek, John R. Cragg, manager Jim Patterson.  Next ranch with Bill Cochrane Ranch C Raymore, with Cyrkle Ranch near Lethbridge.  How Harris, foreman Barley Buck, also McFarlan Ranch on the Kootenty River, Bar U Ranch, George Lane, north fork of Old Man River.  Any further reference any old timer in Macleod who have lived there there since 1874.

Yours truly,

EDWIN LARKIN

---

Dear Sir:

    The Brown Ranch Co. Limited unloaded more than 600 heifers in June 1886 at Medicine Hat.  The heifers were branded B. R. some of their offspring are branded ███████.  A couple of years from now George G. Ross, will be old enough to accept your invitation.

Yours,

WALTER ROSS.

Dear Sir:

Just a line to see if I could join the happy bunch of old-timer cow-punchers.

I rode for John Wilson, the cattle king of Kamloops, B.C., in 1885. His brand was JW on right ribs.

In 1894 I went north and took charge of H. O. Bowe's ranch. His cattle brand was  on the right hip. His horse brand was ꞮB on the right thigh.

Those times were the good old round-up days, and I hope to meet some of the good old boys from that section of the country.

Yours truly,

JAS. D. KIRKPATRICK

Address—3907 15a St. S.W.
   Calgary.

---

Dear Sir.

I was foreman on the Bow Valley Ranch at Midnapore from 1886 to the year 1910. Till I came in to the stockyards at Calgary I was working for W. R. Hull from 1886 to 1902, then P. Burns & Company. Bought the Bow Valley Ranch and have been with them ever since. I rode with the Pincher Creek wagon for three weeks in 1903, Sam Sharp, round-up boss. I also rode for about ten days for ten different summers with the Mosquito Creek wagon with Hunter Powell and Charlie Anderson as foremen, also with the wagon north of the Bow River with Frank Adaman, foreman.

Yours truly,

WM. BANNISTER

Dear Sir:

Received yours of June 21st, saying that the Canadian Pacific Railway Company will act as hosts to the Old Time Ranchmen of the Canadian North West at a dinner they are giving at 6.30 p.m. Tuesday July 9th, at the Palliser Hotel, Calgary, which I have much pleasure in accepting.

My qualifications are, that I arrived here in the spring of 1884, and worked for the British American Horse Ranch, a subsidary of the Cochrane Ranch, the original large one in this country, until July 1885, after which I have been working for myself and took up a ranch west of Nanton in the latter end of the winter of 1886, and have been engaged in ranching since.

For several years the ranching industry that we were particularly interested in, extended from Sheep Creek on the north to the Old Man and Belly Rivers on the south, Rocky Mountains on the west to the junction of the Bow and the Belly Rivers. There were a good many outfits taking part in the round-ups. The one I was particularly interested in, known as "MOSQUITO CREEK" WAGON, was a combination outfit of:

Bar X. Y. Owned by Samson and Harford; C. C. W. E. Cochrane manager. The Two Dot, Harry Alexander, manager. Hull and Trounce, W. R. Hull, manager. The Bar S, Walter C. Skrine, Owner. Bar D. Blunt and Holmes, High River. The P. L. Ranch, George Ross and myself, A-7 Ranch.

I became wagon boss on the round-up on this outfit about 1889 or '90.

Trust the above will fill the bill

I understand that Jack Dempsey, who is now foreman for my Home Ranch, will be eligible for this dinner.

Yours truly,

A. E. CROSS.

Dear Sir

I was talking to P. G. Thomas in High River the other day in regard to the Cowboy Banquet held at the Palliser Hotel, Stampede time, and he told me to write to you regarding same.

I wrangled horses for Lane and Burns beef herd in '98, under Bill McCout, better known as "Slippery Bill", and followed the range for several years after.

Would I require an invitation as I would like to attend.

Thanking you I remain

Yours truly,

J. B. WATT.

---

Dear Sir:

As per your request I am sending my qualifications to dine with you the Palliser at the C.P.R. Expense.

I wrangled horses for the Winder Ranch Roundup Wagon the summer of 1887 which made a big roundup after the very severe and disastrous winter of '86 and '87. Charles Sharples was foreman of the wagon range, Porcupine Hills, Willow Creek and Old Man River. Brands ᛤ on left shoulder on horses and left hip on cattle, ear mark under half crop on each ear. I wrangled for the same wagon some of '88. Then for the well known 76 wagon as cowboy the next, and so on until I had enough money to get a little old ranch for myself.

Yours truly,

F. A. BURTON.

P. S. Wishing you the best of success with your Stampede, and if I get a card will be with you. F. B.

Dear Sir

Seeing by the Herald that you are wanting the names of old Cowboys, I think I am qualified to belong to that class.

I have been in Alberta since 1881 and have lived all my life on a ranch. Have been on the round-ups with the Old (OX) Oxley Ranch, the 76 and ⊙ and DJ. Have put in my share of time both day and night herding and at breaking bronchos.

I hope to be at the Stampede this year. Am a member of the Old Timers so trust you will see fit to enter my name among the "old cowboys".

Yours truly,

W. A. LYNDON, Lieut.-Col.

---

Dear Sir:

Replying to your letter of the 21st re dinner of Old Time Range men.

I have followed cows since 1888 in the Medicine Hat District, from Medicine Hat to Maple Creek and south as far as the Montana line.

The wagon I worked with was known as the "Medicine Hat Pool", owned by about eight or ten medium sized cow outfits. My cattle brands are 7-T on left ribs and also own Z-T on right ribs. Horses brand 🔲 on right thigh.

Will be very pleased to accept the invitation of the Canadian Pacific Railway Co., for Dinner at the Palliser, July 9th.

Yours very truly,

JAS. MITCHELL.

Dear Sir:

I beg to advise you that I hope to be able to attend the "Round Up" Dinner that is to be given at the Palliser during Stampede Week, for men that worked on cow outfits, prior to Dec. 31st, 1899.

I might state that I was punching cows for the 76 outfit when I joined the N. W. M. Police in 1897.

I worked for D. H. Andrews, Roy Cowan of Langdon, Tom Herdon and Fred Craig, son of the late John R. Craig.

Sincerely yours,

P. G. THOMAS.

P. S.   Range that I rode was from East-End, Sask., south to the White-Mud, Mont., U.S.A. mostly.

---

Dear Sir:

I would like to come to the Stampede but am too old to earn my money to pay my fare to Calgary. I am supported by the Government at this place. I was up there in 1924 and had a good time for four days.

With best regards,

EDWIN LARKIN.

Ex-cook.

Dear Sir:

In answer to your request re Old Timers. I may say that I rode on the first round-up in the spring of 1883. G. Emerson, L. Lynch, Fred Stinson of the U͞ were with us.

Duncan Cameron was our night herder, as you know these men are all gone. Previously I went to the Mountains with Mat. Dunn, who had a beef herd supplying the surveyors and engineers who were running the C.P.R. lines forty six years ago. I started the O. H. Ranch and have been in the cattle game ever since, and have ridden the range consistently as long as the range was open.

As far as I can remember all those ranchers that started when I did are gone.

Wishing you every success with the Stampede this year.

Beleive me,

Yours truly,

F. W. INGS.

Dear Sir:

I see by some of the Calgary papers there is to be an Old Time Cowboys Banquet at Calgary on July 9th.

I am writing to see if I am of age and can qualify to be present. I am 63 years of age, came to Alberta the 10th of May, 1883, and have lived here ever since. I worked for the **WR** Ranch in 1884. Dr. Frields was manager at that time, Sam Sharp was round-up foreman. Since then I have managed my own ranch and am still going strong.

Yours truly,

JOHN CLARK.

Dear Sir:

I wish to place my name on the list for C.P.R. Dinner in Palliser Hotel on July 9th.

I came to High River, June 1883 and was employed on HL Ranch round-up Sept. 1884, G. Levings manager and Hunter Powell foreman until Sept. 1885. I then went to work for John Quirk when I made my first purchase of cattle from John R. Craig then manager of the Oxley Ranch and have owned cattle since that time, starting on my own place March 1886 and am still on the job.

Yours truly,

R. A. WALLACE.

Dear Sir:

As for the Cow Boys Banquet taking place in the Hotel Palliser on the 9th of July next. I may say that I have been a cowboy around High River since the year 1897, and on different ranches, viz. A. H. Eckford, T Nichol Bros. OW Sullivan, Bond, Findlay, Spaulding, H. Smith, etc.

Am I entitled to take in that Cow Boys Banquet that day.

Yours truly,

JOHN W. H. BOND.

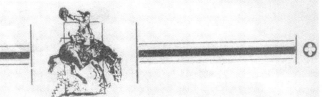

Dear Sir.

*Re Cowboys' Dinner July 9th.*

Rode with Mosquito Creek Round-up Wagon 1897-8-9-1900, for W. R. Hull, brand 25 left hip. Range Mosquito Creek and the west of Nanton, Alberta. Present age 53.

W. TOM BOULTON.

Would like to mention two real old timers.

W. Summers of Nanton, and Ed. Larkin of MacLeod.

---

Dear Sir:

In regard to the Old Timers Dinner at the C.P.R. Hotel on July 9th. I herewith wish to state my qualifications.

I came to Alberta 1896 to 1897, worked on Frank Meade's ranch herding horses etc. at Livingstone, 20 miles from Pincher, wrangled the day herd for the Pod Wagon which shipped beef from Claresholm the fall of 1897 or 1898, worked around that district until fall of 1889, when I went to Montreal with one of the first trains of Waldron beef shipped from Pincher over the Crow's Nest road. These were bought by Archie McLean, he can verify above as he often visited the Mead Ranch.

I was away in Africa, serving in the Strathcona Horse, Reg. No. 651. Came back to Alberta after the war in 1903 and located north of Bassano and have been there 26 years running the Percheron Horse Ranch FH. Sold the land this spring but still have over 100 head of Percherons there.

Mr. E. L. Richardson can verify most of this. I was 20 years of age in 1899 when I went east with the W. R. Cattle.

Yours truly,

BRICE H. BUNNY.

Dear Sir:

I wish to attend the Old Time Cowboys Dinner given during Stampede week, Calgary.

I was born in 1872 and came to High River 1883, worked for fall Roundup 1888. George Lane, Captain.

Yours very truly,

J. L. SEXSMITH.

---

Dear Sir:

*Re Old Time Cowboy Banquet.*

I was on my first round-up as a cowboy in 1882 for the Bar U Ranch and have been with them most of the time since, still going strong. Tom Lynch was the first wagon boss.

Yours truly,

H. MILLAR.

---

Dear Sir:

Would like to attend the Old Time Range Mens' Banquet.

I punched cows in the Cypress Hill country south of Medicine Hat 1893 to 1895, then again from 1898 to 1901, have put in some years as Fire Ranger that is where I got my scars, was 20 years of age 1897.

I might mention I used to go to school with Jas. Mitchell, your bucking horse judge, back in 1888 and '9.

For a good time in a repetition of those good old happy days.

I am, Sincerely yours,

A. J. McCONNELL.

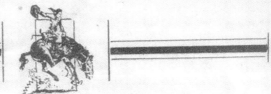

Dear Sir:

I would like to attend the Old Cowboys Banquet. I came to Calgary when I was 16 years of age or June 28th, 1889. I have now been 39 years in Alberta, and I rode on all the Round-ups north of the Bow with D. P. McDonald and Angus Sparrow, who has been dead a good many years, and I also have been captain of the Round-up. The brands were **D. P.** and **75 A-O.**=) and **VL** and hundreds more I can give you. I am now 55 years of age.

Yours truly,

J. C. OSWALD.

---

Dear Sir:

I seen a piece in the Calgary Herald that you wanted the names of old cow punchers that was in the country before 1900.

I came to Calgary the year 1889 and started to work for R. G. Robinson that same year. I worked for him for eight years, the last four years I was foreman for him, and then I started to work for Gordon Ironsides and Freres. I was foreman for them on the =) ranch on the Red Deer river for twelve years, and I was on the 44 ranch for some time.

I would like to meet some of the old boys that I have not seen for years. I would like to join the "Round-up" at the Palliser Hotel on the evening of the 9th of July. I used to know most of the old time boys and would like to meet them all again.

Wishing you the best of good times and good luck at the Stampede.

I remain,

Yours sincerely,

DICK ALLEN.

Dear Sir:

I am not sure just what you want.

The papers said would have to write to you. I suppose all you want to know is where we were in 1899.

I was foreman of the Cochrane Ranch that summer, took over the outfit the summer before, 1898.

Worked for the C. Ranch from 1890 up to Jan. 1st, 1906. The brands were: Cows ═ₗ L. R. C L. H. also K L. R. C L. H. Horses ═ₗ L. T.

If there is anything more you want to know of will be glad to let you have it.

Yours sincerely,

A. FLEMING.

_____

Dear Friend:

I would like to attend your dinner of old Cowboys who worked on the range years ago. I herded cattle for P. Burns in 1893 and was horse wrangler for the "Two Bar" Outfit in 1894. Blue Osbourne was in charge of roundup for Gordon, Ironsides and Freres. Angus Sparrow was western manager for this outfit.

Came to Alberta in 1891. Born 1877.

Yours,

FRANK COLLICUT.

Dear Sir:

I see by an old paper that you want to get in touch with Old Time Cow Punchers, prior to '99, the days of real sport, the open door in the West, and freedom of the range, when the streams sparkled with trout and the prairie one waste flower garden.

Well, I left T. Eaton's, Toronto, August 13th, 1898, armed with a lot of ambition, a suitcase and a christie hat. Worked in the wheat fields of Manitoba and about the 11th of November, 1898, arrived at Cayley with a bunch of Gordon Ironsides Cattle.

I had my first Chinese cooked meal and heard the yip-yapping of the coyotes. The next day I walked to the railroad, and it seemed all the cattle in the south country seen that hat and wanted to inspect it close range. At last I was on the train after having flagged it with a burning torch, got into Calgary and went to bed by the light of a tallow candle. Next day I looked for work. There is a man in Calgary now that ran a sort of real estate and employment office. He tells me I have a job, but for_____sake get a different HAT. I did, but did not get the job, but went out on the Elbow the latter part of November 1898 and fed 100 head cattle for the Cullen family at the Old Man's Place. In March 1899 I started for myself on Tom Cullen's ½ section two miles from Capt. Gardiner. My brother and I bought 11 cows and calves at foot and a Polled Angus boy from Capt. Gardiner and that summer seen my first round-up that took in all south of the Elbow and Indian Reserve from the Chipman ranch R. G. Robinson's to Cow Camp in Foothills.

I helped at different places including my own. I am not positive but feel old man Marshall R. S. Cattle, foreman was Captain. The report of his twenty foot whip would start a stampede or a Mexican Revolution. John Fullman, husband of late famous Lady Fullman that every old timer knew tended the heating of irons. The more whisky he got the hotter the branding irons. At supper there was a great feast. I won't say what it was. If you closed your eyes it tasted O. K. I don't think it will be on the menu at McGuire's dinner.

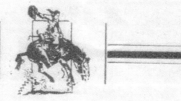

The Gardiner's and Robinson's are all that is left south of the Elbow. Cris. Cullen and Ralph and Clem Dyer are farming at Rock Ford.

Doggin Jack I had not seen for about 15 years until last Stampede week, waiting on beer tables at the Imperial Hotel, Calgary. Tom Cullen died about a year ago, Danny McGillis is at the coast, and some went back to the old country.

I will close, hoping I have not tired you. Wishing you and the Stampede success and Mr. McGuire in the fine spirit he has shown. May they have an enjoyable time. It will be the last for many of them.

Sincerely,

JACK WASSMAN.

---

Dear Sir:

Seen in the Herald about requirements for old time Cow Punchers. I worked for McHugh Brothers from 1894 to the South African War. Broke horses for them all that time. Their brand was H2 left hip. Worked under several wagon bosses during that time among other being Dutch Patrick and Herb Miller. I was under him several times which he can verify himself. After the war went back to McHugh Bros. again and started for myself out here on the Red Deer River and been here ever since, so you see what I have been and you can easily verify this yourself by asking Mr. Christie as he stopped at our ranch out here several times.

Hoping this is satisfactory,

I remain,

Yours sincerely,

JOE HASLETT.

Dear Sir:

I would like to attend the "Old Cowpunchers" Dinner in Calgary's Stampede Week. In 1892 I night herded horses for the North West Cattle Co., F. S. Stinson was manager, and Henry Arnette foreman of the wagon, and Hunter Powel range boss. The range we covered was between the Elbow, the Bow and the Belly and the Mountains.

In '93, '94, '95, and '96 I was working for a horse outfit C. Knox, manager, riding with Felix McHugh, and the Quorn ranch horse round-up wagon, Ted Hills, foreman.

The fall of 1897 I worked for the Oxley wagon, Jimmy Johnson, foreman. In 1898 I went to work for Geo. Emerson and rode every year on the round-up till 1905. During this time I rode with the ⊓ wagon, Herb Miller, foreman until 1902, and then Charlie McKinnon took it over.

Hoping this is the information you require.

I remain,

Yours very truly,

GUY PALLISTER.

---

Dear Sir:

As I anticipate attending your Cow Boy Dinner given at the Palliser Hotel on July 9th, I herewith send my qualifications.

I worked on the Wagon from 1893 to 1897 for George Emerson P and 5 Brands.

Mr. Herb Miller was wagon foreman and J. H. V. Brown captain of range work.

Yours truly,

E. F. THOMSON.

Dear Sir:

Kindly reserve seat for me at the cow boys supper to be given at Palliser Hotel. I worked at the $\overline{U}$ when it was known as The North West Cattle Co., Herb Millar was foreman and Seven "U" Brown was the Captain on roundup.

Yours truly,

E. J. THORNE.

------

Dear Sir:

In reply to your announcement in the Herald, I would like to state my qualifications for attendiing the complimentary dinner for old time stockmen to be held in your hotel next week.

1888 with Y-Z Ranch. Mrs. Ellen McGarry, Fish Creek Assiniboine, 20 miles south Maple Creek, capacity ranch hand.

Following year with James Warnock. Brand forgotten. Ranch hand.

Robert Pollock, Half-moon Ranch, Fish Creek, Ranch hand.

Geo. Newberry, Brand forgotten, Lone Pine, Cypress Hills, Ranch hand.

Rode in four general "round-ups" and rode for strays after round-ups Camp cook for Bob Pollock, six months.

Age during that time nineteen to twenty-two years. At present in charge of advertising T. Eaton Co., Limited, Calgary.

Do these qualify?

Yours sincerely,

G. D. CASSON.

Address: c|o T. Eaton Co. Limited

Dear Sir,

The following is the pioneer's story that you requested from me.

After being coaxed on board the ship with a little oatmeal, we triumphantly crossed the herring pond. At Halifax we boarded the C.P.R. for the wild and woolly west

Seeking adventure, Calgary a real cow town, having stage coaches running north and south quite appealed to me. The first work I secured was freighting to Edmonton. In the Capitol I enlightened my intelligence with the Cree language and Red River Jig (the popular Hobo-hop of those days).

In 1895 I trailed cattle for John Lineham from Edmonton to Dewdaney (Okotoks). Here I became an adherent for three years, of the Round-up with John Weir, better known as Nigger John. My first evening was spent at Weasel Head Bridge on the Elbow River, much too near the town for cowpunchers best interests. Certainly we were a happy crew that night, and it's little wonder, that I was fully resigned this to be the chosen and ideal life for me.

Next evening at Jumping Pond a little stimulant remained and the effects of the previous day were still quite evident. As I rode into camp for supper, a strange and amusing scene was presented to my view, Nigger John, Wheeler Mickell, Sam Howe and others were partaking of a sumptuous evening meal, the tomatoes and Scotch whiskey was apparently greatly relished.

Long since I have recalled the many pleasent incidents of pioneering and am surely anticipating the pleasure of meeting all my old friends once again at the Stampede. This is one of the few opportunities we have of resurrecting many of the interesting occurrances of our early career.

I remain as ever,

Yours truly,

JAMES G. BEWS.

Dear Sir:

As regards to the dinner you are giving the old range men I thought as being an old timer I might come in on it. I came west in 1882 as a N. W. M. Police and after putting in six years in the good old force I took to riding in the cow outfits. Irode and cooked for some years on the round-ups for the old S. F. V. and 7 [ ] Outfits and worked with the 76 at Crame Lake.

I'll be in Calgary for the Stampede so if you think I am entitled to be present at your dinner much oblige.

I remain an old timer,

P. E. RIGGIN.

c|o E. K. Power Co.

Dear Sir

Having noticed by the papers that the C.P.R. is giving a dinner to the Old Time Stockmen and as I have ranched in Alberta for the last forty years. I was for five years where the City of Calgary now is on the North Hill and for the last thirty years at Spring Grove Ranch. I presume I am eligible to join the old timers dinner party should you kindly grant my request

Thanking you in anticipating

I am sir,

Yours truly,

JOHN MACLEOD.

Dear Sir:

*Re Old Time Cowpuncher's Dinner.*

It is not customary in the West for a person to blow their own horn, but if I can "horn-in" to this dinner on these slight credentials it will be considered an honor by myself.

Came west in '89 as a type-slinger on the old Tribune Newspaper, published by the late T. B. Braden. Was of full age of 21. Incidentally, when there was no type to sling, or no cash for slinging it, I at times took to the range.

Broke horses from the old Doc. Lauder ranch, which lay under Nose Hill on the east.

Homesteaded. Worked on the old Begg ranch, at the mouth of High River.

Punched cattle for the B. C. Market Company from the prairies to the Yukon.

Homesteaded again, and at present hold land on the Clearwater River, west of Red Deer.

If these small efforts on the range permit me to shove my feet under the table at the dinner, well and good, if not, just try and slip me a hand-out through the cook-house door.

Yours etc.,

HARRY B. WILSON.

---

Dear Sir:

I have been running beef cattle in Alberta since 1899, having bought the E half of Sec. 13, Tp. 35, Rge. 27, West 4th Meridian from the C.P.R. that year. Am now 58 years of age so am eligible to attend the Dinner given by the C.P.R.

Yours truly,,

CHRIS MOFFAT

Dear Sir:

Received your letter, which we didn't get until today (July 1st). Hope we are not too late.

I was the first man to take the round-up wagon down to Bow River. I lost all of my horses on the trip. Jim Johnson was my horse wrangler. My cook was Niger Green. I also worked for the Corn Ranch, brand R.R., also the Bar U ranch, brand left. I worked for pretty near all the cow ranchers and round-ups.

Mr. Cross of Calgary will tell you all about me if you ask him, also Mr. Dan Riley.

I am thanking you for the invitation to the dinner. I am sure I will be there.

Mr. Weadick, will you please try and get a word to Mr. Christie to try and get a word to some of the cowboys to meet us at the train.

We will be there on the 7th or 8th sure.

Yours truly,,

HUNTER POWELL

---

Dear Sir:

I see by the Calgary Herald of June 29th that you are giving a Dinner at the Palliser Hotel on July 9th for men that have ranched here previous to 1900. I have been ranching since 1892 on the north side of the Bow River, also rode the range from about that time until it was closed up. I rode for the Bar "U" in 1898-99, also several other ranches.

I was with the O. A. Chrichley for seven years. If any other reference I refer you to D. P. MacDonald, Cochrane.

Yours truly,

WILLIAM N. ELLIOTT

R.R. No. 4, Calgary.

Dear Sir:

Have just given you principal details of activities of my early ranch days. Many of the old timers will remember me and can give you any further information you might want.

Yours sincerely,

A. B. MacDONALD.

In 1886—Promoted, organized, selected the land and leases situated in Tp. 12, Rge. 29, West 4th M. of the Glengarry Ranch Company. Was appointed managing director in year of organization of the Company, continuing in that capacity for twenty-four years, when the ranch was sold in 1910. The brand used for cattle and horses was the "44" Following were members of the original company: Sir. Donald Mann, Col. R. R. McLennan, Donald Grant, D. W. Grant, I. M. Ross, Luke Madigan and myself. Sir Donald Mann later buying out original members excepting myself and taking in as new shareholders Sir H. S. Holt and Sir Wm. McKenzie. The present owner of ranch and brand is Mr. Pat Burns, my very old friend. Was president of Alberta Stock Association for some years. Am now in my 87th year.

Allan J. MacDonald, my son, was engaged as foreman of the ranch and ran our wagons with the Willow Creek and Trout Creek round-ups, etc., as early as 1900.

ALLAN B. MacDONALD

---

Dear Sir:

In reference to the Banquet kindly extended to the Rangemen of Alberta, might say I was located on Ghost River Ranch on and after the 6th of October 1884, and shall be pleased to avail myself of the pleasure of being in attendance.

If this is in order please leave my credentials at the office of the Palliser Hotel to be called for.

Thanking you and anticipating the pleasure of meeting you.

Yours truly,,

JOHN GILLIES

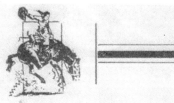

Dear Sir:

Having noticed in the Albertan that you are asking the Old Time cattle men to communicate with you I felt that I was included.

I came from Martintown, Ont., to Alberta in 1886 to work for the Glengarry Ranch, better known as the 44 Ranch, located in the MacLeod district and organized by Mr. A. B. McDonald in 1885, the shareholders included Mr. H. S. Holt, Messrs. McKenzie & Mann, and others, with Mr. A. B. MacDonald as managing director, who is now one of the last of the big ranch managers living. He resides at present in the Dufferin Lodge, Calgary.

For six years I was foreman of the 44 Ranch and Captain of the general round-up in the south country one season, was steer roping champion of the Territorial Exhibition held in Regina in 1896. Ranch owner to 1911 and engaged in the livestock commission business at Calgary since 1912.

Trusting that your plans in connection with the Old Time Cattlemen are a success, I am,

Yours very truly,

D. S. MacINTOSH.

Address—Alberta Stockyards, Calgary

WHOOP-EE-E!